SEVENTH
EDITION

An
Outline
History
of
WESTERN
MUSIC

SEVENTH
EDITION

An Outline History of WESTERN MUSIC

Milo Wold
Linfied College, Emeritus

Gary Martin
University of Oregon

James Miller
University of Oregon

Edmund Cykler
Deceased

 Wm. C. Brown Publishers

Book Team

Editor *Meredith M. Morgan*
Developmental Editor *Raphael Kadushin*
Production Coordinator *Kay Driscoll*

 Wm. C. Brown Publishers

President *G. Franklin Lewis*
Vice President, Editor-in-Chief *George Wm. Bergquist*
Vice President, Director of Production *Beverly Kolz*
Vice President, National Sales Manager *Bob McLaughlin*
Director of Marketing *Thomas E. Doran*
Advertising Manager *Ann M. Knepper*
Marketing Manager *Kathleen Nietzke*
Production Editorial Manager *Colleen A. Yonda*
Production Editorial Manager *Julie A. Kennedy*
Publishing Services Manager *Karen J. Slaght*
Manager of Visuals and Design *Faye M. Schilling*

Cover image: Ihre Fotobestellung an
die Hamburger Kunsthalle,
Werner Gilles: "Engelkonzert"

Cover design by Mary Sailer

Consulting Editor Fred Westphal/University of California, Sacramento

Library of Congress Catalog Card Number: 88–63556

ISBN 0-697-03643-X

Printed in the United States of America by Wm. C. Brown Publishers,
2460 Kerper Boulevard, Dubuque, IA 52001

10 9 8 7 6 5 4 3 2

Contents

Preface

In its original form, the authors conceived this book as a brief historical overview of the development of western music. Numerous narrative histories have provided students and the reading public with detailed accounts of western musical development. Most of these works are long, scholarly narratives containing much detailed information. The authors believed that there was a need for a succinct reference source that would provide students and lay readers with an introduction to the history of western music.

The present outline form will help students gain a clear and logical understanding of the evolution of historical styles in music. With the refinements of its format and sequence, the authors hope students will find it readable and logical.

The authors of the seventh edition considered the problems of twentieth-century music since World War II and concluded that the most manageable way of treating the music of this century was by arbitrarily dividing it into two chapters, the first ending with the close of World War II. For this reason some persons and style have necessarily been treated in both chapters. In addition, the final chapter on popular music has been expanded and brought up to date. A thorough treatment of this vast and important subject deserves an entire book.

A chronology of historical events relating to music and composers has been included again in this edition. Because performers in recent years have become increasingly important as an influence in compositional style, some of the more prominent performers have been included in chapters eight, nine, and ten.

Appreciation for the numerous suggestions for change from the many users who have been kind enough to make their expertise available to the authors is gratefully extended. Special thanks to our colleagues Peter Bergquist and Steven Stone, and to the readers of the manuscript, for their generous help. The reviewers include: Richard Greene, Loyola University; Paul Langston, Stetson University; Robert E. Matthews, Edinboro University.

Introduction

An Outline History of Music has been planned and organized to be used in a variety of ways.

(1) It can be used as a basic text in music history with collateral readings in the many authoritative, specialized studies that are readily available to students. In this manner the text will serve as a practical core from which students can expand their studies to include the vast amount of source material that has been edited and published in recent years.

(2) It is designed to be used as an outline and review for any standard course on the subject. Students can utilize its plan and material to focus attention on the most important musical developments.

(3) The present volume will prove valuable to students who wish to embark on a study of the literature and history of music on their own without the guidance of an instructor. Its information on scores, recordings, and collateral readings can be a guide to further reading and to a selected list of musical examples that will serve as a basis for the understanding of musical styles.

It is the authors' experience that the best source material for teaching music history is the music itself. Consequently, the present volume is designed as a guide to musical examples that illustrate the historical developments relating to music. To facilitate the study of the music of the first five chapters, the authors have included references to recorded examples of music and their scores that are likely to be found in music libraries. This makes it possible to use actual music as source material with a minimum of library facilities. Students are urged to study the music, listen to the recordings, and, when possible, to perform selected examples as a part of the classroom experience. Other music that the instructor might suggest, or the student might seek out, will serve to broaden the student's acquaintance with forms and styles.

In many periods of history the names of composers were subjected to translations into various languages. The authors have followed the preferred spellings of *Baker's Biographical Dictionary of Musicians,* 6th Edition, which is the most common desk reference source for scholars. It is recognized that this is not always in agreement with the spelling in the *New Grove Dictionary of Music and Musicians.*

The authors have avoided the temptation to divide music history into a series of short, specialized periods. Rather, the generally accepted historical periods (Gothic, Renaissance, Baroque, and so forth) are specified. While the music of every composer is unique in specific details, and the earliest music in a style period differs from the later music in the same period, it is the opinion of the authors that a consistent stylistic pattern is often identifiable throughout such a style period. For example, the principal characteristics, patronage, function, performance practice, and musical style in the Renaissance are fairly uniform. Moreover, in spite of the widely publicized "isms" of twentieth century music, there is still a mainstream in modern music that has already lasted over eighty years.

The present volume analyzes each major period of music history with respect to important movements that influence the patronage and function of music, musical devices, forms, and composers. No claim is made to exhaustiveness of the categories or of the items in each category. Only those facts that the authors believe to be pertinent to a basic understanding of the development of music have been included. No doubt teachers and others who use this outline will wish to supplement it with additional material. The following is a brief survey of the plan of each chapter.

I. SOCIOCULTURAL INFLUENCES ON MUSIC

Under this heading important trends and movements in such areas as religion, economics, government, and social and cultural life that seem to have a bearing on the patronage, types, and styles of music are set forth. Because such influences on music are perceived subjectively, only generalizations as to their relationships can be suggested.

II. FUNCTION OF MUSIC

Because composers usually write with a purpose in mind, and because various cultural conditions call for different types of music, the functions of music in a historical period are significant. Moreover, the economic conditions under which a composer lives are partially determined by the demand for, and support of, music with a specific function. Function has a great deal to do with the style and expressiveness of music.

III. STYLE AND PERFORMANCE PRACTICE

Seven fundamental features of music have been identified. Each feature is examined for its general stylistic qualities, as are any special devices or techniques that are prominent in the music itself. The features treated in this book are:
1. Formal organization
2. Melody
3. Rhythm
4. Harmony
5. Texture
6. Instrumentation and tone color
7. Practice and performance

IV. MUSIC FOR VOICES

Each important vocal form is defined, and the general characteristics of its musical substance is commented upon. In addition, specific examples which are representative of the form are suggested, together with available scores and recordings. In the case of more important forms, more than one example is given. The instructor, or student, may substitute or use additional examples as further illustrations. It is realized that no one form can be fully represented by one or two examples.

V. MUSIC FOR INSTRUMENTS

The same procedure is applied to instrumental forms. In those periods of music history in which instrumental forms predominate, this item in the outline will appear before the vocal forms.

VI. COMPOSERS

Composers of major importance are discussed briefly under this heading. They have been chosen because of the quality of their works, as well as for their innovations and influence. Biographies of these composers are presented in chronological order according to their dates of birth. Selected important works, scores, and recordings are mentioned. From the Classic period on, specific scores and recordings are omitted due to the numerous editions and recordings from which to choose.

Other composers are presented in a chronological list by national origin, but without discussion. The authors are aware that this classification is arbitrary, and that it is often only an opinion that places them in one or the other list.

VII. HISTORIANS, THEORISTS, AND MANUSCRIPT SOURCES

Throughout history, writers on music have provided illuminating accounts of the musical environments of their times. These accounts are important sources for understanding musical styles. With few exceptions, only those writers whose works serve these purposes have been included. Title, place, and date of publication information is given. In addition, a brief statement regarding the contents of the writings is made where pertinent.

Especially in the earlier periods, the only sources for music itself are collections of manuscripts, usually preserved in monasteries or universities. These are of great value to the scholar. For this reason manuscripts are identified in chapters up to and including the Renaissance. Music treatises and printed books dealing with music theory and history are cited thereafter.

Supplementary Readings

Collateral readings and current major texts on music history, as well as specialized studies in the various periods, are listed below. In addition, Appendix 3 contains bibliographical entries relevant to each chapter.

Abraham, Gerald. *The Concise Oxford History of Music*. New York: Oxford University Press, 1979.

Austin, William W. *Music in the 20th Century*. New York: W. W. Norton, 1966.

Borroff, Edith. *Music in Europe and the United States*. Engelwood Cliffs, NJ: Prentice-Hall Inc., 1971.

Bukofzer, Manfred E. *Music in the Baroque Era*. New York: W. W. Norton, 1947.

Cannon, Beekman C., Alvin H. Johnson, and William C. Waite. *The Art of Music*. New York: Crowell, 1960.

Crocker, Richard L. *A History of Musical Style*. New York: Dover, 1986.

Einstein, Alfred. *Music in the Romantic Era*. New York: W. W. Norton, 1947.

Grout, Donald Jay, and Claude Palisca. *A History of Western Music*. 4th ed. New York: W. W. Norton, 1988.

Hansen, Peter. *Introduction to Twentieth Century Music*. 4th ed. New York: Allyn & Bacon, 1978.

Hoppin, Richard H. *Medieval Music*. New York: W. W. Norton, 1978.

Lang, Paul Henry. *Music in Western Civilization*. W. W. Norton, 1941.

Machlis, Joseph. *Introduction to Contemporary Music*. 2nd ed. New York: W. W. Norton, 1979.

Reese, Gustave. *Music in the Middle Ages*. New York: W. W. Norton, 1940.

Reese, Gustave. *Music in the Renaissance*. rev. ed. New York: W. W. Norton, 1959.

Rosenstiel, Leonie, ed. *Schirmer History of Music*. New York: Schirmer Books, 1982.

Sachs, Curt. *Rise of Music in the Ancient World, East and West*. New York: W. W. Norton, 1943.

Stevens, Denis, ed. *History of Song*. rev. New York: W. W. Norton, 1970.

Strunk, Oliver. *Source Readings in Music History*. New York: W. W. Norton, 1950.

Wold, Milo, et al. *An Introduction to Music and Art in the Western World*. 8th ed. Dubuque, Iowa: Wm. C. Brown Co., 1987.

Basic References

Baker's Biographical Dictionary of Musicians. 6th ed. New York: Schirmer, 1978. (Dates and spellings in the present volume are according to *Baker's Dictionary*.)

Blume, Friedrich, ed. *Die Musik in Geschichte und Gegenwart*. Kassel: Bärenreiter, 1945.

Hitchcock, H. Wiley, and Stanley Sadie, ed. *The New Grove Dictionary of American Music*. London: MacMillan Press, 1986.

New Oxford History of Music. 10 vols. London: Oxford, 1954–1975. The volumes are: I. Ancient and Oriental Music. (1957); II. Early Medieval Music up to 1300. (rev. 1965); III. Ars Nova and the Renaissance, 1300–1540. (1960); IV. The Age of Humanism, 1540–1630. (1968); V. Opera and Church Music, 1630–1750. (1975); VI. Concert Music, 1630–1750.

(1986); VII. The Age of Enlightenment, 1745–1790. (1973); VIII. The Age of Beethoven, 1790–1830. (1982); IX. Romanticism, 1830–1890. (not yet published); and X. The Modern Age, 1890–1960. (1974).

Randel, Don, ed. *The New Harvard Dictionary of Music.* Cambridge: Harvard University Press, 1986.

Sadie, Stanley, ed. *New Grove Dictionary of Music and Musicians.* 20 vols. London: MacMillan, 1980. This edition of Grove is by far the most comprehensive in the English language. It contains extended articles on every facet of music as well as complete biographical sketches.

Thompson, Oscar, *International Cyclopedia of Music and Musicians.* 10th ed. Edited by Oscar Thompson and Bruce Bohle. New York: W. W. Dodd, 1975.

Scores and Recordings

Burkhardt, Charles. *Anthology for Musical Analysis.* 2nd ed. New York: Holt, Rinehart and Winston, 1972.

Davison, Archibald and Willi Apel. *Historical Anthology of Music.* 2 vols. Cambridge: Harvard University Press, 1946. (Examples nos. 9 through 41 in vol. 1, are recorded on the Orpheus label. Examples 42 through 181 are recorded on the Pleiades label.)

Gleason, Harold and Warren Becker. *Examples of Music Before 1400.* 2nd ed. Van Nuys, CA.: Alfred, 1987.

History of Music in Sound. 10 vols. London: Oxford, 1953. Recorded by RCA. (This anthology contains only partial scores, but the recordings are complete.)

Kamien, Roger. *Norton Scores.* exp. ed. 2 vols. New York: W. W. Norton, 1970.

Lerner, Edward R. *Study Scores of Musical Style.* New York: McGraw-Hill Book Company, 1968.

Parrish, Carl. *Treasury of Early Music.* New York: W. W. Norton, 1964. These examples were recorded by the Haydn Society. (Available in paperback form.)

Parrish, Carl, and John F. Ohl. *Masterpieces of Music before 1750.* New York: W. W. Norton, 1951. These examples were recorded by the Haydn Society.

Schering, Arnold. *Geschichte der Musik in Beispielen.* Leipzig: Breitkopf and Härtel, 1931.

Starr, William J., and George F. Devine. *Omnibus.* parts 1 and 2. Englewood Cliffs: Prentice-Hall, Inc., 1964.

Anthologies

Cohen, Albert, and John D. White. *Anthology of Music for Analysis.* New York: Appleton Century Crofts, 1965.

Fellerer, Karl Gustav, ed. *Anthology of Music.* 47 vol. Cologne: Arno Volk Verlag, begun in 1959.

Hardy, Gordon, and Arnold Fish. *Music Literature.* 2 vols. New York: Dodd, Mead and Co., 1966.

Hoppin, Richard H. *Anthology of Medieval Music.* New York: W. W. Norton, 1978.

Lang, Paul Henry. *The Concerto 1800–1900*. New York: W. W. Norton, 1969.

Lang, Paul Henry. *The Symphony 1800–1900*. New York: W. W. Norton, 1969.

Wennerstrom, Mary H. *Anthology of Twentieth Century Music*. New York: Appleton Century Crofts, 1969.

Norton Critical Scores. New York: W. W. Norton. Various dates. Each volume contains an authoritative study-size score of a major musical work and a comprehensive body of materials for the study of the work.

Norton Anthology of Western Music. 2nd ed. 1988. Two volumes edited by Claude V. Palisca have been published by W. W. Norton to accompany the fourth edition of *A History of Western Music* by Grout and Palisca. The scores found in these two volumes are discussed briefly in the Grout text. A partial recording of the *Norton Anthology of Western Music* is also available.

Recordings of a number of examples of early music are to be found in the *Archive Productions* of the Deutsche Grammaphon Gesellschaft, as well as under *Heritage, Folkways* and *Nonesuch* labels.

SEVENTH
EDITION

An
Outline
History
of
WESTERN
MUSIC

Chinese Musicians: a wall painting from the caves of Tung-chuan in the province of Kan-su from the time of the Tang dynasty (618–907). Pictured above are a variety of Chinese instruments. While no notation or instruments of this period remain today, the picture reveals a high degree of instrumental development. (Bärenreiter-Bildarchiv)

1
Chronology
of Ancient Sources of Western Music

B.C.

c. 1010	David, King of the Jews (c. 1010–c. 974)
c. 974	Solomon (c. 974–c. 937)
c. 582	Pythagoras (c. 582–c. 483)
c. 563	Buddha (c. 563–c. 483)
c. 551	Confucius (c. 551–479)
525	Aeschylus (525–456)
c. 496	Sophocles (c. 496–406)
490	Persian Wars
	Phidias (c. 490–432)
470	Socrates (470–390)
427	Plato (427–347)
404	Athens at war with Sparta

390	Praxiteles (390–330)
384	Aristotle (384–322)
c. 360	Lysippus (c. 360–c. 316)
356	Alexander the Great (356–323)
106	Marcus Tullius Cicero (106–43)
100	Julius Caesar (100–44)
70	Publius Virgil (70–19)
4	Birth of Christ

A.D.

c. 274	Constantine I—The Great (c. 274–337)
313	Edict of Milan
325	First Council of Nicaea
c. 570	Mohammed (c. 570–632)

1
Ancient Sources
of Western Music

I. SOCIOCULTURAL INFLUENCES ON MUSIC

Knowledge of the music of the cultures preceding modern western European culture is at best sketchy. Without some method of notation, the preservation of music must depend on oral tradition. That tradition affects our knowledge of ancient music. Prior to the Romanesque period, no system of notation existed that would enable modern scholars to reconstruct more than a few melodic fragments with any degree of certainty. Music among primitive as well as civilized peoples existed principally as a form of free improvisation.

The best sources of study for music of ancient times are only partially adequate. First, the study of musical practices of twentieth century primitive groups, such as the various African, North and South American Indian, and Oceanic tribes, allows scholars to reconstruct in part the music of early civilizations. Second, insight may be gained by studying the musical practices of ancient civilized peoples whose cultural institutions are in some measure still in existence today, such as the Chinese, Indian, Indonesian, and Japanese. The third source of study for reconstructing ancient music is the study of visual representations of instruments, fragments of notation, writings about music, and the few examples of ancient instruments still intact. Such material has been used particularly in the study of music of the Mediterranean peoples—Egyptians, Hebrews, and Greeks.

During the past fifty years and especially since the middle of the twentieth century, there has been a surge of interest in the musical expressions of folk and non-western cultures. The influence of this music on popular and classical music of Europe and America was apparent in the nineteenth century, but has become more pronounced since 1950. Performances of native groups from those countries where folk music has been able to maintain itself in the face of the widespread dissemination of the western tradition have acquainted the general public as well as creative musicians with rhythms, melodic systems, and timbres which were previously unknown to the world of Western art music.

It is difficult to determine the historical development of non-western music. Over the centuries, most musical expression has been orally transmitted. It is undoubtedly true that ritualistic music is of ancient origin. However, much primitive music that is heard today has been influenced by European tradition, especially through the pervasive presence of radio, recordings, motion pictures, and television.

It seems clear that few cultures prior to that of modern western Europe used music as a purely independent art form. Music as an expressive medium is, however, as old as humanity. Like the pictorial and plastic expressions of cave paintings, rock carvings, sculptures, ceramics, design, and painting, music was closely associated with the rites of the community as well as with the emotional expressions of individuals. Most references to music, whether in written or pictorial form, lead us to believe that its practice was particularly dependent on the attitudes and practices of the dominant religious organization of each culture. This does not exclude, however, a widespread use of music for secular purposes. The attitude of the dominant religion determined not only whether music was to be part of religious worship, banned, or merely tolerated. It also determined the kind of music that was permissible, its manner of presentation, and the instruments to be employed.

Instrumental music was a part of the temple services of the ancient Hebrews, with professional musicians in charge of the musical performance. Scriptural passages from the Old Testament were chanted. There are indications that antiphonal singing as well as sung responses by congregations were commonly used. These practices as well as hymn singing were unquestionably of great influence on the early Christians and the role of music in their religious services, where chant played the dominant musical role for over a thousand years.

Seasonal and geographic considerations often determined features of musical practice. Occupational choices and habits were vitally affected by geographic location, and occupations in turn have been influential on folk music as well as classical music of all peoples. Economic factors such as wealth, natural resources available for musical instruments, and skill of construction has influence in determining musical development as well. Such influences are found in the music of all early cultures, and remnants of these sociocultural forces still determine the use of music in the western world.

antiphone - verse or song to be sung in response

Picture on a Greek urn of a man playing the lyra, a simple form of a harp-like string instrument of the very early Greeks. The amphora or Greek wine jar served as a medium for painting among the ancient Greeks, and remains of these artifacts record many aspects of Greek life, among them musical instruments and performance. The Lyra had a sound box usually made of a tortoise shell and the strings were struck with a plectrum which is depicted here in the right hand of the performer. (The Metropolitan Museum of Art, Rogers Fund, 1922)

m.) Guess - 600-500 BC ?

The Greeks ascribed certain ethical values to their music, depending on the tonal relationships within the scales of the modes on which the melodies were built. Melodies in one mode were considered effeminate and damaging to the morals of youth, while melodies in another mode were thought to be stimulating to warlike action. Plato in his *Republic* and the *Laws* assigned a vital role to the type of music that could be used in education.

II. FUNCTION OF MUSIC

In primitive societies music and ritual were closely connected. Repetitious incantations and instrumental rhythms commonly accompanied religious rites and festivals, achieving a hypnotic or magical character. In ancient civilized societies too, music was mainly associated with religious rituals.

An outgrowth of the combination of music and religious ritual was the musical drama and incidental music in spoken drama. The musical dramas of the Chinese represent a highly developed relationship between music and dramatic presentation. In Greece, music played an important role in the performance of the dramatic works of the classic theater. Unfortunately, there is little or no knowledge of the nature of the music or its precise use.

From paintings, reliefs, and the writings of ancient peoples it also is apparent that secular music existed. Several kinds of secular music, including folk song and dance, were used for festive occasions. Not surprisingly, songs about human experiences such as love and work were present in ancient civilizations.

III. STYLE AND PERFORMANCE PRACTICE

In ancient cultures music was the servant of religious, ritualistic, and festive events that dictated the melodic and rhythmic character of the music. These events also influenced musical structure and the choice of instrumental and vocal timbres. A major difference between music of early Eastern cultures, primitive peoples, and early western European musical tradition was the tendency for Eastern musicians to express themselves in a seemingly unending, repetitive, and rhapsodical manner. In contrast, western composers shaped their music in more clear and formal structures. The repetitive quality of Eastern music was a result of the desire to lend hypnotic expression to their magical and religious rites.

Formal Organization

Generally speaking, the music was based on melodic or rhythmic patterns which constituted a point of departure for the performer, who improvised rather freely. The formal organization was the outcome of repetition and rhapsodic variation.

Melody

Melody was one of two dominant elements of music, the other being rhythm. Although often based on traditional fragments or patterns, the art of the singer consisted of spinning out variations in decorative arabesques, characteristic of most non-western music. Trills, turns, and florid scale passages were the main features of the melodic line. Melody had a seemingly unending character in the music of non-western peoples. This character distinguishes it from the melodic expression of western music.

As far as can be determined, most non-western societies have constructed their melodic patterns on a selection of five tones within the octave, a system of melodic construction known as pentatonic. The music of present-day Oriental cultures is built on such a five-tone division of the octave, closely resembling the relationships represented by the first, second, third, fifth, and sixth tones of the modern major scale. Their music did not include the half-step interval found between the third and fourth and the seventh and eighth tones in the modern major scale. However, many Oriental systems divided this pentatonic scale into very small intervals representing one-fourth, one-eighth, and even one-sixteenth of a modern whole step. On the other hand, some Indian cultures divide the octave into as many as twenty-two intervals.

Writings of the Greeks indicate a vast knowledge of music theory. They had available, through scientific discovery, the twelve tones of the octave which constitute the modern chromatic scale. Their melodies were based on a system of tetrachords which, when performed in sequence, resulted in an octave scale of seven tones similar to those in the modern major scale. Since each of the seven tones might be used as the fundamental tone, a series of seven different modal scales was theoretically possible for the construction of a melody. These were the scales or modes to which the Greeks ascribed ethical values.

Rhythm

The second important element of non-western music was rhythm. In many respects, rhythmic patterns among primitive as well as civilized groups achieved a complexity that western civilization did not cultivate until the present century. Rhythm in music includes quantitative—long and short—beats, as well as qualitative—strong and weak—beats. Irregular rhythmic patterns of seven, ten, and fourteen, for example, are common, especially in India.

Among some African groups the development and cultivation of rhythmic expression resulted in extremely complicated patterns, some of which conveyed specific meanings. In addition to the music of Africa, polyrhythmic expression is frequent in the music of the Javanese and Balinese.

Harmony

In the modern sense of the term, harmony was nonexistent in ancient music. However, drones and ostinato patterns were probably more widely used than heretofore realized. This is particularly true of the music of southeastern Asiatic societies such as Java and Bali.

Texture

A variety of musical textures resulted from the combinations of voices and instruments performing the same melody. Accounts and pictures of hundreds of instrumentalists and singers points to an interest in heterophonic texture. Such performances likely duplicated the same melodic patterns at the unison or octave, or even at other intervals.

Instrumentation and Tone Color

Music and words were closely connected in early musical performance, and it is obvious that the voice was an important medium of expression. Wind, string, and percussion instruments accompanied the voice, generally at the unison or octave. Percussion instruments were made of wood, metal, stone, and even of vegetable fiber such as gourds. They were divided into groups which were accurately pitched according to chosen scales and those which had no such pitch differentiation. Many of the tuned instruments of these cultures made use of pitches based on intervals smaller than the half steps common to western music.

Bowed string instruments were of relatively simple construction, normally made with only one string. Plucked strings reached a high state of perfection second only to percussion instruments. Much skill was required in both their construction and performance.

The least developed of the non-western instruments were the winds that correspond to our present brass and woodwind types. The brasses never advanced beyond a simple natural form (i.e., without valves or slides). They were made of metal, bone, and wood, the primitive mouthpieces being part of the horns themselves. There was a great variety of woodwind instruments, including flutes and reeds. Some were simply made folk instruments; others were elaborately constructed.

All performance practices in ancient music relied on the oral traditions of their cultures. This was necessary because there was no fixed system of written musical notation. The selection of instruments, voices, dynamics, and tempi was determined by contemporaneous taste and tradition. In ancient writings, references to musical performance indicate that particular instruments were used only for certain occasions due to the association of their timbre with moral and ethical values.

It is probable that the voice also was used in a different fashion from the European tradition. Judging from practices now in use in cultures other than those of western Europe, various tonal qualities were cultivated by such practices as tightening of the throat passage, falsetto, and guttural grunts. Among most non-western peoples, especially the east Asians, the use of the voice suggests that it is desirable to make singing as different from speech as possible. The eastern singer's vocal technique results in sounds that persons in the western world associate with nasality and restricted resonance. In contrast, vocal technique in western singing attempts to produce a sustained, refined, and fully resonant speech. Based on the evidence of present-day performance of African, Indian, and western Oriental music, it is probable that a strikingly high perfection of performance skill was achieved in the use of percussion instruments in ancient cultures.

IV. MUSIC FOR VOICES

The improvisational character of ancient vocal music precluded most set formal structure. Furthermore, the absence of notated examples gives us no basis for reconstruction of formal designs, if any existed. It is therefore impossible to speak about vocal forms beyond the fact that vocal music, both sacred and secular, was used. It is likely that the narrative nature of the vocal texts influenced the musical form. The written and pictorial records of the time give evidence of accompanied vocal music as well as helpful information about instrumental music.

V. MUSIC FOR INSTRUMENTS

In ancient times instrumental music, like vocal music, was improvisational, with no set forms. Purely instrumental music, unrelated to song or dance, was found in some instances. The orchestral groups of percussion instruments used in Java and Bali are notable examples. Instrumental music was usually descriptive and illustrative of poetic or pictorial ideas, as illustrated by the flute and zither music of China and Japan.

VI. COMPOSERS

There is no written record of any composers or extant musical works from this period. Accounts of performers such as David in the Old Testament are the only records which would give any indication of composers as such, since every performer was in fact a composer.

While there are no specific composers to whom compositions can be attributed, examples of ancient music do exist. Volume 1 of *The History of Music in Sound* gives fifty-two short examples of the music of ancient cultures from the early music of China to that of Greece and Islam. (Rec. 1.1)

Examples of recorded non-western music can also be found in the UNESCO collections of *Music in the Orient and Africa* issued under the labels of Bärenreiter-Musicaphon and Phillips. (See Schwann Foreign Catalog.) Numerous further examples can be found under the Folkways label.

VII. HISTORIANS, THEORISTS, AND MANUSCRIPT SOURCES

Early writers dealt with music either as a mathematical-theoretical system or as a philosophical-ethical matter. Among the former the most important are those who based their theories on the work of Pythagoras, the early Greek mathematician and theoritician concerning the harmony of the spheres. Among the latter the most extensive writings are those of the Greek philosophers, although references to music can be found in the works of many ancient writers—Chinese, Indian, Hebrew, and others. What few examples of notated Greek music there are have been deciphered from inscriptions on stone.

Pythagoras (c. 582–B.C.–c. 500 B.C.) was a Greek philosopher and mathematician to whom is ascribed the discovery of pitch ratios. For centuries only the octave and fifth were considered pure consonances. There is no record of any of Pythagoras' writings and his theories are known only as they were developed by his followers.

Plato (427 B.C.–347 B.C.) was the great Greek philosopher whose concern with music was almost entirely with its ethical values. Passages in *Timaeus* and the *Republic* state his concepts of music and its place in society.

Aristotle (384 B.C.–322 B.C.), a pupil of Plato, also concerned himself with the ethical values of music in several of his writings, notably in the *Politics.*

Aristoxenus (354 B.C.–?) was the most important of the Greek writers on music. Two works, *Harmonic Elements* and *Elements of Rhythmics,* have come down to us, the first complete, the second in fragmentary form. An English edition of these works translated by H. S. Macran was published in 1902.

Cleonides (first half of the second century A.D.) was a Greek writer whose *Harmonic Introduction* was a source of information for Renaissance musicians on classic Greek music. An edition of it was published in Venice in 1497.

Aristedes Quintillianus flourished around 200 A.D. His treatise *De Musica Libri VII* provides a basic source for knowledge of the music of ancient Greece. A German translation by Schafke was published in 1937.

Athenaeus (200 A.D.) was a Greek writer who lived in Rome. While he was not a musician his descriptions of musical performance in *Sophists at Dinner* are a valuable source for insight into the place of music in Roman life.

Excerpts from most of the foregoing writings may be found in Strunk, *Source Readings in Music History.*

King David playing the rotta; an eighth century miniature from the Canterbury Psalterium. The rotta was a medieval instrument referred to in very early sources. It was probably a psaltery on which the strings, like those of the harp, were plucked by the fingers. Other medieval instruments are pictured: four zinks or cornetti and two small straight flutes or recorders. The clapping dancers at the bottom of the picture suggest that the music being played is secular in nature. (British Museum)

2
Chronology
of the Early Middle Ages

354	St. Augustine (354–430)	912	Otto the Great (912–1073)
c. 480	Boethius (c. 480–524)	c. 997	Guido of Arezzo (c. 997–1050)
c. 540	Pope Gregory (c. 540–604)	1073	Winchester Troper (1073)
	Gregorian Chant (c. 540–1100)	1079	Abelard (1079–1142)
650	Rise of Monasteries	1100	St. Martial Organum
742	Charlemagne (742–814)	1150	Troubadours
787	Second Council of Nicaea (787)		School of Notre Dame

2
Romanesque
Early Middle Ages (500-1100)

I. SOCIOCULTURAL INFLUENCES ON MUSIC

The term Romanesque is generally used to describe the medieval style of art that was influenced by the Roman Empire. While the term is more accurately used to designate architecture, it is also commonly used to refer to that period of music that was dominated by monophony. While the monophonic chant continued its development beyond 1100, it began to lose its preeminence as a compositional style after the development of polyphony and the consequent introduction of harmony in Gothic music. Sacred monophony is generally referred to as plainsong, or chant, and as a performing style continues up to the present, especially in monastic settings.

Our knowledge of Romanesque music in general is based upon rather meager evidence. While we have examples of early sacred music which were notated and preserved by the Roman Catholic Church, its interpretation is open to question. This is due to a somewhat primitive system of notation, particularly in relation to rhythm. We have even fewer authentic examples of secular monophony because virtually all writings from the period were by monks, whose function it was to transcribe sacred texts and music.

Under the patronage of the Roman Catholic Church, music was organized according to the needs of the liturgical service. The many monastic orders that flourished during this period influenced that development and organization of sacred music. In keeping with liturgical practice, the music was set to an ecclesiastical Latin text.

In general, the music of the Byzantine church took its forms and liturgical order from the early Apostolic church and the Jewish service, but modern scholarship is in doubt as to the exact details of such connections. There is also doubt about the degree to which instrumental music was employed in church services. This derives from the fact that only music with texts was sanctioned by the church fathers, and notated in the manuscripts of the period. The apparent absence of instrumental music in the church has been interpreted by some as evidence of the medieval ascetic denial of the physical.

The most important influence on music outside the church during the middle ages was feudalism, which gave rise to a society with a well-developed social consciousness. A large body of secular music and poetry in the vernacular was derived from society's entertainments and the desire for self-expression outside the confines of the Church.

II. FUNCTION OF MUSIC

In keeping with the "other-worldly" spirit of early Christianity, sacred plainsong in the Romanesque period expressed a simple faith in God. This function was achieved by the musical setting of portions of all rituals of the Church, the most important of which was the Mass. Other rituals that also used music were the Divine Offices or canonical hours, such as matins, lauds, and vespers. The music of the vespers, which includes the Magnificat, was to become especially important.

The liturgy of the Roman Catholic Mass called for the musical setting of eleven texts; the remaining texts were spoken. The musical settings were divided into two parts. One part, the Ordinary, consisting of the Kyrie, Gloria, Credo, Sanctus, Agnus Dei (Benedictus), and the Ite missa est, used an invariable text. The other part, the Proper, used variable texts in accordance with the church calendar. It consisted of the Introit, Gradual, Alleluia, Offertory, and Communion.

In addition to the Mass and the Divine Offices, plainsong was used extensively in musical settings of hymns, psalms, and tropes. These tropes, nonliturgical texts and music, were inserted between words of liturgical texts.

Much less is known about secular music. It did exist and was used for dancing, to chronicle news events, and as a vehicle for the expression of folk tradition.

III. STYLE AND PERFORMANCE PRACTICE
Formal Organization

The organization and forms of sacred plainsong were determined by the Latin text of the liturgy. In a few instances, mainly in tropes and sequences, the organization was based on freely composed melodic configurations, with little regard for the natural accents of the

Example 1. Chart of modes

language. The forms of secular monophony were also determined by the text, but these texts were most often poetic, and consequently, the music reveals such patterns as verse with refrain or repeated melodic phrases.

Melody

Plainsong consists of a monophonic melody set to a sacred text. It has a restricted range, seldom extending beyond an octave.

Plainsong melodies were constructed on the intervallic relationships of the church modes (Ex. 1). These modes differ from one another by the order of steps and half steps within the octave. All the modes are organized around a dominant or reciting tone, and a final or ending pitch. Four modes: I, III, V, and VII are the authentic modes. The order of steps and half steps in these modes corresponds to the diatonic octave scales based on D (mode I), E (mode III), F (mode V), and G (mode VII) as illustrated in Example 1. These modes, however, can be transposed to begin on any pitch. Each authentic mode had a corresponding plagal mode. Each pair of modes, I and II, III and IV, V and VI, and VII and VIII, had the same final. The overriding difference between an authentic mode and its corresponding plagal mode was the range or ambitus. The authentic mode had a range within the octave of its final. The plagal mode had a range within the octave of the fourth below its final to a fifth above. The secondary principal tone in each mode was called the dominant.

Some plainsong chants, especially those for psalm settings, made use of a reciting tone. This is a tone upon which most of the syllables of the chant are executed and is usually the dominant of the mode. This syllabic chant is one of three plainsong types. In it each note is set to a syllable of the text. A second type, called neumatic, is one in which a small group of notes are sung to one syllable. Florid, or melismatic chant, is a third type in which extended groups of notes are set to one syllable.

Secular monophony often used a wider range of notes than plainsong. This melodic type was not restricted by the church modes and often approaches tonality. It was usually cast in regular phrases, while plainsong was more irregular.

Rhythm

Plainsong rhythm was determined by the rhythmic flow of the prose, which includes the long and short syllabic values of ecclesiastical Latin. As a consequence, metric patterns are absent in sacred monophony. In contrast, secular monophony used the vernacular in which there are more qualitative accents, and its rhythm is most often metric.

Harmony

There was no systematic harmonic practice during the Romanesque. However, both sacred and secular monophony were accompanied on occasion by instruments and consequently some performance practices, such as drone bass and ostinato figures, were probably present.

As early as the ninth century a practice of singing in parallel fourths and fifths began and was called *organum*. Several types developed that were variously named. They all had the common characteristic of using a preexisting chant (*vox principalis*) to which was added one or more melodic lines. Parallel organum added a second voice (*vox organalis*) fixed at the interval of a fifth or fourth below the vox principalis (Ex. 2).

Example 2. *Sit gloriosa* (parallel organum)

King David playing the organ and *Pope Gregory dictating music.* The organ was one of the few acceptable instruments for religious services in the Middle Ages. King David is often represented as a performer on the organ. Pope Gregory is shown receiving the inspiration of the Holy Spirit, portrayed as a dove, as he dictates the music of the chant. In actuality, he did not write chants, but was responsible for their codification and preservation. (The Bettmann Archive)

Free organum employed contrary and oblique motion in the vox organalis (Ex. 3), whereas a later type, melismatic organum, used elaborate decorative note groups in the vox organalis against the very slow

Example 3. *Cunctipotens genitor* (free organum)

moving values of the vox principalis (Ex. 4). All styles of organum emphasized the use of the perfect intervals of the unison, fourth, fifth and octave at cadential points.

Example 4. *Cunctipotens genitor* (melismatic organum)

Texture

Since sacred plainsong was monophonic, there was no texture in the sense of a combination of lines or tonal coloring of later music. However, the austere line of plainsong sung by the priest, or the chant sung in unison or organum by a choir, created a mystic simplicity of linear sound that complemented the stark simplicity of the Romanesque cathedral. A fuller texture was created in secular monophony with its frequent use of instruments. Combined with a wider range, more definite rhythmic patterns, and vernacular texts it expresses a widening range of human feelings and emotions.

Instrumentation and Tone Color

Sacred plainsong was always vocal. While there is some evidence that instruments were occasionally used as accompaniment, as a rule instruments were prohibited in the Romanesque church. The preponderance of secular monophony was vocal, but it was often accompanied by instruments, especially when used as dance music. The instruments used in secular music were plucked and bowed strings, and a variety of wind and percussion instruments.

IV. MUSIC FOR VOICES

There were five important types of sacred plainsong, or chant in this era. Collections of these chants formed the basis of musical practice in the areas of their origin. (Rec. 2.1–2.7) (1) Byzantine chant was the earliest form of chant developed after the establishment of the Eastern church by Constantine. It is still sung in the Greek Orthodox church. (2) The Ambrosian chant, named for Bishop Ambrose of Milan, comes from northern Italy. (3) Gallican chant was used in France until about 800; no notated manuscripts of it survive. (4) Mozarabic chant was the chant of Spain, with origins prior to the eighth century. (5) Gregorian chant has been the most widely used, and is so named because it was collected and organized under the leadership of Pope Gregory (c. 540–604). As religious power was consolidated in Rome, Gregorian chant became the prescribed form of chant for liturgical services throughout the Roman Catholic world.

Psalm settings constitute one of the most important bodies of plainsong literature for the Mass and the Divine Office hours. There are three types of psalm settings, defined according to the practice of performance: (1) In responsorial chant a soloist sings the verse and is answered by a choir; (2) In antiphonal singing the choir is divided into two groups singing alternately; and (3) In direct psalmody the psalm is sung with no refrain by a soloist or a choir.

It is probable that sacred plainsong was sung with little or no vibrato and with the falsetto male voice. Only male singers were permitted to participate in the liturgy. Chants of the Mass and hours of the Divine Office were sung by the clergy, but the congregation joined in the singing of hymns and some processional chants.

A technique to aid sight-singing, called the hexachord system, was perfected by Guido d' Arezzo in the eleventh century. The six tones of the hexachord were designated by six syllables in order, from the lowest to the highest—ut, re, mi, fa, sol, la—corresponding to the first syllables of successive lines of a hymn to St. John the Baptist (Ex. 5). A system of overlapping hexachords was devised that enabled the singer to sing melodies that lay outside the range of a single hexachord.

Example 5. *The hymn "Ut queant laxis,"* the source of Guido's solmization system

The practice of singing in parallel fifths and fourths, called organum, was probably improvised. While it is generally associated with sacred music, there is evidence that it was also practiced in secular music as well. Later developments brought the practice of contrary motion and the use of nonperfect intervals. (See Examples 3 and 4.) By the end of the eleventh century, organum was so well established that it was referred to in theoretical treatises. Rules were established for avoiding the tritone (the augmented fourth), for arriving at unison cadences, and for identifying those parts of the liturgical chant that were permitted to be used in this manner. The practice of organum led directly to the development of polyphonic forms in the Gothic.

Single Movement Forms and Structural Procedures

With few exceptions, the musical form and organization of specific plainsong chants were based solely on the form of the text. Any suggestion of A B A or similar formulae was the result of textual considerations. There were some traditions that placed specific texts in certain of the church modes and naturally those chants set to the same texts show a degree of similarity. However, there are few distinguishable forms as such. The monophonic Mass is not a true musical form, but rather a composite, a collection of appropriate chant settings of the Ordinary and Proper of the Mass. (Rec. 2.8)

Among these single movement forms or procedures are the following:

Antiphon. A short sentence of scripture or other sacred verse sung both before and after the psalm, and after each pair of verses within the psalm. The formal effect was that of a refrain to the psalm. It was mostly in syllabic style. (Rec. 2.9–2.10)

Alleluia. The alleluia is added at the ends of sections of many chants. It consists of a refrain on the word *alleluia,* and is followed by a verse or section with the refrain repeated. The *jubilus* is a vocal elaboration on the final vowel of the *alleluia* that provides a strong impetus for musical form. (Rec. 2.11–2.12)

Trope. Music with a nonliturgical text inserted between phrases of liturgical text is called a trope. The words provide a commentary on the liturgy. The trope is a musical type that allowed for creative musical expression within the rather rigidly defined liturgy of the church. The practice of interpolating tropes gradually fell into disuse, and they were finally abolished by the Council of Trent in the middle of the sixteenth century. (Rec. 2.13–2.15)

Sequence. The sequence evolved from the practice of troping, and consisted of added poetic words to the final jubilus of the alleluia, replacing the verse that followed the alleluia. The texts that provided the musical incentive were usually long and in a free style with repeated sections. Such formulas as A BB CC DD E were common and represented independent compositions. Like the trope, the sequence evolved toward secularism. Eventually only five sequences were retained in the body of Church music. (Rec. 2.16–2.18)

Conductus. The monophonic conductus was probably first sung while a participant in the Mass or liturgical drama was "conducted" or moved from one place to another in the altar area of the church. The text was metric, and not liturgical. The melody was not taken from a chant collection, and was freely composed. While this form was first associated with the Church, it soon became a secular form, and the title was applied to almost any Latin song of a serious nature. (Rec. 2.19)

All of the foregoing types had their origins in sacred music. Secular monophony of the period up to 1100 has not been preserved as well as that of sacred music. No doubt this was largely due to the fact that there was no institution whose duty it was to maintain and preserve this music, as was the case in sacred music.

It is known that secular monophony flourished during the Romanesque period through the songs of the goliards, jongleurs, and minstrels. Some of the most important of these songs were those of the goliards who were wandering scholars. The most noted collection of goliard poems is *Carmina Burana,* made famous in modern times by Carl Orff. Of the goliard songs that survive today, most exist only as poems without music. Among these is *O Admirable Veneris,* which dates from the tenth century. Its melody also appears as *O Roma Nobilis.* It is metric and in strophic form with a refrain. (Rec. 2.20)

The jongleurs and minstrels were itinerant performers who entertained with song, dance, tricks, and juggling. While they cannot be considered either poets or composers, they sang verses in the vernacular. One of the early types of jongleur song was the *Chanson de Geste,* a narrative song telling of heroic deeds. The most famous of these is the *Song of Roland,* which became a national epic of France. Unfortunately no authentic music has survived. It is probable that the jongleurs and minstrels helped spread the folk song tradition that ultimately made its way into art music.

V. MUSIC FOR INSTRUMENTS

While instrumental music was generally banned in the Church, it is known that organs existed in churches as early as 800. We do not know, however, how they were used, or what music was played. It is evident from manuscripts and pictorial representations that instruments were used in secular music both as accompaniment to song and independently as dance music. As is the case with all Romanesque secular music, we have little information about specific forms, as none of the music has survived in decipherable notation.

VI. COMPOSERS

Because of the improvisatory nature of early music, almost every performer was a composer. This was especially true in secular music and no doubt the same procedure was responsible for the origin of most of the chants that later became traditional. It is known, however, that the following were composers of some stature and influence during the Romanesque period.

Notker Balbulus (c. 840–912) was one of the earliest composers identified by name. (The word "balbulus" is the Latin word for stammerer.) He was especially known as a composer of sequences. (Rec. 2.21)

Wipo of Burgundy (d. 1048) The sequence for Easter, *Victimae paschali laudes,* still in use today, is by Wipo. (Rec. 2.22)

Hermannus Contractus (1013–1054), also known as Herman the Cripple, was a theorist as well as a composer. His *Alma Redemptoris Mater* achieved great popularity and became the basis for numerous monophonic and polyphonic works. (Rec. 2.23)

Abelard (1079–1142) is known to have made a collection of hymns for monks and nuns. One of these nuns, for whom his love is legendary, was the famous Heloise. Their love story has held the interest of the public for many centuries.

VII. HISTORIANS, THEORISTS, AND MANUSCRIPT SOURCES

Most early theoretical writings on music were either interpretations of the music theory of the ancients and the subsequent concept of music as a science or attempts to link music and religion by means of allegorical writings. They were not derived from contemporaneous musical practices.

Boethius (c. 480–524), one of the earliest theorists was also a philosopher and mathematician. His chief work was *De Institutione Musica,* in which he related the music of his time to the theories of the Greek philosophers.

Cassiodorus (c. 485–c. 580) was a historian, philosopher, statesman, and the founder of a monastery. His important contribution to the history of music was *Institutiones musicae,* written between 550 and 562.

Isidore of Seville (c. 560–636) was a Spanish scholar. His *Etymologiarum sive originum libri XX* is an encyclopedia of the arts with an account of liturgical music.

Odo of Cluny (879–942), an abbot in France, was a music theorist whose *Dialogus de Musica* contains an account of modes and medieval notation. He was the first to use letters to indicate pitches.

Guido d'Arezzo (c. 997–c. 1050), a Benedictine monk, was the most important writer of his time concerned with the actual practices of music. He dealt with the problems of notation and especially with the technique of singing. His numerous writings have been an important source for modern scholars in interpreting medieval music.

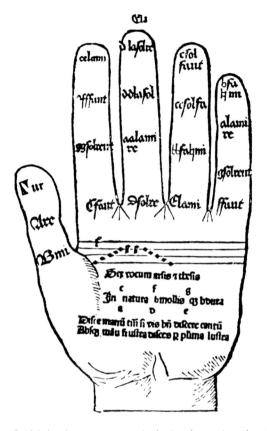

Guido's hand was a mnemonic device that assigned scale degrees (ut, re, mi, fa, sol, la) to various parts of the hand. It was used to help singers and other musicians with various aspects of music theory. Attributed to Guido, it remained in use for several centuries. (Art and History Archive)

He is popularly known today for the system of solmization based on the hymn *Ut queant laxis*. Related to it was the teaching aid known as the Guidonian Hand.

Musica enchiriadis (c. 900) is a treatise noteworthy for its description of early organum. Its authorship has never been established. For a long time it was thought to have been written by Hucbald (c. 840–930), but recent scholarship has determined that he is not the author. *Musica enchiriadis* covers the whole range of musical knowledge. Most of its material was borrowed from the ancients, including the concept of music as mathematics, the acceptance of Pythagorean theory of numbers, and the division of the scale according to intervallic ratios.

(The writings of the previously mentioned theorists are not readily available in English. Important excerpts from each can be found in Strunk, *Source Readings in Music History*.)

Winchester Troper: There is only one important extant collection of original manuscripts prior to 1100, the *Winchester Troper*. It is a liturgical book containing tropes and organum. These are part of the great literature of plainsong melody that has been in the process of being collected, edited, and published by the Benedictines of Solesmes since 1889. Sixteen volumes have been published in the *Paléographie Musicale*.

Further readings on these subjects are identified in the books included in the *Supplementary Reading List*, found in the Introduction, and in Appendix 3.

Cathedral at Amiens, France (c. 1225). An excellent example of the great thrust of Gothic architecture. The pointed arches which frame the massive entrance doors and cover the niches of the sculptured figures above the doorways, the greatly elongated openings of the belfry towers, the pointed decorated spires adorning the facade, and the topmost roof all give a breathless feeling of heavenly lift to this massive building.

3
Chronology
of the Late Middle Ages
(Ars Antiqua — Ars Nova)

1098	Abbess Hildegard von Bingen (1098–1197)	1265	Dante Alighieri (1265–1321)
1100	Crusades (1100–1300)		Ars Nova
c. 1155	Perotin (b. 1155–1160, d. 1200–1250)	c. 1290	Jean de Muris (c. 1290–c. 1351)
1160	Leonin (fl. 1160)	1291	Philippe de Vitry (1291–1361)
1182	St. Francis of Assisi (1182–1226)	1300	Guillaume de Machaut (c. 1300–1377)
	Organum (fl. 9th–12th century)		Marchetto da Padua (fl. 14th century)
1200	Trouvères, Troubadours, and Minnesingers (c. 1200)	1304	Francesco Petrarch (1304–1374)
	Ars Antiqua	1304	Papacy in Avignon
1227	St. Thomas Aquinas (1227–1274)	1313	Giovanni Boccacio (1313–1375)
c. 1237	Adam de la Halle (c. 1237–1287)	1325	Francesco Landini (1325–1397)
1250	Franco of Cologne (fl. 1250–1280)	c. 1340	Geoffrey Chaucer (c. 1340–1400)
c. 1260	Jacques de Liège (c. 1260–c. 1330)	c. 1348	The Black Death

3
Gothic — Late Middle Ages
(Ars Antiqua — Ars Nova)

I. SOCIOCULTURAL INFLUENCES ON MUSIC

The period from 1100 to about 1430 has been designated as Gothic mainly to describe architecture that is characterized by pointed arches, ribbed vaulting, and flying buttresses. The term was introduced by seventeenth century writers who looked upon this style as unclassical and vulgar. They associated it with the medieval Goths of northern Europe. At present, the term merely identifies the artistic style of the period without derogatory implications.

Two major musical contributions of the Gothic era are the rise and development of polyphonic forms and the merging of secular and sacred musical styles. In fact, many Gothic forms and musical practices relating to sacred music survived into the twentieth century. Because a system of notation was devised during this period, much Gothic music has been preserved. Consequently, modern scholars are able to recreate much of the music with authority and accuracy. The Gothic system of notation made it possible to represent accurately both rhythmic (mensural) and pitch notation.

The development of Gothic music was accelerated by a number of varied sociocultural movements that took place between 1100 and 1430. Among these was scholasticism, a medieval philosophy that systematized all intellectual and religious experience according to rigid rules of medieval logic. Its effect on religious music was two-fold. First, it regulated the theory and practice of music according to canons of acceptable practice in the Church. For example, triple rhythm was held to be more perfect than duple rhythm, and perfect intervals were ruled necessary on all strong beats, while dissonant intervals were generally avoided whenever possible. Second, scholasticism also controlled and codified the emotional content of sacred music. Church officials frowned upon ornate melodies because they felt such melodies obscured the meaning of the texts. Any move to make music more emotionally expressive was avoided because it appealed to the senses and not to the soul. Only after a long period of development were expressive qualities allowed in sacred music. Although scholasticism had little direct effect on secular music, there was an indirect influence inasmuch as church composers who rebelled against strict control found freedom in the secular style.

Western society was becoming more and more independent economically, intellectually, and artistically. People became skeptical of the authority of the Church to order and control all of life's activities. Communication with the East, the result of the Crusades (twelfth to the thirteenth centuries), opened new channels of trade, brought new wealth, new ideas, and new incentives for living. New social customs and cultural practices were eventually integrated into western civilization. As a consequence, a favorable climate for artistic development existed during the Gothic in contrast to the rather severe asceticism of earlier times. Entertainment outside the Church became widely cultivated. Even religious music was infused with the new humanism.

The rise of towns stimulated centers of learning in newly established universities, especially in England, the Netherlands, and France. Music became an integral part of education, first as a science and eventually as an art. As well as being associated with the church, the leaders and innovators of Gothic music were either at the universities or associated with the courts, where music was given great importance. Beginning with the Gothic period, musical leadership came from northern Europe instead of Italy where musical activity had been centered up to this time.

The Gothic period also saw the beginning of the struggle between church and state which, in effect, was a struggle between asceticism and humanism. In music it took the form of a conflict between the sacred and the secular, a conflict in which each style reached new heights of musical expressiveness.

II. FUNCTION OF MUSIC

Romanesque and Gothic sacred music served the same religious functions. In the Gothic era the same liturgical texts were set to music, but in polyphony instead of monophony. An important addition to sacred music was the motet, a form that was later to become one of the most important vocal polyphonic forms. The Gothic spirit precipitated a great program of church building, an activity that in turn led to an increased demand for church musicians. This demand lead to the establishment of schools such as St. Martial and Notre Dame where sacred music was especially cultivated.

Music took on increased importance in the fabric of Gothic society. The rise in the social status of secular music, demonstrated by the nobility of the troubadours and trouvères, shows the wide interest in vernacular secular song. The establishment of courts and the growing power of other secular institutions encouraged strong centers of secular culture in many medieval cities. This was the age of chivalry and the time when courtly love became the subject of lyric love songs. For the first time in music history, individual composers achieved recognition for their creative efforts. Moreover, the most significant developments in music have been traced to these secular composers.

III. STYLE AND PERFORMANCE PRACTICE

Although sacred plainsong and secular monophony continued in the Gothic, the growth and refinement of polyphonic style was the major concern of Gothic composers.This concern for a defined polyphony marked the beginning of the emancipation of music from its dependence on preexisting materials such as plainsong, a process that was to continue through the Renaissance.

In the twelfth century the Ars Antiqua composers of the School of Notre Dame, mainly Leonin and Perotin, were among the first to develop the basic rules of polyphony (counterpoint). A new movement emerged in France and Italy during the fourteenth century. It was called Ars Nova. In the new movement, rhythm was expanded by the acceptance of duple patterns. In harmony, the use of thirds and sixths were introduced and treated as dissonances.

Formal Organization

All vocal music was organized according to the poetic and syllabic considerations of the text. However, these were frequently made secondary to rhythmic and harmonic considerations. Less is known about instrumental music of this period, but it bears many of the characteristics of vocal forms.

Composers of sacred polyphony organized sections of text into complete units by means of short repeated rhythmic patterns called rhythmic modes. In the fourteenth century longer sections were combined on the basis of the isorhythmic principle, a repetition of longer and more complicated rhythmic patterns throughout a composition. Organum continued to be an important organizational principle, even after the introduction of contrary motion and elaborate melismatic settings.

Monophonic and polyphonic secular forms such as the rondeau, virelai, and ballad were known as "forms fixes." They were organized on the basis of two musical phrases combined in repeated patterns such as AB AB AB. Some other secular forms also contain a two-line refrain both at the beginning and at the end of each stanza. Those forms which used more than one stanza (strophe) of text to the same musical setting are referred to as strophic.

Secular polyphony made extensive use of canonic imitation as a means of formal organization. The most obvious example is the rondellus.

Melody

Gothic melody was vocal in style; that is, it tends to move stepwise within a limited range. Secular melodies and fourteenth-century sacred forms expanded that range somewhat. Sacred melody in polyphonic forms other than plainsong usually consisted of short phrases in repeated metric patterns, while secular melody, both monophonic and polyphonic, was often cast in longer phrases and was more lyric. There was no attempt to express the meaning of the text in sacred melody, but secular melody often captured the mood of the text.

All Gothic melodies, both monophonic and polyphonic, were modal. In the Ars Nova, however, secular songs had a tendency toward intervals that suggested tonality. A common melodic practice of many Ars Nova composers was to move from the leading tone to the sixth tone before proceeding to the tonic. This has been given the name Landini cadence even though the composer Landini did not initiate the practice (Ex. 6).

Example 6. A Landini cadence

Rhythm

Rhythmic development held the attention of all Gothic composers who were concerned with extending the expressiveness of music. To emancipate musical form from the rhythm of text and to gain some agreement of accent among the voices of polyphonic forms, it was necessary to invent some sort of rhythmic system that was independent of poetic rhythm. To that end composers devised a system by which rhythmic cohesion could be brought to a melody through repeated notational patterns called rhythmic modes. These rigidly repeated rhythmic patterns were usually separated by a rest before their repetition. There were six rhythmic modes, each identified by a number (Ex. 7). Some of these rhythmic modes are related to the rhythmic feet used in the analysis of poetry (e.g., iamb, dactyl, trochee). In some instances each polyphonic line was set to its own rhythmic mode. In the late Gothic (Ars Nova) these modes were extended to longer patterns which formed the basis of isorhythmic compositions. While the principle of rhythmic modes involved a series of exact repetitions, the practice was to introduce a degree of flexibility by varying the patterns.

Example 7. Rhythmic modes

Rhythmic patterns in triple meter were used extensively in sacred music, while secular forms had the freedom of employing either triple or duple meter. Many kinds of beat subdivisions appeared in the fourteenth century (Ars Nova) giving the rhythmic flow more freedom and subtlety. An especially remarkable device of the period was the "hocket," an alternating interruption of the rhythmic and melodic flow among the voices.

Harmony

All Gothic harmony was the result of polyphonic texture. Because there was no systematic chordal structure, there were often sharp and unresolved dissonances among the voices. This was partly due to the fact that, in the early Ars Nova, each of the upper voices related to the lowest voice and not to one another.

Because melodies were composed in modes, harmony was also modal, although secular polyphony on occasion tended toward major and minor tonality. The harmonic vocabulary was largely limited to the use of perfect fourths, fifths, and octaves. All other intervals were considered dissonant. In the Ars Nova, thirds and sixths were considered imperfect consonances and were utilized, first in secular forms and then in sacred music.

Chromaticism was generally avoided as an expressive device. Chromatic alterations were often introduced in cadences (Ex. 8), and were used to avoid the intervals of the augmented fourth or diminished fifth (called tritones) above the lowest tone. One aspect of chromaticism, the practice of *musica ficta* or false music, enabled performers to introduce flats or sharps into the modes in order to avoid certain intervals, or to make intervallic adjustments for the sake of "beauty."

Example 8. Avoiding a tritone using *musica ficta*

Texture

Polyphonic texture prevailed in almost all Medieval music after 1300. Prior to this time, secular music was monophonic and religious music was either set to traditional plainsong or organum, an early form of polyphony. Three-voice polyphony was the most common, but four voices were in frequent use by the end of the fourteenth century.

Crucifixion of St. Andrew. This page of a Flemish-Rhenish Antiphonary (circa 1230–40) illustrates the art of illumination practiced in the manuscripts of the Gothic period. The elaborate "U" depicting the martyrdom of St. Andrew serves as the first letter of the word *Unus* (one) which begins the text of this antiphon. The notation and the four line staff of the late Gothic era became the official notational style of the Gregorian Chant for the Roman Catholic Church. The translation of the Latin text is: "One of the two who followed the Lord was Andrew, the brother of Simon Peter, alleluja, e u o u a e. Walking by the sea of Galilee, Jesus saw Peter and his brother Andrew and said to them, 'Follow me and I will make you fishers of men.'" The vowels following the word "alleluja" are an abbreviation often used in chant manuscripts for the Latin words "seculorum, Amen." (The Saint Louis Art Museum)

In three-voice polyphony the cantus firmus was normally the lowest voice. The other voices usually moved more rapidly and were often ornamented. In four-voice polyphony the cantus firmus was assigned to the tenor, and the lowest part was the contratenor, later named the bassus. It had approximately the same range as the tenor and frequently crossed the tenor line. The voice immediately above the tenor was called altus, and the voice above the altus was designated sovrano or superius.

There was no distinction between the textures of sacred and secular polyphonic music of the period. The different voices retained their melodic independence and frequently crossed. At the same time, there was an openness about the sound of early polyphony due to extensive use of the intervals of the fourth, fifth, and octave which lack the harmonic direction of dissonant intervals.

Notation

The most vital innovation in Gothic music was the development of a system of notation. After the emergence of a system of lines and spaces in the eleventh century, pitch designation was fairly accurate, although there was no practical means of notating duration and stress. By the thirteenth century mensural (measured) notation had been developed, principally by Franco of Cologne, introducing for the first time a codified system for recording notes of varying duration and emphasis. This system, with many variations, was to remain in use until c. 1600. Black notes used in the thirteenth and fourteenth centuries were changed to white notes in the fifteenth century. The relative durational values of these notes within the mensural system and their modern equivalents are illustrated in the following example. (Ex. 9) Unlike modern notation, which assumes a division of any note into two notes of the next smaller degree, mensuration divided the notes into either two or three notes of the next smaller degree. The divisions of the longa, breve, and semi-breve were named as follows:

Mensural Divisions into 3	**Mensural Divisions into 2**
Modus perfectum	Modus imperfectum
1 longa = 3 breves	1 longa = 2 breves
Tempus perfectum	Tempus imperfectum
1 breve = 3 semi-breves	1 breve = 2 semi-breves
Prolatio major	Prolatio minor
1 semi-breve = 3 minims	1 semi-breve = 2 minims

Example 9. Mensural notes—their names and modern equivalents

Black notes	White notes	Modern equivalents
Maxima	Maxima	Double whole note
Longa	Longa	Whole note
Breve	Breve	Half note
Semi-breve	Semi-breve	Quarter note
Minim	Minim	Eighth note

The division of the longa, breve, and semi-breve into two or three smaller units was indicated by the use of symbols of mensuration as follows:

1. A circle indicated tempus perfectum, the division of the breve into three semi-breves. In prolatio minor the semi-breve was divided into two minims. (Ex. 10A)

2. A broken circle indicated tempus imperfectum, the division of the breve into two semi-breves. Here again in prolatio minor the semi-breve was divided into two minims. (Ex. 10B)

3. As stated above, the circle indicated tempus perfectum. However, the addition of the dot within the circle indicates the further division of the semi-breve into three minims, prolatio major. (Ex. 10C)

4. As stated above, the broken circle indicated tempus imperfectum. When the dot was added within the broken circle prolatio major was indicated. (Ex. 10D)

Instrumentation and Tone Color

Music for voices dominated both sacred and secular music. Melodic instruments of all kinds could be substituted for the cantus firmus in polyphonic forms. No doubt instruments also doubled vocal parts, especially in secular polyphony. Secular monophony was usually ac-

Example 10A. Tempus perfectum   Prolatio minor

which corresponds to the modern notation of 3/4

Example 10B. Tempus imperfectum   Prolatio minor

which corresponds to the modern notation of 2/4

Example 10C. Tempus perfectum   Prolatio major

which corresponds to the modern notation of 9/8

Example 10D. Tempus imperfectum   Prolatio major

which corresponds to the modern notation of 6/8

companied by instruments, most commonly the lute, viol, and harp. Combinations of instruments were also used for dances and out-of-doors music, but because this kind of music was either improvised or played from memory, few actual written examples have survived.

The instruments of the Gothic era in many instances bear little similarity to the instruments of today. (A description of these and other instruments may be found in Appendix 1.)

IV. MUSIC FOR VOICES

Single Movement Forms and Structural Devices

Secular monophony was music of the troubadours, trouvères, and minnesingers. It included many forms of secular monophony such as the virelai, rondeau, and ballad. The troubadours were poet-musicians of southern France who wrote in Provençal French. They were often gentlemen of high birth and wealth who could afford to hire performers to sing their songs. Trouvères, who lived in northern France, were the counterpart of the troubadours. The songs of both the troubadours and trouvères were mainly of an amorous character, including love songs to the Virgin Mary. The minnesingers were German poet-musicians who were inspired by the troubadours and trouvères. Their songs were often of a didactic or devotional nature. Individual songs were poetic types designated according to subject matter. Minnesingers limited themselves to four formal types, each derived from a well-known strophic form already in existence: the hymn type, the litany type, the rondel-type, and the sequence type.

The **canzo** is an example of the hymn type. Each stanza has six or seven lines with the melody of the first two lines repeated for the second two. The last two or three lines use a different melody. For example, AB AB CD. The German version, found in the literature of the minnesingers, is called bar form. (Rec. 3.1–3.3)

The **rotrouenge,** an example of the litany type, is a form in which the same melody is used for all the lines of the poem except for the last two. The pattern would be AA AA BB. (Rec. 3.4)

The **virelai** is a form of the rondel type, incorporating the refrain and stanza principle. The general musical pattern is: AB CC AB AB. The verse pattern is: AB CD EF AB. The *cantiga* and *lauda* also used this pattern. (Rec. 3.5–3.8)

The **lai** is derived from the sequence with one melody to every two lines of poetry. The lai text is usually addressed to the Virgin Mary and is cast in irregular stanzas of from six to sixteen or more lines. The musical form consists of AA BB CC DD. In Germany it was called *leich*. This form was commonly used by the trouvères and minnesingers. (Rec. 3.9–3.10)

In the thirteenth century, a type of polyphony called **Notre Dame Organum** was developed. The principle of organum was restricted to those portions of the chant which were normally sung by a solo voice. Other sections were sung in plainsong. In the organum, the tenor sang the plainsong melody in long pedal tones while the upper voice or voices sang free, usually metric, melodies above it. (Rec. 3.11–3.12)

The **clausula** was a polyphonic form which used a melismatic section of a chant as a cantus firmus. It was often only a section of an organum. The upper voices move in a quick but measured rhythm against the tenor, which moves in notes of even lengths. Because the melisma used only a few syllables or at the most two or three words, there was no meaningful text to the clausula. All parts were vocalized on the vowel sounds of the tenor line. (Rec. 3.13–3.15)

The **conductus** is a two-, three-, or four-voice form in which the lowest voice is a freely invented melody on a Latin text. One of its important features is the syllabic and rhythmic unity among the voices giving the effect of chords. (Rec. 3.16–3.17)

The **motet** was the most important vocal form in the thirteenth and fourteenth centuries in both secular and sacred practice. In the earlier motet the lowest voice, the tenor or cantus firmus, is a melody selected from plainsong or secular sources in a slow-moving rhythmic mode. The two upper voices, the duplum or motetus and the triplum, move more quickly, each with its own text. At times, even the language of each text was different. Due to the fact that the tenor notes were an elongation of the original cantus firmus, its text was unimportant and it was common practice to play the tenor line on an instrument. The titles of motets are made up of the *incipits* of the several voices. (Rec. 3.18–3.20)

The **isorhythmic motet** was developed in the fourteenth century and had much the same characteristics as the earlier motet. One difference was that the rhythmic modes were extended. Isorhythm consists of a rhythmic pattern, called *talea,* which was repeated a number of times to form the rhythm of a melody, called *color.* The melody was usually repeated, but its repetition did not always coincide with the beginning of a talea (Ex. 11). This led to a much more complex and interesting rhythmic structure. While the isorhythmic principle was first applied to the tenor, in later works it was often present in all voices. (Rec. 3.21–3.22)

The **rota** is a medieval round, or canon, in which each singer returns from the end of the melody to the beginning. The phrases of the melody are so composed that their interaction makes functional harmony. All voices end on a cadence at the completion of any phrase. The rota is usually a secular form. In the famous example, *Sumer is icumen in,* the rota is accompanied by an ostinato bass line in canonic style. (Rec. 3.23)

The **ballata** is an Italian secular form for two or three voices derived from the virelai. The ballata consists of a chain of stanzas, each with six lines. A two-line refrain precedes and follows each stanza.

Example 11. Tenor from three-part isorhythmic motet: *S'il estoit nulz*

A: Original cantus firmus   Machaut

B. Machaut's isorhythmic treatment of the cantus firmus

Color *   to   * *

Talea └── ───┘

The ballata has two melodies, one for the refrain and one for each of the two first pairs of lines from each stanza. The third pair of lines uses the refrain melody. The resulting pattern is A b b a A. (Rec. 3.24–3.26)

The **caccia** is a hunting song that appeared in the fourteenth century. It often has three voices, and when it does, the two upper voices move in strict canonic imitation. The lower voice was independent and was probably performed on an instrument. The French version of the form is called *chace*. (Rec. 3.27–3.29)

The fourteenth century **madrigal** is a lyric poem in which each stanza consists of three lines followed by a two-line couplet called a ritornello. The entire text is set for two or three voices. The same music is used for each stanza while the ritornello is set to different music. The upper voice is usually ornamental. Instruments frequently doubled or substituted for the lower voice parts. (Rec. 3.30–3.31)

Composite Forms
Polyphonic Mass

The polyphonic setting of the sung portions of the Mass is the only music of the Gothic that can be likened to a composite, or multiple form. While the Mass was not a musical form in itself, late Gothic composers began the practice of setting the liturgical texts of the Ordinary of the Mass with some semblance of unity among the various sections. This unity is achieved by means of motives common to each section, by similarity of moods and by similarity of imitative devices. (Rec. 3.32–3.35)

V. INSTRUMENTAL COMPOSITIONS

Single Movement Forms and Structural Devices

Notated instrumental forms were slow to develop. Most dances during the Gothic were still improvised, as they had been earlier. Many medieval dances were cast in two sections—dance and afterdance. There was usually a slow-moving section in duple time followed by a faster section in triple time. Sometimes the section in triple time was based on the same melody as the first or duple section. Because of the improvisatory nature of these dances, very few have come to us in notation. (Rec. 3.36)

Conducti, motets, and even polyphonic sections of the Mass were sometimes played instead of sung. It was common practice to perform vocal music on instruments. Many vocal forms derived from dance melodies. (Rec. 3.37–3.38)

The dance form most commonly notated in the thirteenth and fourteenth century was the *estampie*. It is similar to the vocal sequence and consists of a number of sections called *puncti* which were repeated. Its form is AA BB CC. (Rec. 3.39–3.41)

VI. COMPOSERS

Leonin (fl. 1160) was the first of the great masters of the Notre Dame School. Noted for his style of organum, he made extensive use of the syllabic technique, and foreshadowed the motet principle by lengthening the notes of the plainsong as a cantus firmus with a freely moving voice above it. He wrote a cycle of two-part liturgical settings for the church calendar known as the *Magnus Liber Organi*, (The Great Book of Organum). (Rec. 3.42)

Perotin (twelfth century) succeeded Leonin at Notre Dame. He developed organum from the Leonin style by instilling a greater rhythmic accuracy, and by making additions and modifications to the *Magnus Liber Organi* attributed to Leonin. His tenor voices were written in a series of rhythmic motives that were the precursors of the rhythmic modes. He expanded organum to three and four voices. In addition, his music shows evidence of canonic imitation. His most famous work is *Sederunt principes,* a quadruple organum. (Rec. 3.43)

Adam de la Halle (c. 1237–1287) is one of the best known trouvères. He was both a poet and a composer. Many examples of his monodic as well as his polyphonic compositions survive. Besides many rondeaux and virelais, his musical play *Le jeu de Robin et de Marion* written for the entertainment of the Aragonese court at Naples is still performed. (Rec. 3.44)

Guillaume de Machaut (c. 1300–1377), leader of the French Ars Nova, was the most important composer of the fourteenth century. In addition to being a musician, Machaut was also a theologian, holding many important ecclesiastical posts, including that of Canon of Rheims. He was also secretary to King John of Bohemia. Among Machaut's musical innovations was the development of more lyric melodies and a more suave harmonic texture using thirds and sixths to soften the dissonance of earlier organum. He was the first to compose a complete polyphonic setting of the Ordinary of the Mass with some degree of unity between sections. He wrote in all the musical forms of his time, sacred and secular. Among the secular forms, he excelled in the ballad, bringing to it an ingenuity of imitation, a sonorous harmony, and an expressive melody that foreshadowed Renaissance style. (Rec. 3.45–3.46)

Francesco Landini (1325–1397) had the distinction of being the most famous Italian Ars Nova composer of the fourteenth century. Blinded in his youth, he became a virtuoso performer on a number of instruments, but was best known as an organist. His skill as a performer and as a composer won him legendary fame in the annals of Italian music. Landini's compositions number over 150, and include every form of secular music, although the greater portion are two-part and three-part ballatas. His melodies are very expressive and the resulting harmonies are exceedingly smooth and fluid. (Rec. 3.47–3.48)

ADDITIONAL COMPOSERS
A. France
   Franco of Cologne (fl. 1250–1280)
   Philippe de Vitry (1291–1361)
B. Italy
   Giovanni da Cascia (Giovanni da Firenze, fl. 1330–1350)

VII. HISTORIANS, THEORISTS, AND MANUSCRIPT SOURCES

Gothic writers still considered music the servant of the Church, and their philosophy is mainly a repetition of the earlier authors. However, major portions of their writings are concerned with practical problems of music, mainly those of rhythm and notation. An especially important subject was the interpretation of rhythmic notation.

The conflict between the more conservative style of early medieval music with that of the fourteenth century Ars Nova (new art) was made articulate by Gothic writers. This controversy is made especially clear in the writings of Jacques de Liège and Jean de Muris. The former was an ardent foe of the new style and a champion of the more traditional manner of composition.

Franco of Cologne (fl. 1250–1280) was a medieval theorist and a practical musician. A number of medieval writings were attributed to Franco, but only *Ars cantus mensurabilis* has been authenticated as genuine. Franco made an extraordinary contribution to notation which in its earliest stages was known as "Franconian." In other areas of musical knowledge his writing is based on the earlier theorists.

Marchetto da Padua (fl. fourteenth century), an Italian who wrote an account of the musical practices in Italy, was also the author of a theoretical treatise, *Pomerium*, that was a justification of duple time in music.

Jacques de Liège (c. 1260–c. 1330), a Belgian, was the author of *Speculum musicae,* written about 1325. It was an attack on modern musical practices and more particularly an attack on the writings of Jean de Muris. In addition to its controversial nature, the *Speculum* is a compendium of all medieval knowledge about music.

Jean de Muris (c. 1290–c. 1351) was a writer on music, astronomy, and mathematics. He was the author of *Musica speculativa secundum boetium* and the important treatise, *Ars nove musice.* He championed the cause of the "new style" and also dealt with the interpretation of rhythmic notation.

Philippe de Vitry (1291–1361) was the first writer to theorize on the "new art." His treatise, *Ars nova,* in which he describes the new way of measuring time, gave the name to this period first in France and then in Italy. De Vitry was also known as a composer.

(The writings of the foregoing Gothic theorists and historians are not readily available in English. However, important excerpts from these can be found in Strunk, *Source Readings in Music History.*)

There are a large number of manuscript collections from the twelfth to the fourteenth centuries. The following are generally recognized as the most important:

(a) St. Martial MSS of the twelfth century is a collection of early organum.

(b) Two important collections of motets from the thirteenth century are the Codex Montpellier and the Codex Bamberg.

(c) Fourteenth century Italian secular music is adequately represented by the Codex Squarcialupi. It contains works by Francesco Landini and other Italian composers. Forms included are madrigals, ballatas and caccias.

Further source readings are identified in the *Supplementary Readings* list at the end of the Introduction to this volume.

(fol. 142.b)   Die geschicklheit in der musiken und was in seinen ingenien und durch
in erfunden und gepessert worden ist.
(Cod. 3033.)

Sixteenth century woodcut from Der Weisskunig, depicting a large number of Renaissance instruments. The number of instruments and the conditions of performance indicate the great rise in instrumental performance and the secular nature of court music in this period. (The Metropolitan Museum of Art, Harris Brisbane Dick Fund)

4
Chronology
of the Renaissance

c. 1400   Guillaume Dufay
(c. 1400–1474)

c. 1420   Johannes Ockeghem
(c. 1420–1496)

1430   Rule of the Medici family
(1430–1495)

1440   Sandro Botticelli
(1440–1510)
Meistersingers in
Germany (c. 1440)

1449   Lorenzo de Medici
(1449–1492)

c. 1450   Josquin des Prez
(c. 1440–1521)
Heinrich Isaac
(c. 1450–1517)

1452   Leonardo da Vinci
(1452–1519)
Jacob Obrecht
(c. 1452–1505)

1454   Gutenberg (1398–1468)
invented printing from
moveable type. Bible
printed.

1469   Niccoló Machiavelli
(1469–1527)

1471   Albrecht Dürer
(1471–1528)

1473   Nicolaus Copernicus
(1473–1543)

1475   Michelangelo Buonarroti
(1475–1564)

1480   Mathis Grünewald
(1480–1528)

1483   Raphael Sanzio
(1483–1520)
Martin Luther
(1483–1546)

c. 1490   Adrian Willaert
(c. 1490–1562)

1496   Johann Walter
(1496–1570)

1501   Ottaviano Petrucci
(1466–1539) printed The
*Harmonice musices
odhecaton.*

c. 1520   Andrea Gabrieli
(c. 1520–1586)

c. 1525   Giovanni Perluigi
Palestrina (c. 1525–1594)

1532   Orlando di Lasso
(1532–1594)

1534   Church of England
separates from the
Papacy.

1540   Founding of the Jesuit
Society.

c. 1540   Maddalena Casulana
(1566–1583)

1543 William Byrd
(1543–1623)
1545 Council of Trent
1553 Luca Marenzio
(1553–1599)
c. 1557 Giovanni Gabrieli
(c. 1557–1612)
c. 1560 Don Carlo Gesualdo
(c. 1560–1613)
1564 William Shakespeare
(1564–1616)

4
Renaissance
1400-1600

I. SOCIOCULTURAL INFLUENCES ON MUSIC

In its narrowest sense, the term Renaissance means a rebirth of interest in the ideas and forms of classic antiquity as applied to the artistic and cultural life of Italy during the fifteenth and sixteenth centuries. In its wider sense, however, Renaissance implies a general renewal or rebirth of interest in the dignity and inherent value of man, a trend already indicated in the Gothic period. This trend is reflected in all the political, religious, and social institutions of the period as well as in the several arts. It is most adequately expressed in the philosophy of humanism. Music reflected the movement only in the broader sense, and found its greatest expression in the works of the Burgundian and Netherland composers until the final half of the sixteenth century. At that time the Italians, educated in the style of the period by the long influx of northern composers, blossomed into a dominating school. With the contributions of these later schools of composition, the Renaissance witnessed a rebirth of music.

The Roman Catholic church retained its important position as leading patron of musical production even though there was a growing tendency toward secularization. Evidence of this deep concern in counteracting the increasing secularization of religious music as well as the influence of Protestantism can be seen in the abolition of two things, tropes and sequences (except for four), and secular canti firmi for the composition of motets and masses by the Council of Trent (1545-1563). The Council's determination to stem the great wave of secularization almost resulted in the banning of all polyphonic settings of liturgical music and a return to the exclusive use of traditional plainsong.

The Protestant Reformation exercised a greater influence upon religious music specifically, and European music generally, than any other movement initiated in the Renaissance. Both the Huguenot and

English Reformations gave rise to musical expressions appropriate to these movements. It was, however, the positive inclusion of music by Luther as a vital and important part of the religious liturgy in the form of congregational chorale singing that contributed substantially to the musical renaissance in German-speaking lands. It was this movement that ultimately led to the supremacy of German and Austrian music from the middle of the seventeenth to the end of the nineteenth century.

The rise of wealthy and powerful aristocratic patrons in the ruling courts of Burgundy in the fifteenth century, the Holy Roman Empire of Charles the Fifth and Philip the Second, and the princely courts such as those of Florence, Mantua, and Venice were powerful influences on music. Usually these aristocratic rulers were as influential in religious as in secular affairs, since they maintained important chapels within the courts and became patrons of composers for their religious as well as secular compositions.

The invention of printing in the fifteenth century led to mechanical means for printing music, and the first successful music printing from moveable type took place at the beginning of the sixteenth century. Ottaviano Petrucci (1466–1539), an Italian, was the first to print an edition of part music, the *Harmonice musices odhecaton*, in 1501. Pierre Attaignant, a Frenchman, published the first collection of French chansons with moveable type in Paris in 1528. Thomas Tallis (c. 1505–1585) and William Byrd (1543–1623) published the first English collection of motets in 1575. By the end of the sixteenth century, large numbers of printed musical works were available, particularly editions of secular music such as madrigals, airs, and chansons. While the artistocracy and wealthy upper middle class were the principal purchasers of such works, the multiplicity of printed copies tended to spread the musical works of important composers over a wider area than was heretofore possible through limited manuscripts.

II. FUNCTION OF MUSIC

The primary purpose of sacred music in the Renaissance was liturgical. It served both the traditional Roman Catholic service and the newly founded service. The Roman Catholic church had the more highly organized musical service, and therefore, the greater body of religious music was composed in the service of Catholicism.

Secular music provided a highly cultivated group of amateur performers among the aristocracy and upper middle class with appropriate music for singing and playing. Cultivated ladies and gentlemen of the Renaissance were often capable singers or players, and frequently both.

During the last half of the sixteenth century, instrumental music was employed to provide a select society with entertainment performed by professional and skilled amateur players. These performances took place in the salons of the nobility and the homes of wealthy burghers. Music was written in response to the demand for dancing at formal court functions. Popular songs and dances of folk-like character supplied the great mass of people with music that was appropriate to festivals and other social occasions, both religious and secular.

III. STYLE AND PERFORMANCE PRACTICE

Much of the music of the Renaissance was based on polyphonic practices. There was a unity of style in both secular and religious music which applied to vocal and instrumental compositions as well. The Renaissance represents the last period of music history in which there is such unity of style in all forms.

Formal Organization

Renaissance music shows a unity of formal organization except in the case of small poetic and dance forms of a secular nature. One unifying technique employs a cantus firmus derived primarily from plainsong literature or from folk song sources, giving rise to works which were basically polyphonic elaborations of a preexisting melodic idea. The cantus firmus was generally placed in the tenor voice which in the early Renaissance was the lowest pitched voice.

The imitative use of melodic material became an increasingly important organizational device. In order to give variety to such practice, several forms of imitation were used:

(1) In canonic imitation all voices use the same melodic material, but each voice begins at a different time. Canonic imitations vary from strict to free imitation of the original melodic materials, and can be constructed so that the pitches of each voice are at the same or at different intervals (Ex. 12).

(2) In imitation by inversion, the direction of the original melodic intervals was changed so that the ascending interval in the original melody becomes a descending one in the inverted version and vice versa. In the excerpt that follows (Ex. 13) the middle and upper voices present the ascending five-note melody, while the other three voices invert the pattern.

Example 12. Canon in three voices at the unison: *Illumina oculos meos*

Palestrina

(3) In imitation by retrogression the original melody is repeated note for note in the reverse order. This device is also called *crab* or *cancrizans* imitation. It can also be used in combination with imitation by inversion.

In Machaut's *Ma fin est mon commencement* (My end is my beginning) voice 1 (beginning to end) is identical to voice 2 (end to beginning). Continuing with the intent of the title, voice 3 is a true retrograde, reading identically from beginning to end and from the end to the beginning. (Ex. 14)

(4) In imitation by augmentation a melody is presented in two voices, one of which is in longer note values than the other (Ex. 15).

(5) In imitation by diminution the original melody is answered in a second voice with the same melody, but in shorter note values (Ex. 16).

A different kind of imitation employed preexisting material in new compositions such as the Parody Mass, which went so far as to employ complete short polyphonic works in larger works.

Example 13. Canon in inversion: from *Jeremiae Prophetae Lamentationes*
(1585) *Orlando di Lasso*

Example 14. Imitation by retrogression: *Ma fin est mon commencement*

Guillaume de Machaut

Example 15. Imitation by augmentation

In strictly polyphonic works, both secular and religious, formal organization was episodic. Compositions consisted of a number of sections, each treating its thematic material individually and exhaustively. In highly developed polyphonic forms such as the motet and Mass, there was rarely any repetition of a previously used musical section or text. Each section constituted the complete treatment of a line of text.

Example 16. Imitation by diminution

Secular poetic song forms were often characterized by a formal organization which used a principal refrain in contrast to its other musical phrases. Dance forms were based on folk idioms and generally consisted of an application of the principle of repetition and contrast. Contrasting with the Mass, all these works are in single rather than multiple movements.

Melody

All expression in Renaissance music was the result of varied melodic treatment. Melodic form is determined by textual rather than musical considerations. Harmony and rhythm cannot be analyzed apart from melodic structure. Melodies were modal, largely vocal in conception, and limited to a range which rarely exceeded the octave. Wide skips were avoided, and most melodic movement was diatonic or restricted to the tones of a particular modal scale. Chromaticism is rare in the early works of the Renaissance, but is frequently found in the secular music of the late Renaissance. (See musica ficta, page 62.)

Rhythm

The restrictive isorhythmic devices of the Gothic period disappeared in the fifteenth century although there are some examples of this method of rhythmic organization among early Renaissance compositions. Renaissance rhythm was free from strict metrical phrasing, although many rhythmic formulas were used, including syncopation. Rhythmic phrases were generally long, free from metrical accent. The rhythms of the polyphonic voices often overlapped (Ex. 17).

Example 17. Zwischen Berg und tiefem Tal

Heinrich Isaac

The rhythms of Renaissance music are often complex as a result of the polyphonic writing and the metric intricacies of the texts. One aspect of this complexity is exemplified in the musical puzzles that delighted Renaissance composers. These musical puzzles were based upon a variety of clefs and mensural signatures, leaving the performer to find the key to their solution. They varied from the rather simple to the very intricate, often with instructions for their solution (Ex. 18). In its original notation, the puzzle appears simple. However, when transcribed into modern notation its rhythmic complexity becomes more apparent (Ex. 19).

Example 18. *Agnus Dei "Ex una voce tres":* a mensuration canon from *Missa L'Homme armé*

Josquin des Prez

A   -   gnus   Dei

Example 19. A transcription of example 18

Josquin des Prez

Harmony

In Renaissance music, harmony results from the simultaneous sounding of more or less independent lines of melody, and not from planned harmonic progressions. Composers did not build their music on chordal assumptions within a tonal system. Such a predetermined function of harmony gradually made its appearance at final cadences, however, and began to point the way to the dominance of harmonic considerations over melodic voice leading. One of the most common is the authentic cadence (Ex. 20). Other cadences that were commonly used are the plagal, Landini, Lydian, and Phrygian.

Harmony was essentially intervallic rather than chordal. The relation between the tones of the melodic lines, particularly in reference to the cantus firmus, was of prime importance in determining the melodic progression and the treatment of dissonance. Since rules

Example 20. An authentic cadence

and conventions governing voice leading were determined by the treatment of intervals among the voices, that which strikes the ear as harmonic progression today is a result of voice relationships rather than harmonic construction.

Texture

Polyphony was the predominant texture of Renaissance music. Even in the late Renaissance, where a tendency toward homophonic treatment was found in secular songs, the accompanying voices were treated more or less as independent melodies rather than as chordal accompaniments. In the sixteenth century there were works in which harmonic texture was used as a contrast to the predominating polyphonic texture. These homophonic passages were called the *familiar*

Example 21. Familiar style, from the motet: *Magnus es tu, Domine*

Josquin des Prez

style (Ex. 21), suggesting that this might have been a practice generally used in folk or popular music.

Instrumentation and Tone Color

The human voice, both in solo and ensemble, was the generally accepted medium of performance for all Renaissance music. Voice ranges, cantus or superius (soprano), altus, tenor, and bassus became the framework for all vocal compositions. The voice was reinforced by instruments of all kinds in both sacred and secular music. Instruments such as the organ, harpsichord, and clavichord were used independently in the sixteenth century, and both string and wind ensembles became increasingly popular.

An engraving of equestrian musicians. This ensemble is performing festive out-door music on what appear to be sackbuts, cornamuse, and shawm. (The Bett-mann Archive)

The English *full* consort was an ensemble in which a consistency of tone color was achieved. These were most commonly groups of viols or recorders in different ranges. Variety in tone color was accomplished by mixing the various types of instruments in performance. This was referred to as a *broken* consort. The lute, which held a place of importance parallel to the piano in the nineteenth century, was the most popular instrument. (A description of these and other instruments may be found in Appendix 1.)

Practice and Performance

Composers rarely indicated specific voices or instruments for their music. This was left to the judgment of the performers. Notation indicated relative pitch because at the time there was no absolute or fixed pitch such as A = 440 cps. Accommodation to vocal and instrumental ranges determined the actual pitch of any given performance.

Clefs were used before the Renaissance to designate the pitch names and relationships of the notes on the staff. By the sixteenth century, however, regular use was made of the C and F clefs to designate the ranges corresponding to our modern soprano, alto, tenor, and bass voices. The G or treble clef began to displace the soprano C clef in the latter part of the sixteenth century.

No interpretive directions as to tempi, dynamics, or phrasing are to be found in the music of the period until the time of Giovanni Gabrieli. The use of sharps or flats written above the notes in modern editions indicates the editor's decision that these were included in performance, but not in notation, a practice known as *musica ficta*, as described in the chapter on Gothic music. The performers understood this common practice, and added appropriate accidentals to avoid inappropriate voice leading and dissonance. This dependence on the common practice explains the chromatic differences occurring between the notated and performed music of the Renaissance. Another term, concerning which there is little agreement, is *musica reservata*. Several of its interpretations suggest that performance was often regulated by commonly understood practices of improvisation for which no detailed directions were necessary at that time.

The fifteenth century French practice of using a succession of first inversion triads or sixth-chords was known as *fauxbourdon*. The composer duplicated a soprano melody at the sixth below, and a singer extemporized a fourth below the soprano resulting in a series of $^6_4$ chords. This practice marked the beginning of the use of the third and the full triad as a basic harmonic element (Ex. 22).

Polychoral singing was a practice that was particularly cultivated in Venice, due in part to the architecture of St. Mark's Cathedral. The large choral compositions of the Venetian School of the late Renaissance lent themselves to a division of the choral forces into intervals of two or more groups which were placed in different parts of the

Example 22. Fauxbourdon from a *Magnificat*

cathedral. The success of this practice gave rise to many compositions for divided choral groups, and their placement in various parts of the church was widely adopted by choir directors throughout Europe. Two choral groups alternating in performance results in antiphonal singing.

IV. MUSIC FOR VOICES

Single Movement Forms and Structural Devices
Motet

The motet continued to be an important vocal form during the fifteenth and sixteenth centuries. The isorhythmic motet (see the chapter on Gothic music) continued in use until the middle of the fifteenth century. (Rec. 4.1)

Many new methods of composition were applied to motet writing, but the cantus firmus in long note values continued in use through the last half of the fifteenth century. However, the principal motet form of the Renaissance was developed by Josquin des Prez, and consisted generally of a work in four to six voices with imitative treatment. The motet was usually made up of a number of sections, nonrepetitive, each of which treated a portion of the text. The texts were always in Latin and taken either from the liturgy of the Mass or from the Bible. In polyphonic writing of this period, the voices seldom concluded textual lines simultaneously. Consequently, well-defined harmonic cadences were few, except at such marked divisions in the music as occur with changes in meter or at the conclusion. (Rec. 4.2–4.7)

Hymn

These were polyphonic strophic settings of Latin poetic religious texts in which each verse of text was repeated to the same musical setting. The upper voice was usually melodic. (Rec. 4.8–4.9)

Chorale

The hymn tunes and their four-part chordal settings, which were adopted for use in the German Protestant church by Luther and his musical collaborators, are known as chorales, German Protestant Chorales, or Lutheran Chorales. The texts were in the vernacular language, principally German. The tunes were often taken from older Latin hymns or specifically composed to appropriate texts, but a rich source was the secular folk melody. These chorales in their simple form are usually binary, with a repeated first section. The melodies, predominantly in the upper voice, are slow moving, and the cadences are very marked and strong. (Rec. 4.10–4.11)

Psalms

The psalm compositions were the music of the French Protestant movement, the Huguenots, were simple settings, generally in chordal style, with some free polyphonic treatment. The dominant melody, as in the German Chorale, was in the upper voice. Rhythmically, these psalm settings were somewhat more lively than the German Chorales, and the texts were French metrical translations. (Rec. 4.12–4.13)

Anthem

Similar to the motet, anthems were introduced by the Anglican church. They followed the general structure of the Renaissance motet, but were sung in English. Two types evolved. The *full anthem* was sung in motet style, that is, with the entire choir participating throughout. In contrast, the *verse anthem* presented soloists and chorus with instrumental forces in varying combinations. (Rec. 4.14–4.17)

Frottola

This derivation of a dance form represents the most important of the strophic forms developed in the late fifteenth and early sixteenth centuries in northern Italy. It is a sophisticated folk song, generally chordal in structure, and characterized by variously arranged patterns of two contrasting musical ideas. One pattern commonly used is ABAABAB. The frottola was written for three or four voices. The lower voices were probably played on instruments, as well as sung. (Rec. 4.18–4.19)

Madrigal

The madrigal is the most highly developed of all the Renaissance secular vocal forms. It originated in Italy and flourished in the latter half of the sixteenth century. Composers of all schools, even outside Italy, set the lyrics of Italian poets in madrigal form. Three stages of development are discernible—the chordal style represented by Arcadelt and Verdelot, the more highly developed imitative polyphonic style often in five voices represented by Palestrina, Lasso and Rore, and the highly dramatic and expressive madrigals of the late Renaissance, represented by Monteverdi, Marenzio, and Gesualdo. The madrigal became very popular in England where an independent school of composers rivaled the Italians in quantity and quality for a short time. The largest body of madrigals by English composers was set to English lyric poetry though some was written in Italian.

The Renaissance madrigal was a through-composed (nonrepetitive) polyphonic composition contrasting with the verse-refrain madrigal of the fouteenth century. It varied from the chordal, much as in the frottola, to the imitatively polyphonic. In some respects the madrigal was a secular counterpart to the sacred motet, as were all these highly developed secular forms.

There were madrigals that were humorous, and others of a more serious nature, often treating the subject of unrequited love. Instances of the deliberate use of musically expressive devices to fit the text are frequent. These so-called *madrigalisms* consisted of textual interruptions by rests, chromaticisms, naive attempts to make the music illustrate the text by means of rhythmic and melodic tone painting. Frequent changes of rhythm are often used. Madrigals were commonly written in three to five voices. Toward the end of the sixteenth century there was a distinct tendency to write madrigals in homophonic style with a predominating or solo voice. The *ballet* madrigal, most common in England, was a strophic form with a "fa-la" refrain. (Rec. 4.20–4.24)

French Chanson

Fifteenth century chansons were generally in the repetitive fixed forms of the rondeau or virelai. In the sixteenth century, the fixed forms were abandoned and there was a truly polyphonic treatment in imitative style. The term *chanson* embraced the whole of the polyphonic secular writing to French texts of the fifteenth and sixteenth centuries. Like the motet, the chansons were usually sectional and were through-composed. The sections, however, were short and marked with simultaneous cadences in all voices, and tended to be homophonic. Their rhythms were faster and lighter than in the motet. Most of the sixteenth century chansons were in four voices and the top voice usually carried the principal melody. (Rec. 4.25–4.27)

Polyphonic Lied

The German counterpart of the Italian and English madrigal as well as the French chanson is the polyphonic lied. Almost without exception, they were polyphonic settings of folk song melodies. In some instances these settings were predominantly chordal. However, an imitative polyphonic treatment developed in the last half of the fifteenth and first half of the sixteenth centuries. (Rec. 4.28–4.29)

Quodlibet

The quodlibet was a polyphonic composition in which several popular or folk songs were combined to make a humorous polytextual unit. (Rec. 4.30–4.31)

Ayre

In England the ayre was a late development of the Renaissance. These largely homophonic songs were strophic. The accompanying voices were normally played on the lute, though in some instances (such as Dowland) they were sung as vocal ensemble music much as the madrigal was. Its most distinguishing characteristic was its strophic form. (Rec. 4.32–4.33)

Miscellaneous Secular Forms

A large body of traditional strophic forms such as the villancico, virelai, ballata, or rondeau employed both monophonic and polyphonic styles in the fifteenth and sixteenth centuries. They retained their fixed forms though they were often more simple in form and rhythmic structure than earlier. The principal melody was placed in the uppermost part, and settings were generally chordal with little imitation. The formal musical structure of these songs was determined by their strict poetic forms. (Rec. 4.34–4.37)

Composite Forms

Mass

The Mass is the only important composite form used in the Renaissance. It is built up of a series of movements, each of which is similar in structure and form to the motet. Each of these movements provides a musical setting for one of the five principal parts of the Ordinary of the Roman Catholic Mass: Kyrie, Gloria, Credo, Sanctus, and Agnus Dei. As in the motet, the composer employed secular, sacred, and freely invented canti firmi, as well as imitative techniques for organizational purposes. Renaissance masses, for the most part, were based on preexisting material: plainsong, folk song, motets, or polyphonic secular works.

One type, often called the *Plainsong Mass,* was constructed on appropriate and different canti firmi for each of the parts of the Mass (e.g., the Kyrie on a plainsong Kyrie, the Gloria on a plainsong Gloria). This procedure was in use since the late Middle Ages.

The *Cantus Firmus Mass* was the most frequently composed type in the Renaissance. It used a single cantus firmus that appeared in each of the several parts of the composition. The cantus firmus might consist of an entire preexisting melody or only a portion of it. It might be quoted literally or paraphrased in all movements while reserved for the tenor voice. In contrast, it may be paraphrased throughout each movement and appear in all voices imitatively. (Rec. 4.38–4.40)

A special type of Mass, the *Parody Mass,* was developed in the sixteenth century. This form is an even more complex extension of the technique of basing the parts, as well as the whole, on a preexisting form. In the Parody Mass a polyphonic motet was used as a basis for imitative development. The motet could be used in its entirety or in fragments throughout the several movements of the Mass.

A motet was often selected from among the composer's own works as the basis for Parody Masses. (Rec. 4.41)

Names given to the preceding mass types were taken from the motets or canti firmi from which they were derived (i.e., *Missa Pange Lingua*). Relatively few masses were composed entirely on original, freely invented material. (Rec. 4.42)

V. MUSIC FOR INSTRUMENTS

Single Movement Forms and Structural Devices

While instruments were popularly used in musical performance in the Renaissance, there was no independent instrumental writing until very late in the sixteenth century. Consequently, there are very few purely instrumental forms that are unrelated to the polyphonic style of vocal music. Except for dance music, the greatest amount of instrumental performance was either in duplication of, or substitution for, voice parts in polyphonic vocal music. Some works written specifically for instruments in the sixteenth century displayed a consideration for the special technical capabilities of those instruments then in use.

Ricercar

The instrumental equivalent of the vocal motet, the ricercar, like the motet, was constructed in several sections. Each section had a musical theme which was treated imitatively and contrapuntally. The ricercar written for instrumental ensemble was closely patterned after the vocal motet with numerous sections and melodic themes. The fact that many such works were published with instructions "to be sung and played" indicated their affinity to vocal forms.

The organ ricercar, while basically the same construction, tended to use fewer themes and sections, and therefore the treatment of the themes was longer and more elaborate. Contrapuntal imitation was its principal formal ingredient.

There were nonimitative ricercars for the lute, organ, and instrumental ensemble. They seem to have been written more for study purposes, since they tend to exploit the technical possibilities of the instruments. (Rec. 4.43–4.45)

Canzona

The instrumental canzona, which appeared in the sixteenth century, was at first a mere instrumental arrangement, or transcription, of the vocal chanson. It was written for either lute or keyboard. Subsequently, composers wrote original instrumental works in the style of the vocal chanson that also borrow the name *canzona*. Keyboard canzonas, as well as those for instrumental ensembles, varied from the conventional imitative and sectional character of the vocal chansons to the spectacular polychoral type of the Venetian school. These Venetian compositions presented alternating sections in varying rhythms and textures, and were performed by alternative choirs of instruments. (Rec. 4.46–4.47)

In Nomine

The *In nomine* compositions were instrumental works based on the antiphon *Gloria tibi Trinitas,* which was derived from a cantus firmus mass of the same name by John Tavener. They were written exclusively in England. (Rec. 4.48)

Toccata

A form of keyboard composition deriving its name from the Italian *toccare,* to touch. The toccata exploited a rather improvisatory style in which florid homophonic scale and chord passages were combined with imitative sections. Most characteristic of the toccata is its adherence to keyboard idiom and its unchanging tempo. (Rec. 4.49–4.50)

Fantasia

This was a rather ambiguous title given to instrumental compositions in the sixteenth century. The name probably referred to the improvisatory nature of such works as the ricercar, which combined a free form with strict contrapuntal style. The title "Fantasia" was used to cover a wide variety of compositions published at the very end of the sixteenth century, many of which were free ricercars and chansons printed in tablature form. (Rec. 4.51–4.52)

Prelude

This term was applied very loosely to a variety of compositions which originally served to introduce a liturgical ceremony. In the fifteenth and sixteenth centuries it was used to designate free idiomatic keyboard music. The prelude was often very short and in homophonic style, and usually exploited the technique of the keyboard. Unlike the canzona or ricercar, the prelude does not derive from any vocal form, but represents the first truly instrumental music. English virginal composers often used the term to describe virtuoso keyboard compositions. (Rec. 4.53)

Variation

This form is basically repetitive using a newly invented, or a preexisting melodic idea, presented in a succession of altered versions. Composers of variations faced the problem of maintaining the relationship among the successive versions and at the same time providing interest through the alterations. In the sixteenth century early versions of this form altered the contrapuntal texture by the use of imitative figures, or by embellishing the melody by ornamentation and rapid scale passages.

Variations for vihuela (lute) or keyboard in the early sixteenth century Spanish school illustrate the contrapuntal type, while the keyboard variation of the English school is representative of the figured type. (Rec. 4.54–4.56)

Dance Forms

There are only a few instrumental dances in polyphonic style to be found in the fifteenth century. Those which are known come from the *Münchener Liederbuch* and the *Glogauer Liederbuch*, the two large collections of dances and songs dating from c. 1460. The sixteenth century, however, is a period dominated by dance forms and is often called the century of the dance. These dances are characteristically paired like the pavane-galliard and the passamezzo-saltarello. In these pairs, the first dance is in slow duple meter followed by the second in fast triple meter. In many instances the second dance is a rhythmically changed version of the first dance. This was particularly true of the German *Tanz* and *Nachtanz*, or *Tanz* and *Proportz*. In this case the second dance assumes the characteristics of a variation on the first. The form of the dance is binary. (Rec. 4.57–4.60)

Composite Forms

At the end of the sixteenth century the pairing of dances and the grouping of several dances indicated a desire to write instrumental works of larger scope. These combinations are among the first examples of the instrumental suite which became a standard form in the Baroque period. (Rec. 4.61)

VI. COMPOSERS

In the Middle Ages artworks in all media were for the most part anonymous efforts. Renaissance composers commonly began to be identified by name with their works. Moreover, many of those whose names we now know were innovators in style, or leaders of particular schools of composition. During the Renaissance there were two distinctive schools, the Burgundian and the Flemish, or the Netherlands school. The Burgundian school flourished during the first half of the fifteenth century and included Dufay and Binchois. The Flemish school, from about 1450 to 1600, included such composers as Ockeghem, Obrecht, Josquin des Prez, and many others who were to spread the Flemish innovations to various sections of Europe. While their works represent Renaissance music of high quality, mention of them here does not mean that their works were always superior to composers whose names have been omitted. In addition there were vital musical centers or schools in England, Spain, Germany, and Italy, particularly in Rome and Venice.

John Dunstable (c. 1380–1453) was an English composer and early master of counterpoint. He is especially noted for his interesting contrapuntal lines composed around the plainsong melody. He was an important influence on the composers of the Burgundian school. (Rec. 4.62–4.63)

Guillaume Dufay (c. 1400–1474) is considered the master of the Burgundian school. His works show a strong preference for the upper voices, both melodically and rhythmically. The use of instruments is often implied. He wrote in all the religious and secular forms of his time. (Rec. 4.64)

Gilles Binchois (c. 1400–1460) was also one of the Burgundian group, and is best known for the excellence of his secular works, especially the chanson. Like others of his time, his stylistic features were essentially the same in both sacred and secular polyphony. (Rec. 4.65)

Johannes Ockeghem (c. 1420–1496), a pupil of Dufay and the leader of the Flemish school, developed devices of imitation that served as models for those who later perfected the *a cappella* style. He was also one of the first to write four-part polyphony that created a seamless fabric. His writing was generally for low voices. (Rec. 4.66–4.69)

Josquin des Prez (c. 1440–1521) of the Flemish School, was one of the greatest composers of all time, and the first to make music a personally expressive art. He was fortunate to have the majority of his compositions published during his lifetime. Because of this fact, coupled with his genius, he was well known and had great influence on other composers. In general his sacred works are contrapuntal, but many of the secular works tend toward homophony, perhaps due to the influence of the Italian frottola. (Rec. 4.70–4.73)

Heinrich Isaac (c. 1450–1517). Though Isaac was a Flemish composer, he was at one time court composer to Maximilian in Vienna, bringing the Flemish style to Austria. He wrote many masses and motets, but it was his polyphonic settings of chorale melodies that make his music memorable. (Rec. 4.74–4.75)

Jacob Obrecht (c. 1452–1505) was born in the Netherlands. He carried on the innovations of Ockeghem, adding an expressive quality that followed the meaning of the texts. In his four-voice writing the

Dufay (c. 1400–1474) and Binchois (1400–1460). A fifteenth century illuminated manuscript depicting Guillaume Dufay and Gilles Binchois, two outstanding composers of fifteenth century Burgundy. On the left is a portative organ, on the right an early harp. (The Bettmann Archive)

lowest part became a true bass line, leading to frequent authentic cadences. He was also one of the first composers to have a large number of his works published during his lifetime. (Rec. 4.76–4.77)

Adrian Willaert (c. 1490–1562) was a Flemish composer who became the founder of the Venetian school, numbering among his pupils such masters as Andrea Gabrieli and Zarlino. He held the post of Master of the Chapel at St. Mark's where he introduced a style of writing for two antiphonal choirs. While his sacred music is of high quality, he is perhaps best known for his madrigals, a form which he raised far above the level of the popular frottola. (Rec. 4.78–4.79)

Ludwig Senfl (c. 1486–1543), whose name means "little mustard" was Swiss, but held musical positions in Germany. He was known as a singer and a composer of church music. As a pupil of Isaac, he cultivated the Flemish style. He was also known for the charm of his polyphonic settings of the German Lied. Luther praised Senfl as the "Prince of all German music." (Rec. 4.80–4.81)

Thomas Tallis (c. 1505–1585), an English organist and composer, was the first to use the English language in settings of the liturgy of the Anglican church. He also wrote a large number of motets and masses in Latin. (Rec. 4.82–4.83)

Jacobus Clemens (c. 1510–c. 1556), a Flemish composer known as "Clemens non Papa" to distinguish him from a pope of similar name, was one of the more progressive composers of the early sixteenth century in his use of chromatic harmonization. His best works are masses and motets, but he is also important as the first composer of settings of psalms in the vernacular (*Souterliedekens*). (Rec. 4.84)

Antonio de Cabezón (1510–1566), an important Spanish composer and organist, was a strong influence on many European composers for the organ and other keyboard instruments. He also made keyboard arrangements of the vocal music of Josquin des Prez and other Flemish composers. (Rec. 4.85)

Andrea Gabrieli (c. 1520–1586) was an Italian composer of the Venetian school, a pupil of Adrian Willaert, and uncle and teacher of Giovanni Gabrieli. After extensive travel in Germany and Bohemia, Andrea became organist at St. Mark's in Venice where he achieved a great reputation as organist. He was a prolific composer of both choral and instrumental music, ranging from massive sacred works to the madrigal. Many of his larger compositions exhibit the polychoral tradition of the Venetian school established by Willaert. (Rec. 4.86–4.87)

Philippe de Monte (1521–1603), a Belgian, was a friend of Roland de Lassus (Orlando di Lasso) and was influenced by the Flemish style. He is best known for his expressive madrigals. (Rec. 4.88–4.89)

Giovanni Pierluigi Palestrina (c. 1525–1594), an Italian composer, was generally considered the greatest master of Renaissance Catholic music. His most important post was that of director of the Cappella Giulia at the Vatican. Palestrina is noted for the perfection of a purely vocal style, commonly known as the *a cappella* style. His music is characterized by a high degree of technical perfection, with diatonic melodies and smooth textures that culminated in a rare beauty of sound that is almost transcendental in its sound. His *Missa Papae Marcelli* became a model of pure Catholic music. (Rec. 4.90–4.92)

Roland de Lassus or Orlando di Lasso (1532–1594) was also a product of the Flemish school, but was international in his music. He wrote over two thousand compositions. His fame rests mainly on his religious music. However, his writing was equally effective in Italian madrigals, German polyphonic Lieder, and French chansons. Historians rank him as the greatest of the Flemish composers, and along with Palestrina, one of the most important of the Renaissance composers. (Rec. 4.93–4.95)

William Byrd (1543–1623) was one of the greatest composers in English history. He is best known for his superb polyphonic settings of sacred texts, including masses for three, four, and five voices. He was equally skilled in keyboard music for both the organ and virginal. His *Carmen's Whistle,* a set of variations for virginal, was very popular during his lifetime. (Rec. 4.96–4.97)

Tomas Luis de Victoria (c. 1549–1611), a leading representative of the Roman school in Spain, studied in Rome, probably with Palestrina. However, his music has a dramatic intensity and spiritual fervor that is thoroughly Spanish. He is best known for his motets, of which there are many in four, five, and six parts. He also wrote a large number of other works including a *Requiem Mass,* considered his masterpiece, and a book of hymns for four voices. (Rec. 4.98–4.100)

Luca Marenzio (1553–1599) was an important Italian madrigalist. His writing demonstrates the work of a progressive composer who made many innovations in chordal relationships and expressive chromaticism. (Rec. 4.101–4.102)

Giovanni Gabrieli (c. 1557–1612) was a nephew and pupil of Andrea Gabrieli. He was the greatest composer of the Venetian school and extended the grand musical tradition at St. Mark's Cathedral. He was one of the first to write expressly for combined voices and instruments. Among his best known works in this medium are the collections called *Sacre Symphoniae.* He achieved massive sonorities with his polychoral technique. He is often regarded as the first to develop orchestration, and to indicate varied dynamics as in his *Sonata Pian'e Forte.* (Rec. 4.103–4.104)

Thomas Morley (1557–1602) was an English composer of madrigals and ballets. He was the publisher of the *Triumphs of Oriana,* a set of twenty-five madrigals by twenty-three composers—each madrigal in honor of Queen Elizabeth. He was also the author of the first treatise on music printed in England, *A Plaine and Easie Introduction to Practicall Musicke.* (Rec. 4.105–4.106)

Don Carlo Gesualdo (c. 1560–1613) was an Italian madrigalist whose works represent the extreme of chromaticism reached in the last years of the Renaissance. The harmonic results achieved by Gesualdo, while often described as mannerism, are indicative of a growing consciousness of the strength of musical expression and of the ideals of the dawning Baroque era. (Rec. 4.107–4.108)

Hans Leo Hassler (1564–1612) flourished in the period that bridged the Renaissance and the Baroque. He was a German who studied in Italy with Andrea Gabrieli, adapted the Venetian style to the German Lied, and created a strong German musical style. He wrote in all the current vocal and keyboard forms, both Renaissance and early Baroque, but was best known for his settings of German polyphonic songs and chorales. (Rec. 4.109–4.110)

Claudio Monteverdi (1567–1643), like Hassler spans the final years of the Renaissance and the beginning of the Baroque. He was one of the first composers to employ consciously two different practices: a *prima prattica (stile antico)*, and a *seconda prattica (stile moderno)*. While he wrote works such as sacred choral music and madrigals in the first practice, typical of the Renaissance, it was his use of the second practice which marked his contribution to the emerging Baroque and made him historically important. (Rec. 4.111)

Thomas Weelkes (c. 1575–1623) was one of the greatest of the English madrigalists. He was well in advance of his time in his characterization of text. He wrote numerous anthems and services for the Anglican liturgy. (Rec. 4.112)

ADDITIONAL COMPOSERS

A. Austria
   Paul Hofhaimer (1459–1537)
   Jacobus Gallus (Handl) (1550–1591)
B. England
   John Taverner (c. 1490–1545)
   Giles Farnaby (c. 1565–1640)
   John Bull (c. 1562–1628)
   John Dowland (1562–1626)
   John Wilbye (1574–1638)
   Orlando Gibbons (1583–1625)
   John Farmer (fl. 1591–1601)
   John Bennet (c. 1570–c. 1614)
C. Germany
   Conrad Paumann (c. 1410–1473)
   Heinrich Finck (1445–1527)
   Johann Walter (1496–1570)
   Johannes Eccard (1553–1611)
   Melchior Franck (c. 1579–1639)
D. Italy
   Annibale (Il Padovano) (c. 1527–1575)
   Claudio Merulo (1533–1604)
   Marco Antonio Ingegneri (c. 1545–1592)
   Orazio Vecchi (1550–1605)
   Giovanni Gastoldi (d. 1622)

E. Burgundy-The Netherlands
   Pierre de La Rue (c. 1455–1518)
   Philippe Verdelot (d. 1552)
   Nicholas Gombert (c. 1490–1556)
   Thomas Crécquillon (d. 1557)
   Clement Janequin (c. 1485–c. 1560)
   Claudin de Sermisy (c. 1490–1562)
   Jacob Arcadelt (c. 1505–1568)
   Cipriano de Rore (1516–1565)
F. Spain
   Luis Milan (c. 1500–1561)
   Cristóbal de Morales (c. 1500–1553)

VII. HISTORIANS, THEORISTS, AND MANUSCRIPT SOURCES

The theoretical treatises on music written during the Renaissance were generally in Latin, the language of scholars, and in a learned style that often obscures rather than illuminates. These treatises are the sources of most of our knowledge of Renaissance music not revealed by the music itself. Without these sources little would be precisely known about Renaissance notation, rhythm, tempo, tuning, performance, instrumental construction, or rules of theory. Many of these works contain examples from the music of the times that would otherwise be unavailable. In cases in which more than one treatise was written by a theoretician, the most important has been listed below with its original title and date of writing or publication, as well as any modern edition or translation.

Bartolome Ramos de Pareja (c. 1440–1491) was a Spanish theorist. His *Musica practica* (Bologna 1482) is a landmark in the science of harmony, particularly concerning intonation. Ramos, through his division of the monochord, established the ratios of 4:5 and 5:6 for the major and minor thirds.

Johannes Tinctoris (1435–1511) was a Belgian theorist and composer. His *Terminorum musicae diffinitorium* (Naples 1473) is the oldest known dictionary of musical terms. An English translation appeared in London in 1849. Several of his writings were published in Coussemaker's complete edition of the writings of Tinctoris in 1875.

Franchino Gaforio (1451–1522), an Italian theorist, deals with rules of counterpoint and compositional practice, as well as the current performance styles in his magnum opus, *Practica musicae Franchino Gaforio Laudenis . . . in IV libris* (Milan 1496).

Pietro Aaron (1489–1545) is one of the most important Italian theorists of the early sixteenth century. *Thoscanello della Musica* (Venice 1523) contains descriptions of contrapuntal rules, the chord formations employed in his day.

Martin Agricola (1486–1556) was a German theorist whose *Musica instrumentalis deudsch* (Wittenberg 1529) remains an authoritative work on the instruments of the time. It is a valuable source for the history of notation.

Henricus Glareanus (1488–1563) was a Swiss philosopher, theologian, historian, poet, and musical scholar. His *Dodechachordon* (Basle 1547) advocated the completion of the modal series to twelve and greatly influenced the concept of modality and tonality. A German translation of this work was published in 1888.

Gioseffo Zarlino (1517–1590) discussed various topics concerning music of his day in the four books that make up his major work *Instituzioni harmoniche* (Venice 1558). This treatise includes rules of counterpoint, intonation, treatment of text, and the general excellence of music.

Thomas Morley (1557–1602) wrote and published the earliest treatise on music published in England. *A Plaine and Easie Introduction to Practicall Musicke* (London 1597) is a discourse on all phases of music making. Reprinted in 1937, this is the most important English book on musical theory from the Renaissance. Another modern edition was published in 1952.

(Important excerpts in English from several of the foregoing works can be found in *Source Readings in Music History* by Strunk.)

Until music printing became a practicality in the sixteenth century, the manuscript collections constituted the most valuable source of actual music of the Renaissance. These manuscripts were usually made by anonymous copyists, and were treasured in the libraries of monasteries, churches, and royal courts. Of the countless manuscripts written before the end of the fifteenth century, when the printing of music had not yet displaced the collecting of musical works in handwritten form, certain monumental collections stand out as important. In many cases these are the sole sources of folk and composed music.

Old Hall MS, written about 1450 at the Catholic College of St. Edmunds in Old Hall, England, contains a large number of mass compositions and hymns. A modern edition of this work was published in 1935–38 by Ramsbotham and Collins.

The *Trent Codices* contain polyphonic music of the fifteenth century, both sacred and secular, in six volumes. They include perhaps the richest collection of music by most of the masters of fifteenth century polyphony. A large part of this collection has been printed in modern notation in the *Denkmäler der Tonkunst in Oesterreich* (vols. 7, 11, 19, 27, 31, and 40).

Among the collections of purely secular songs, the *chansonniers* and *Liederbücher* of France and Germany respectively are especially noteworthy. The *Copenhagen Chansonnier* of the fifteenth century contains thirty-three polyphonic chansons, and is representative of a number of such collections. It is available in modern edition also. Of the German collections, the *Glogauer Liederbuch*, the *Lochaimer Liederbuch*, and the *Münchner Liederbuch* contain vocal and instrumental polyphonic and monophonic settings of German folk songs and composed works. All three of these are published in modern editions.

Further source readings are identified in the *Supplementary Readings* list at the end of the Introduction to this volume.

*   *   *

Exuberantly decorated organ cases were the hallmark of Baroque organ builders. This example includes typical angel musicians high on the organ case. (Historical Pictures Service, Chicago)

5
Chronology
of the Baroque

1547	Miguel de Cervantes (1547–1616)	1602	Pier Francesco Cavalli (1602–1676)
c. 1550	Giulio Caccini (c. 1550–1618)	1605	Giacomo Carissimi (1605–1674)
c. 1557	Giovanni Gabrieli (c. 1557–1612)	1606	Rembrandt van Rijn (1606–1669)
1561	Jacopo Peri (1561–1633)	1616	Johann Jakob Froberger (1616–1667)
1562	Jan Pieterzoon Sweelinck (1562–1621)	1618	Beginning of the Thirty Years' War
1564	Galileo Galilei (1564–1642) William Shakespeare (1564–1616)	1620	Pilgrims landed at Plymouth
		1623	Marc' Antonio Cesti (1623–1669)
1567	Claudio Monteverdi (1567–1643)	1630	Boston founded
1571	Michael Praetorius (1571–1621)	1632	Jean-Baptiste Lully (1632–1687)
1577	Peter Paul Rubens (1577–1640)	1634	Marc-Antoine Charpentier (1634–1704)
1583	Girolamo Frescobaldi (1583–1643)	1637	Dietrich Buxtehude (1637–1707) First public opera house opened in Venice
1585	Heinrich Schütz (1585–1672)		
1586	Johann Hermann Schein (1586–1630)	1640	Publication of the *Bay Psalm Book*
1587	Samuel Scheidt (1587–1654)	1653	Arcangelo Corelli (1653–1713) Johann Pachelbel (1653–1706)
1598	Giovanni Lorenzo Bernini (1598–1680)		

1659   Henry Purcell
       (c. 1659–1695)
1660   Johann Kuhnau
       (1660–1722)
       Alessandro Scarlatti
       (1660–1725)
1661   Reign of Louis XIV
       (1661–1715)
1668   François Couperin
       (1668–1733)
1678   Antonio Vivaldi
       (1678–1741)
       First public German
       opera house opens in
       Hamburg
1681   Georg Philipp Telemann
       (1681–1767)

1683   Jean-Philippe Rameau
       (1683–1764)
1685   Johann Sebastian Bach
       (1685–1750)
       George Frideric Handel
       (1685–1759)
       Domenico Scarlatti
       (1685–1757)
1700   Sauveur measures
       musical vibrations
1709   Cristofori builds the first
       pianoforte
1710   Giovanni Battista
       Pergolesi (1710–1736)
1730   Guarneri family makes
       violins in Cremona

5

Baroque
1575-1750

I. SOCIOCULTURAL INFLUENCES ON MUSIC

The term Baroque probably derived from the Portuguese word *barroco* meaning an irregularly shaped pearl. It was first used as a term of scorn for works of art, particularly architecture, produced from the end of the sixteenth century to the middle of the eighteenth century. The word no longer carries a derogatory meaning, and is widely used to designate the arts and music of this era. The term applies to a long period of history and to such diverse countries as Italy, France, England, and the vast territories that came under Germanic influence. So generous was the artistic output of the Baroque that it is normally divided into three phases: early, middle, and late. In general, Baroque art is considered elaborately decorative, dramatic, flamboyant, and emotional. There is a tendency to fuse the arts wherever possible. Architecture, painting, and sculpture, for example, are combined in the domed ceilings of seventeenth and eighteenth century churches. Music, literature, painting, architecture, and sculpture are all combined in the opera or *dramma per musica*. The intense desire to express an idea, a feeling, or the artists' own deep convictions and emotions often led to excesses in all forms of art. The tendency to ascribe these violent expressive qualities to lack of taste or to the desire to cover poor workmanship placed the arts of the Baroque in disfavor in the late eighteenth and nineteenth centuries. A reappraisal of the Baroque in the twentieth century as representative of a period of violent and revolutionary upheavals, however, gives new insight into the deep-lying motives which found expression in what seems at first to be the arts of excess.

The whole Baroque movement had its inception in Italy as a part of the Counter-Reformation. Its influence and spirit spread rapidly into all parts of Europe, particularly into southern Germany and Austria where the Roman Catholic Counter-Reformation was most successful in its struggle with the Protestant North. Despite its first association with the Counter-Reformation, the Baroque spirit became an equally vital part of the Protestant Reformation, and in fact pervaded both spiritual and secular forms of artistic expression. Several important movements in religion, government, economics, and science influenced the artistic activity of the Baroque.

The Thirty Years' War was brought about by the struggle between Roman Catholics and Protestants over religious issues, political power, and the ownership of land. It dominated the first half of the seventeenth century, especially in northern and central Europe, widening the cultural and musical differences between Roman Catholics and Protestants. The Roman Catholics in the south were influenced primarily by the Italian style, while the Protestants in the north worked to expand and elaborate on the chorale tradition. This devastating war delayed the development of Baroque musical life in the German lands for more than a generation. However, both the Roman Catholic church, which in this series of wars partially regained its political influence, and the Protestant church which developed a clear cut form of its own, adapted the prevailing magnificence of Baroque style for their own purposes.

The rise of absolute monarchies and the unification of national states played an important part in the creation of national styles, since the monarchs and princes were among the most important patrons of a lavish musical life. The courts of Louis XIV and Louis XV of France and the Hapsburgs of Spain and Austria were centers that stimulated the production of large, spectacular forms of musical expression like the opera. Smaller courts, such as those of the German princes and dukes, were influential in cultivating intimate music for salon and chapel. The courts of the Dukes of Weimar and the Princes of Anhalt-Cöthen are examples of these smaller but highly cultural courts.

Worldwide intensive colonization during the seventeenth and eighteenth centuries gave rise to a wealthy merchant class. This wealth supplied the basis for the rich independent cities that were to provide a suitable climate for the establishment of a commercial theater and its musical production, the opera. Cities like Venice and Hamburg are good examples of such a concentration of merchant wealth and their musical theaters became internationally famous during the period.

Scholarly inquiry became much more important in the Baroque era. Discoveries through the application of inductive reasoning were most spectacular in the sciences of physiology, astronomy, mathematics, and physics. The success of scientific examination in these fields influenced musicians to apply methods of science to problems of music, and led to a systematic development of the techniques and materials of musical art. Such works, discoveries, and devices as Bach's

Art of the Fugue, Rameau's *Treatise on Harmony,* the practice of well-tempered tuning, and the perfection of the violin family are all examples of the urge to systematize and to investigate through scientific inquiry.

Literature and music abounded in affectations and expressive feeling. Architecture achieved these by means of such devices as the arch without a keystone and the twisted stone columns as decorative elements whose function no longer was architectural but expressive. Music achieved these same qualities in the tension created by dissonance within the tonal system of Baroque harmony. Related to this was the *doctrine of affections,* a philosophical position that assumed that the arousal and sustaining of feelings and affections was the primary purpose of music. This doctrine expected that a consistent emotion be evoked and sustained throughout a movement or composition. As the doctrine was practiced, numerous musical formulae were devised for the evocation of particular emotions. It was a calculated and planned emotional music.

II. FUNCTION OF MUSIC

While a great deal of religious music was written for purely liturgical purposes, especially for the Lutheran church, an increasing amount of religious music for instruments was used for nonliturgical purposes. Some of this nonliturgical music was used for preludes, postludes, and musical background for quasi-religious purposes such as marriage ceremonies, dedication of new buildings, and the installation of civil or religious officials.

Much music in the latter part of the Baroque was written for amateur musicians who performed in the households of the aristocracy and the wealthy class. Music for private entertainment was cultivated in these households where small bands of musicians provided both the compositions and performances of dinner music, dances and even ensemble concerts that ranged in style from the purely utilitarian to that of real aesthetic quality. While a substantial portion of this music was instrumental, vocal music was also very important. This was truly chamber music, meant more for the pleasure of the performer than for an audience.

In the large wealthy courts, ballet and opera were first performed as special entertainment for princes and courtiers. The opera soon developed into a very popular form of public entertainment. This occurred first in Italy and in private theaters, and thereafter in public theaters throughout Europe. Performances of purely instrumental character were rarely given for the general public.

The oratorio was the religious counterpart of the opera. Because of its subject matter and presentation without staging, gesture, costumes, or lighting, it was not as popular as opera, but it found success as a public choral concert.

Special festive occasions called for vocal music as well as instrumental music. The secular cantata was often presented for such events with texts that referred directly or allegorically to the occasion.

There was no institutional organization for teaching the musical arts. Young boys who showed interest and talent either were taught by their own musical fathers or relatives or were attached to the household of a composer-performer. Without doubt many compositions were written for the teaching of such prospective musicians. Such works as the *Orgelbüchlein* (Little Organ Book) by J. S. Bach was in part to provide exercise material for his four musical sons. The *Art of Playing on the Violin,* long erroneously attributed to Geminiani, was a systematic approach to instrumental pedagogy. Instruction in performance and composition was restricted to the aspiring musician and to the households of the aristocracy and wealthy burghers.

III. STYLE AND PERFORMANCE PRACTICE

For the first time in the history of western European music, two styles flourished side by side: (1) the Renaissance style, the *stile antico* or *prima prattica* which carried over into the Baroque period; and (2) the new Baroque style itself, often called *stile moderno* or *seconda prattica.* The following characterizations apply to the *stile moderno* or *nuove musiche,* which is typically Baroque. It must be realized, however, that many composers, including some of the most important, continued to use characteristics of Renaissance style.

The *stile moderno* was characterized by several stylistic compositional devices peculiar to the Baroque itself. One of these devices was given the Greek name of *monody.* This was a manner of writing in which melodic line was supported by a very simple chordal accompaniment. Strictly speaking, therefore, it is in homophonic style. Originally the melodic line was something midway between speech and song and was called *stile rappresentativo.* It was characterized by freedom of rhythm, dramatic pauses, and asymmetric phrases. The alleviation of the monotony of the musical declamation by means of passages that were more melodic eventually gave rise to the distinction in monodic style between recitative and aria.

Another characteristic of Baroque music was the *stile concertato.* In concertato style the composer used instrumental and vocal forces in compositions that were harmonic or contrapuntal in style. The style includes planned contrasts of instruments or voices against one another either as soloists or as groups. Many of the vocal and instrumental forms of the later Baroque are derived from this style of writing.

The *stile concitato* or excited style was a practice in which music illustrated the words or moods of the dramatic action. The use of tremolo in the strings of the orchestra or rapidly sung syllables to a repeated note by the voice are typical of this style.

Formal Organization. Contrapuntal development of thematic material continued to be used in works which were wholly or partially contrapuntal—the fugue, toccata, and the chorale prelude. The new homophonic forms, particularly in instrumental music, generally depended upon simple statement and contrast of melodic material. The variation principle was a logical expansion of these forms, and evolved homophonically and contrapuntally into the theme and variation, passacaglia, or chorale variation.

A great number of solo instrumental works for keyboard instruments, especially organ and harpsichord, were written in a style which suggested improvisation. Rapid scale passages, decorations, or chordal figurations in a free style were characteristic of such compositions, often called *fantasias*. Sometimes such improvisatory passages were used for a display of a brilliant technique, and were dictated by this consideration rather than purely musical ones.

As in the Renaissance, text continues to dominate vocal musical forms, but in different ways. In the new recitative the text was declared in an almost theatrical style thought to replicate vocal delivery in the Greek theater.

The establishment of major and minor tonalities led to distinct phrase and period construction in formal design. This was common to instrumental and vocal music, as was the frequently used device of sequential patterning in formal organization.

Melody. Melodic writing varies from the declamatory style of the recitative to the extremely florid style of the late Baroque arias and instrumental melodies. An example of the latter is referred to as *fortspinnung*, a process of melodic writing in which short figures are developed into melodic lines of substantial length and complexity. In recitative, the declamatory style, which to modern ears may appear to be a negation of melody, dominated the formal structure.

The recitative, a creation of early Baroque composers, represented a melodic idea whose structure was determined solely by verbal considerations. Two forms of recitative were employed. One was known as *recitativo secco* (dry recitative) in which only a thorough bass accompanied the voice (Ex. 23). The second, *recitativo accompagnato* accompanied recitative) was more dramatic, and was accompanied by

Example 23. Recitativo Secco from the *Passion according to St. Matthew*

Heinrich Schütz

Example 24. Recitativo accompagnato from *Unser Mund sind voll Lachens*, Cantata # 10

J. S. Bach

an ensemble of instruments (Ex. 24). Accompanied recitative style was usually used to introduce an aria in cantatas and the dramatic forms of opera and oratorio.

In a real sense the opera was the progenitor of the *bel canto* (beautiful singing) style which emphasized beauty of vocal sound and brilliant florid technique. Composers provided for this demand by writing melodies which were musically scintillating and often dramatically expressive. In conformity with this demand, melodies often deteriorated into spectacular vocalises with ornamentation either written in or left to the discretion of the singer.

In the Baroque, melody gradually assumed vocal and instrumental idiomatic styles, but these were often interchangeable. However, in the early decades of the seventeenth century, publications appeared which designated specifically whether the music was to be sung or played. It was not uncommon to find purely vocal design applied to instrumental writing and vice versa. Both instrumental and vocal music employed melodic line of extended range. The desire for

Example 25. Tenor aria from *Ich hatte viel Bekümmernis*, Cantata # 21

J. S. Bach

vocal display and the use of homophonic style account for this phenomenon, while the continued perfection of keyboard and stringed instruments made an extended instrumental range possible.

In homophonic music, melody was essentially one of balanced phrase and period, usually in four or eight measures. While the upper melodic line was dominant, there existed a kind of polarity between the melody and the bass line which was in itself a melodically conceived part (Ex. 25).

Rhythm

Except for recitative, repeated metrical units became the standard in Baroque music. Tempos were more constant in part because of the importance of the moving basso continuo, which gave a certain driving, almost motoric, feeling to both instrumental and choral works written in contrapuntal style. The rapid change of harmony induced by the basso continuo also made for a driving harmonic rhythm, the movement given to music by changes in harmony, which added its force to the total rhythmic motion.

Harmony

A fundamental change in harmony occurred during the Baroque. The reliance on modal systems of the past gradually yielded to the major-minor system of tonal relationships. This system dominated western music until the twentieth century. Even in works which were essentially contrapuntal, Baroque counterpoint was based on major-minor tonality rather than the modality of the Renaissance.

The chordal nature of harmony was reflected in a system of numbers placed under the notes of the bass line. The harmonic figurations of the bass line, suggesting rapid changes of harmony, especially in the works of the late Baroque, were then realized by the keyboard performer. The bass line and its performance were called by various names: thorough bass, figured bass, basso continuo, or continuo. (Example 26 illustrates the use of figured bass and Example 27 is a possible realization of the same bass.)

Example 26. Soprano aria from *Ich hatte viel Bekümmernis*, Cantata #21, showing unrealized figured bass

J. S. Bach

Example 27. Soprano aria as in example 26, showing realized figured bass

J. S. Bach

Seuf -zer, Trä - nen,Kum - mer,

Chromaticism and dissonance were freely employed in Baroque music for expressive purposes. Tempered tuning of keyboard instruments was introduced and made possible the chromatic changes that were necessary for extended modulations. Bach's *Das Wohltemperierte Klavier* (The Well-Tempered Clavier) illustrates, in a series of forty-eight preludes and fugues, how tempered tuning made it possible to play in all keys, both major and minor, without retuning the instrument.

Texture

Homophonic textures began to predominate in vocal and instrumental forms. There are abundant examples in opera and in solo arias of all kinds, as well as in instrumental forms such as the sonata da camera, keyboard sonatas, and suites. The tendency in purely homophonic forms to include contrapuntal techniques and the harmonic richness of contrapuntal forms tended to make the texture of most Baroque music rather thick and opaque.

The interest in homophonic texture did not exclude polyphonic textures, which were achieved by tonal counterpoint. Such counterpoint was used in religious choral works as well as in many types of instrumental compositions such as the fugue, chorale prelude, or variations on a ground.

There was great emphasis on contrasting textures, especially in the concertato style. The common contrast of large and small groups was enhanced by the general use of contrapuntal treatment for the large group and homophonic treatment for the smaller group.

Instrumentation and Tone Color

Many of the instruments of the Baroque era were forerunners of modern instruments. The violin family, for example, was perfected and gradually displaced the viols by the end of the period. Composition became increasingly idiomatic as composers wrote for the possibilities and limitations of specific instruments.

Trio sonatas were written for one of the most popular chamber music ensembles of the Baroque. Despite its title, it most frequently consisted of four instruments: two treble melodic instruments (often interchangeable), a bass instrument to play the continuo part (wind or string instrument), and a keyboard instrument to realize the figured bass (usually a harpsichord or organ). Such instrumentation is not always employed. For example, Bach wrote six trio sonatas for organ as well as solo sonatas for violin which are essentially trio sonatas as well.

In the Baroque, the *solo sonata*, whose name again belies the instrumentation, consisted of three instruments—a melody, a bass, and a keyboard instrument which comprised the continuo.

The instrumentation of the orchestra was not fixed. Orchestras accompanied vocal dramatic works and performed as independent musical organizations. The Baroque orchestra was smaller than the modern orchestra and consisted mainly of strings and woodwinds, with brass and percussion added for special effects. At the beginning of the period the brass instruments were natural, that is, without valves. Much solo music was written for the high or *clarino* register of the natural trumpet, often called the *clarin trumpet*.

The Baroque organ was an instrument of great clarity and mellowness of tone, but it could only execute crescendos by adding stops. In general, however, this was not done because terraced dynamics were the practice of the period. Contrasts in dynamics generally followed the Baroque practice of contrasting sonorities, achieved on the organ by changes in registration. Its limited volume and pureness of tone quality made the Baroque organ an ideal instrument for realizing the transparent contrapuntal texture of the organ music of the period. Many of the great composers of the Baroque wrote for the organ and were organ performers.

The term *clavier* referred to all types of keyboard instruments, especially the harpsichord and the clavichord. The former, known variously as *clavecin, cembalo, gravicembalo, spinet,* and *virginal,* was the more widely used instrument. The harpsichord was displaced by the *pianoforte,* invented in 1709 by Cristofori, but not universally adopted until after the Baroque era. Much solo and ensemble music was written for the harpsichord, especially in the last half of the Baroque.

In addition to the traditional vocal classifications of soprano, alto, tenor, and bass, which have persisted throughout history, the Baroque added male or artificial sopranos known as *castrati.* The power, range, and technical facility of the castrati voices made them a great favorite with Baroque opera audiences and accounts for many arias in Baroque operas which are extremely difficult for modern singers. The *counter-tenor,* or male alto, which used a falsetto voice in singing, continued from the Renaissance, but now in a solo role as well as in sacred ensemble music.

(Appendix 1 includes further information on instruments.)

The Baroque was the last period in which improvisation was a definite requisite of every performer. Such improvisatory techniques as the realization and actual addition of ornaments in both vocal and instrumental performance were not only tolerated but expected. In fact, in both instrumental and vocal music composers often only outlined the melodic line with the full expectation of having the performer add not only ornamentation but passing tones, scale passages, and even melodic fragments to the notated melody. Vocal music was particularly given to such improvisatory additions at highly expressive points, often dictated by the texts, and known as *gorgia.* In the later Baroque, brilliant rapid ornamentation of a virtuoso type was known as *coloratura,* and it sometimes designated a particular soprano voice type.

The high altar, Augustin Church of Freibourg, Switzerland (1592–1601), by Peter Spring. Four of the angelic host from this central group are playing instruments which are clearly identifiable; left upper, a harp; left lower, a zink (cornetto); right upper, a lute; right lower, a sackbut (trombone). The sculptured group represents the acceptance of secular music into the church art and music of the Baroque era. (Courtesy of Bärenreiter-Bildarchiv)

In all music performers were expected to extend cadences, especially climactic cadences near the end of a movement or work, with elaborate improvisation. Such improvisations came to take the name of *cadenzas*. In solo arias of operas and in solo instrumental concertos, cadenzas became integral parts of the works, and performers used them not only to exhibit their ability at improvisation but also their command of technical skill. Organists practice improvisation to the present day.

Closely allied to pure improvisation was the realization or completion of the harmonies indicated in the figured bass by keyboard performers. Where figuration was present the realization consisted of improvising suitable chordal and rhythmic patterns or even contrapuntal lines. (See Ex. 27.) Much music, however, was not even figured so that the keyboard realization demanded the choosing of both the proper harmony and its patterns.

Various systems of tempered tuning were adopted during the Baroque. Mean-tone temperament was the most consistently employed, but by the end of the Baroque period the tendency toward a system of equal temperament was indicated by the ever increasing modulatory practice of composers. Tuning of some instruments varied, such as the altered tuning of the violin, known as *scordatura*, a tuning used to achieve unusual chordal effects and note combinations which would otherwise be impossible.

While writing for instruments became more and more idiomatic, there was still freedom given to the choice of instruments in certain compositions. Flutes, both recorder and the new transverse or German flute, as well as oboes and violins were often interchangeable in ensemble music. Tremolo and pizzicato were string instrument performance techniques introduced in this period. Dynamic markings such as p., f., cresc., dim., were introduced, but were used very sparingly. Most dynamic variations were achieved by contrasting instrumental groups of varied size or quality.

Signs and symbols were increasingly used to designate particular ornaments in the Baroque. Performers were expected to improvise ornamentation even though it was not marked by the composer. While some of the signs were in common usage, many of them took on the personal meaning of the composers or schools to which they belonged. This has given rise to many differences of interpretation in the works of the Baroque. Tempo designations such as *allegro, andante,* and *grave* were also introduced, but bore imprecise meanings.

Almost all composers were recognized as virtuoso performers as well. This was especially true of keyboard performers. Both Bach and Handel were celebrated as skillful performers of the organ. Corelli,

Tartini, and Biber made notable advances in the technic of violin playing, with double stops, triple stops, arpeggios, and so forth. In the performance of opera, the castrato, Farinelli, became internationally known as a virtuoso singer of opera.

IV. MUSIC FOR VOICES

Single Movement Forms and Structural Devices
Recitative

Vocal passages written in a style of highly inflected declamation are known as recitatives. This is the declamatory form of the *stile rappresentativo* which came to be separated from the lyrically melodic parts of the monody. By the end of the seventeenth century the clear distinction between recitative and aria had been accomplished. The recitative served to carry the narrative and acted both as a prelude to and the connecting material between the highly emotional points represented by the arias. Recitatives took no formal structure such as the aria. They were rhythmically free and served as a vocal vehicle for the prose dialogue. In some situations recitative might be accompanied by full orchestra. In quick moving operatic narrative, it was often accompanied only by the continuo that performed from the figured bass. In the former case, it was known as *recitativo accompagnato* (accompanied recitative). The latter was called *recitativo secco* (dry recitative). (Rec. 5.1, 5.2)

Aria

The more melodic passages of the *stile rappresentativo* took on a formal character and finally separated from the declamatory parts as arias. The most typical form which these arias assumed was the three part or *da capo aria* in which a musical statement was followed by a contrasting section, that was in turn followed by a repetition of the original section with ornamentation. This form was almost universally adopted by the writers for all musical dramatic works, secular and religious. The aria form was often applied to ensembles such as the *chamber duet* or the trio. (Rec. 5.3, 5.4)

Arioso

The *arioso* was a free vocal form for solo voice that emerged from the declamatory style of the recitative and moved toward the lyrical style of the aria. Like the aria, the arioso was accompanied by full orchestra, often with repeated figures. The arioso was often used to express rapid changes of mood by means of the vocal line and the orchestral accompaniment. More brief than the aria, the arioso was not cast in any formal design. (Rec. 5.5, 5.6)

Chorus

Choral and ensemble works or passages took on no new formal characteristics. Contrapuntal texture generally prevailed in the oratorio and mass, while homophonic texture frequently invaded operatic writing. Because of the emphasis on solo singing, choral passages were infrequent in Baroque opera and occurred only when dramatic incidents required it as part of the action. (Rec. 5.7)

Motet

Baroque composers continued the Renaissance tradition of the unaccompanied choral motet. Typically, however, the motet was moving toward tonal counterpoint as opposed to the modal counterpoint of the past. The motet was generally liturgical, and was used in both the Roman Catholic and Lutheran services. (Rec. 5.8)

Spiritual Concerto

Works variously known as *concerti ecclesiastici* and as *Geistliche konzerte* were frequently composed in concertato style. They were restricted to a few voices with continuo or sometimes a few concerted instruments. Many of them were for only a single voice. German composers of the seventeenth century used spiritual concertos most frequently since it could be used in much the same manner as a cantata in the Lutheran service. (Rec. 5.9, 5.10)

Anthem

Baroque composers continued to write anthems (see Renaissance vocal compositions) for the Anglican church. The verse anthem with an introduction of dramatic style was most typical of the Baroque era in England. (Rec. 5.11)

Solo song

Solo songs, though not constituting a major form, were being written especially by German composers. They were strophic, usually of folk character, in binary or ternary form similar to arias, and with instrumental accompaniment. The English lute song is sometimes associated with the Renaissance, but it is arguably an expression of the Baroque as well. (Rec. 5.12)

Composite Forms

Opera

The most significant composite vocal form originating in the Baroque period was the dramatic opera, first called *dramma per musica*. The first impulse toward this form was given by certain intellectuals, noblemen, poets, and musicians who met in Florence. They formed a group known as the Florentine Camerata who wished to create a drama in which words would dominate the music and dictate the rhythm. This was a seventeenth century attempt to recreate what was thought to be the role of music in the classical tragedies of ancient Greeks. The expression of this desire came to be called the monodic style. Opera generally concerned itself with secular themes shaped into dramatic form. Early opera was based on Greek myths but later works dealt with historical, legendary, and fictional heroes and heroines, and were referred to as *opera seria*. The comic entr'actes of the opera seria were brought together at the end of the seventeenth century constituting an independent comic opera form, *opera buffa* (comic opera). The *opera buffa* (Italy), and the parallel forms of *opera comique* (France), *Singspiel* (Germany), and even the *ballad opera* (England) became commercially successful to a large degree due to their use of the vernacular, their focus on comedy, and on characters of greater realism than those of opera seria.

Opera was written for soloists, chorus, and orchestra, and was staged with appropriate scenic settings and dramatic presentation. Elaborate stage machinery was often a dominant part of the stage decor. While the first operas were performed for private groups in such surroundings as palace halls and theaters, opera houses were soon built for public presentations.

Musically the opera used a variety of formal sections such as arias, choruses, dances, duets, and other ensemble numbers. The music was largely homophonic in texture. Choral passages, generously used in the early operas, were finally reduced to insignificance, while solo arias received more and more attention.

Because of the great public appeal of opera by the end of the seventeenth century, certain characteristics were attached to it by virtue of its national origin. Four general schools of opera can be discerned, namely Italian, French, English, and German.

The Italian school was the first and most widely disseminated. Its main centers were Florence, Venice, Rome, and Naples, from which it spread to all the great political and economic centers of Europe. By the end of the seventeenth century, most Italian opera had become little more than an elaborate display of solo singing. Arias in *bel canto* style, displaying elaborately embellished and virtuoso passages were held together loosely by dramatic narrative sung in recitativo secco. The orchestra provided an overture and an unobtrusive accompaniment for the vocal passages which added little to the dramatic intensity of the work. (See orchestral overture.) (Rec. 5.13–5.15)

The centers of French opera were the royal courts of France, especially under the reigns of Louis XIV and Louis XV. It differed from Italian opera in language and general emphasis. French composers, influenced by the great popularity and prestige of classic French drama, tended to emphasize dramatic sincerity and action, and wrote arias of simpler melodic line with less demands on virtuoso technique. A clear difference was the inclusion of ballet episodes, an attempt to give national character to French opera by continuing the tradition of the *ballet de cour*. In French opera the orchestra provided an overture in the French style. (See orchestral overture.) It also provided the music for the dances as well as accompaniment for the singing. (Rec. 5.16–5.18)

English opera is represented by very few works. The general characteristics were adopted from French and Italian models. The tradition of the English dramatic form of the masque to which music was often added was influential in the few operas written. (Rec. 5.19)

In Germany, opera found wide acceptance, and while the Italian style was well entrenched, a considerable number of important German composers were active. Most of their works were in the Italian style, even when written to German texts. The *Singspiel*, a native German form in which songs of a popular nature were combined into a new musical entertainment, was the only original form comparable to opera. (Rec. 5.20, 5.21)

Oratorio

The oratorio employed the same forces as the opera, but was distinguished from it in that it usually did not use dramatic action, costumes, or stage settings for presentation. Originally performed in the oratory of the church in Italy, by the end of the Baroque it had become a musical dramatic form based on a religious but nonliturgical theme, and presented in concert form. The oratorio, while it employed soloists, tended to emphasize the chorus and usually contained a number of large choral movements.

The forms of the solo and small ensemble movements were identical with those of opera, though often of more reserved character. The choral movements, however, were almost exclusively contrapuntal, ranging from strict to free fugal forms. The oratorio frequently used a dramatic character known as the narrator (*storicus or testo*) who introduces and often narrates the story of the work by means of recitative. (Rec. 5.22–5.24)

Passion Music

The settings of the passion of Christ as narrated in the four gospels of the New Testament were frequently set for both Roman Catholic and Lutheran use. These settings were actually oratorios whose texts were restricted to Biblical quotations concerning Christ's trial and crucifixion, and such other commentary as the composer might select in keeping with this subject. A narrator took the part of the evangelist and sang all the narration that was not in direct quotation in recitative style. Other soloists took the parts of Biblical characters or sang solos which were commentary on the story. The chorus (*Turba*) represented people, soldiers, and priests, and its members also sang choruses based on the commentary. In many passion settings for the Lutheran church, German Protestant chorales were used. Otherwise these works were constructed in the same manner as the oratorios of the period. (Rec. 5.25)

Cantata

In the publications of the early Baroque, title pages would use the word *cantade* and variants thereof to instruct that the contents were to be sung. From that beginning the cantata developed in several forms and for several purposes. Solo and choral cantatas were written for liturgical and nonliturgical religious purposes, as well as secular occasions.

The structure of these cantatas was essentially the same in all instances. Small instrumental groups were employed for accompaniment with solo instruments often used in obligato fashion with the voice. Soloists and chorus provided the vocal forces. The forms of the aria, ensembles, and choruses were the same as those used in opera and oratorio. Cantatas might be regarded as miniature oratorios. The primary difference between solo cantatas and choral cantatas was the forces employed. While solo cantatas were obviously written for a single solo voice, choral cantatas, in addition to the chorus, employed soloists as well.

While Roman Catholic and Protestant composers both wrote cantatas, those written by Lutheran composers in the sixteenth and seventeenth centuries comprise the greatest wealth of church music of this period. These were liturgical cantatas and might be said to represent a kind of musical sermon since most cantatas were written for specific holy days in the church calendar. (Rec. 5.26–5.30)

Mass

The Roman Catholic mass continued to be set, now in typical Baroque style, taking on a dramatic character with the addition of orchestral accompaniment and frequent division of its various sections into solo and ensemble as well as choral settings. Even the da capo aria form was employed in some instances. (Rec. 5.31)

V. INSTRUMENTAL COMPOSITIONS

In general there were no specific instruments designated for much of Baroque instrumental music. Instruments were interchangeable. For example, keyboard compositions could be performed on the harpsichord, clavichord, or even the organ. In ensembles, violins, flutes and oboes were often interchangeable, as were the bassoon, cello and string bass. In some works instruments such as the natural trumpet or oboe d'amore, for example, were specified, but could be substituted by other instruments of the same range.

Single Movement Forms and Structural Devices

Toccata

The toccata, frequently called *prelude,* grew out of the improvisatory style and was a continuation of the Renaissance toccata. In mature Baroque style the improvisatory toccata was coupled with a section in imitative contrapuntal style. A final crystallization of form was revealed in the toccata, which framed a fugue middle section between two rhapsodic improvisatory parts. The toccata was frequently treated as a single movement independent of the fugal with which it was often paired. In this case it was likely to be of purely improvisatory nature. (Rec. 5.32)

Prelude

This name is freely used to describe an introductory movement, usually one of improvisatory character. It is often applied to the toccata form itself. In the late Baroque, preludes coupled with fugues were usually free and in indefinite form. (Rec. 5.33–5.35)

Ricercar

The ricercar is an imitative contrapuntal form for harpsichord or organ. The Baroque ricercar, in contrast to that of the Renaissance, is a work in which one theme is developed imitatively throughout. The distinction between ricercar and fugue is more one of rhythmic drive than of formal organization. The ricercar is frequently modal exploiting its thematic material with less climactic contrast, making less use of sequential treatment, and using thematic material that is slower moving and potentially less significant rhythmically. (Rec. 5.36)

Fugue

The fugue is an imitative contrapuntal texture built on a single theme or subject repeated in two or more individual voices. The presentation of the subject alternately on tonic and dominant pitch levels (the latter form of the subject is known as the answer), emphasizes the tonic-dominant relationship as a means of achieving formal development. Fugues, in contrast to the ricercars from which they were developed, used subjects of more melodic and rhythmic character. Fugues commonly employ the imitative devices of stretto, inversion, augmentation, and diminution. They often employ a persistent countersubject along with the principal subject and develop the subject through various key changes, rhythmic treatments, or sequential appearances. Episodes, or sections in which the subject does not appear in its entirety, alternate with repeated appearances of the subject in some or all of the voices. While the fugue is generally a single movement of comparatively brief duration, it is possible to present the fugal material in a great variety of key relationships so that the single movement can be drawn out to considerable length. A fugue with two subjects is called a double fugue.

While the fugue is essentially an instrumental form, especially well adapted to organ and other keyboard performance, fugal writing is found in many other instrumental forms and also in large choral works of the Baroque period. It represents the highest development of harmonic contrapuntal technique of the period. (Rec. 5.37–5.39)

Fantasia

An instrumental composition, the fantasia was originally closely related to the ricercar. In the Baroque it became a loosely structured, improvisatory-sounding composition for various solo instruments or small ensembles. Some composers, such as Telemann, wrote solo fantasias which were more on the order of Italian sonatas than the early ricercar.

The term *fancy* was used in England to designate works of this general nature written for an ensemble or consort of viols or wind instruments. The name fantasia was also given to improvisatory single movement works which were later paired with fugues, as were preludes and toccatas. (Rec. 5.40–5.41)

Orchestral Overture

While this term was used variously, two forms growing out of Italian and French opera are typical of the multiple section works generally called overtures. The French and Italian overtures differ mainly in the order of their three sections. The French overture consists of a slow section with pompous dotted rhythms and rich harmonies followed by a lively, driving fugal section. It concludes with a return to the opening slow section or at least a part of it. The Italian overture reverses the order of movements to fast, slow, fast. Both types were used as pure orchestral forms as well as orchestral openings to operas. (Rec. 5.42, 5.43)

Theme and Variation

An extension of the same form used in the Renaissance in which a melody either original or preexisting, more often the latter, is presented in a number of variations. In the Baroque, theme and variation writing became more idiomatic, exploiting the technical possibilities of specific instruments. Two kinds of variation were employed. One was of a contrapuntal character in which the melody remained intact as it wandered from voice to voice while the counterpoint changed in each variation. The other was essentially homophonic, in which the harmony remained the same throughout while the melody above the harmony was ornamented or changed in subsequent variations. (Rec. 5.44, 5.45)

Passacaglia and Chaconne

While there are those who contend these two names designate different forms, both are variations on a repeated bass line (basso ostinato) of four to eight measures. Sometimes this ostinato melody can be found in voices other than the bass, or disappear altogether, leaving only a repeated harmonic progression. Passacaglias and chaconnes were written for all types of instruments and combinations although those for keyboard are the more frequent. (Rec. 5.46, 5.47)

Chorale Prelude

This is generic organ music in which a chorale tune is the basis of the composition. In some instances the chorale tune acts as a theme for a set of variations. Such works are known as *chorale partitas* or *chorale variations*. In other instances the chorale tune forms the basis for a fantasia, and the work is then known as a *chorale fantasia*. By far the most popular, however, was a single setting of the chorale tune which might vary from a highly developed fugal treatment to a rather simple homophonic presentation. This last form probably originated as a prelude to the singing of the chorale by the congregation in the Lutheran church. (Rec. 5.48–5.50)

Composite Forms
Suite

The idea of extending an instrumental piece by joining a number of dance movements of different rhythms and tempos is an extension of the Renaissance device of pairing dances. The typical early suite was written for harpsichord and combined four dances to form a complete work. These dances are the *Allemande, Courante, Sarabande,* and *Gigue.* Generally, each dance is in binary form, with the first part ending in the dominant key and the second half returning to the tonic. Each dance retains its original rhythmic character but is cast in an idealized form with no practical use in mind. The dances have no thematic relationship to one another and the only unifying factor is the constancy of key among all the dances. While the four dances named were considered the basic dances of the suite (*partita* in German, also *ordre* in French), other dances, even those in then current ballroom use, were often added to, or substituted for, the original dances. Such optional dances, frequently following the sarabande, might include the *Minuet, Bourrée, Gavotte,* and *Loure.* This is especially true of the French ordre. (Rec. 5.51, 5.52)

Orchestral Suite

As in the chamber sonata, there was no set number or order of dances in the orchestral suite. The orchestral suite was often called an overture because the first movement was frequently in the form of the French overture. (Rec. 5.53)

Sonata da Chiesa (Church sonata)

These compositions evolved from the sectional canzona of the Renaissance into a rather freely designed multimovement form which became one of the most important in the chamber music of the Baroque period. While there are no definite forms for individual movements, these compositions generally used alternating slow and fast tempos with contrapuntal or fugal style in one or more movements. The sonata da chiesa was written for various instrumental combinations: any solo melodic instrument with continuo, or more frequently, for two violins or other melodic instruments and continuo (trio sonata). While dance forms were regularly found in the sonata da camera, movements of the sonata da chiesa were sometimes in dance forms though not necessarily so designated. The sonata da chiesa often went by the simple name *sonata*, especially in the late Baroque. (Rec. 5.54, 5.55)

Sonata da Camera (Chamber sonata)

This is the ensemble form of the suite written as a solo sonata or trio sonata, but often using larger groups. Adherence to the basic four dances was less likely to be found in the chamber sonata. Additional and substitute dances were often used. A prelude frequently preceded the chamber sonata, and movements other than dances, such as the aria, were often present. (Rec. 5.56, 5.57)

Keyboard Sonata

The original use of the term sonata to differentiate instrumental from vocal works was often retained in the Baroque period. A number of keyboard compositions therefore bear the title sonata, though they do not resemble either of the two typical sonata types of the Baroque, sonata da chiesa or sonata da camera. Some of these sonatas consisted of several movements, while others had only one. Generally, simple binary or ternary forms were used for individual movements, which varied from dance-like character to song types, usually homophonic in texture. The greatest exponent of the keyboard sonata in the Baroque was Domenico Scarlatti. (Rec. 5.58)

Concerto and Concerto Grosso

Two forms of the concerto, the solo concerto and the concerto grosso, were the final instrumental contributions of the Baroque period. These two forms differed only in that the solo concerto used a single instrument as soloist, while the concerto grosso used a group of soloists, generally three, in contrast to the larger mass of orchestral sound.

Three movements are most frequently employed: first, an allegro; then a slow movement in a closely related key; and finally, a shorter fast movement in the original key. Each of the movements is constructed on the concertato principle, alternating soloist or soloists (concertino) and full orchestra (tutti or ripieno). While soloists and orchestra may be given different themes, usually the entire thematic material is presented by the full group and then developed by the soloist or soloists in turn. The solo concerto and the concerto grosso were at times designed to display the technical virtuosity of the soloists. As well, they offered the Baroque composer the possibility of combining the concertato idea, the polarity of bass and treble melody, the concept of clear major-minor tonality, and the use of a number of separate movements into a single idealized instrumental form. (Rec. 5.59–5.62)

VI. COMPOSERS

Giulio Caccini (c. 1550–1618) was an Italian singer and composer associated with the Florentine Camerata. His performance of the new type of monodic composition, *musica in stile rappresentativo*, was looked upon as the idea of his style. His most important work was the collection of madrigals and arias published under the title *Le Nuove musiche*. Its preface contains one of the clearest and most detailed descriptions of the manner of performance of the new monodic style. (Rec. 5.63)

Jacopo Peri (1561–1633), a member of the Florentine Camerata, composed the opera *Dafne*. It is one of the earliest operas in the new monodic style. Peri was known for his masterly handling of pedal-point basses, a device which suited his delight in somber subject matter. (Rec. 5.64)

Jan Pieterzoon Sweelinck (1562–1621) was a celebrated Dutch organist and composer. His two outstanding contributions to organ literature are the development of the organ chorale variation, leading to the organ prelude, and his use of monothematic treatment in the ricercar, which resulted in the form known as the fugue. While he also wrote a great number of vocal works in Renaissance style, his organ compositions belong to the early Baroque. As the teacher of many German pupils he was to become the founder of the famous north German organ school. (Rec. 5.65)

Claudio Monteverdi (1567–1643), the greatest of the early Italian Baroque composers, was the creator of the first operatic masterpiece in modern style. In *Orfeo*, he adapted the Florentine recitative style to closed forms of the aria and dance song. He was equally at home in the Renaissance polyphonic and the Baroque monodic idioms. His madrigals are among the finest of the Italian school, but even here he shows his association with the modern school of the Baroque through his close attention to word and mood expression. Monteverdi expanded the orchestra and in some cases scored for specific instruments in his dramatic works. His harmonic writing was for expressive purposes, and caused much adverse criticism, particularly by one Giovanni Artusi. Among his works are eight books of madrigals, dramatic scenes, religious music, and a number of operas. The most important operas are *Orfeo*, *Il Ritorno d'Ulisse in patria*, *L'Incoronazione di Poppea*. He also wrote dramatic scenes and religious music. (Rec. 5.66)

Michael Praetorius (1571–1621), a German composer and theorist, devoted himself extensively to the writing of Lutheran choral works. His most important contribution to music history was made in his treatise, *Syntagma musicum.* (Rec. 5.67, 5.68)

Girolamo Frescobaldi (1583–1643), an Italian organist and composer, was an important link in the history of fugal form. While he wrote no works that were actually called fugues, his monothematic ricercars were among the most important forerunners of the fugue. As a teacher of Froberger his influence in the development of composition and performance of the south German organ school was equalled only by Sweelinck's influence in the north. He was recognized as one of the greatest organists of his day, and was appointed organist at St. Peter's in Rome. His compositions include toccatas, capriccios, ricercars, and canzonas, typical organ forms of the early Baroque. A collection of these works for church use appeared in his *Fiori musicali* (Musical Flowers). (Rec. 5.69)

Heinrich Schütz (1585–1672) was the greatest German composer before J. S. Bach. Evidence of his importance is the oft repeated designation of Schütz as the father of German music. He was the composer of the first German opera, *Daphne.* His contacts with Italian music of the late sixteenth and early seventeenth centuries led him to write a great number of dramatic religious vocal works to German texts that introduced the new Baroque style into Germany. He adapted the recitative, the thorough bass and the concertato principle to works for the Lutheran service, and laid the foundation for the great art of dramatic church music in his *Symphoniae sacrae* (Sacred Symphonies), *Cantiones sacrae* (Sacred Songs), and *Kleine geistliche Konzerten* (Little Sacred Concerti) which later blossomed into the cantatas and passion music of Bach and his contemporaries. Recent performances based on research into Schütz's music have revealed a starkness and simplicity of dramatic presentation. These characteristics are apparent in such works as *Die Sieben Wortte . . .* (The Seven Last Words), *Historia, der freuden-und gnadenreichen Geburt Gottes und Marien Sohnes, Jesu Christi* (The Christmas Oratorio), *Auferstehungs Historie* (The Resurrection of Our Lord), and his passion settings to the Gospels of Matthew, Luke, and John. (Rec. 5.70)

Johann Hermann Schein (1586–1630), another German, also helped introduce Italian monody and instrumental music into Germany. His choral adaptations for organ were representative of the great interest in this form. A collection of twenty suites for strings called *Banchetto musicale* represents some of the earliest instrumental works written in Germany. Schein also wrote numerous vocal compositions. (Rec. 5.71)

Samuel Scheidt (1587–1654) is often considered the most important German organ composer of the first half of the seventeenth century, particularly in his treatment of the chorale in true organ style. His greatest published work, *Tabulatura nova,* was a collection of figured chorales, toccatas, fantasias, hymns, and other works for the organ. Though his main contribution was in organ composition, he wrote many choral works as well. (Rec. 5.72)

Pier Francesco Cavalli (1602–1676) was celebrated as an opera composer in his native Italy, where he held the position of Maestro di Cappella at St. Mark's in Venice. He was also well known in France and Austria. Though he wrote church works, it was his forty-one operas that gained him wide recognition. His greatest operatic successes were *Jason, Cerce,* and *Ercole amante* (Hercules, The Lover). Cavalli's wide recognition attests to the rapid rise and acceptance of Italian opera in other countries. (Rec. 5.73)

Jacques Champion Chambonnières (c. 1610–1672) is regarded as the founder of the French clavecin school. As the teacher of Couperin the Elder, d'Angelbert, and others, his influence was felt not only in France but throughout Europe. He was first chamber musician to Louis XIV. His wide recognition influenced German harpsichord composers from Froberger to J. S. Bach. His compositions were exclusively for harpsichord. (Rec. 5.74)

Giacomo Carissimi (1605–1674), an Italian composer, applied the new devices of the monodic style to religious music, particularly the oratorio. His masterpiece, *Jephte,* is a composition of the highest musical and dramatic quality. He is regarded as the founder of the oratorio form. (Rec. 5.75)

Johann Jakob Froberger (1616–1667) was a German organist and pupil of Frescobaldi, whose techniques he introduced in Vienna. He wrote many works for the organ, and is credited with having created the keyboard suite and established the order of dances within it: Allemande, Courante, Sarabande, and Gigue. (Rec. 5.76)

Marc' Antonio Cesti (1623–1669) gained wide recognition as an Italian opera composer. *Il pomo d'oro* (The Golden Apple), produced in Vienna in 1667, is regarded as his masterpiece. (Rec. 5.77)

Jean-Henri d'Angelbert (c. 1628–1691) was a French composer and pupil of Chambonnières. His collection, *Pièces de clavecin* (Pieces for the Harpsichord) contains suites, arrangements of airs from Lully's operas and variations, as well as instructions on how to play figured bass. (Rec. 5.78)

Jean-Baptiste Lully (1632–1687) was the most distinguished opera composer of seventeenth century France though he was actually an Italian by birth. He succeeded in establishing a true French opera which was in effect a reform of the traditional Italian opera with its many musical excesses. He was able to give French opera a greater measure of dramatic sincerity through his handling of dramatic recitative, arias, and instrumental accompaniment. He established the French overture as well as the ballet as parts of French opera. His musical production was not exclusively operatic, however. He composed a great number of ballets for Molière's plays, some independent instrumental music, and religious choral works. Among his operatic masterpieces are *Cadmus et Hermione, Alceste, Armide et Renaud, Thésée,* and *Persée.* (Rec. 5.79)

Marc-Antoine Charpentier (1634–1704), a French composer and pupil of Carissimi, was mainly concerned with writing masses, motets, and oratorios. He also wrote operas and smaller dramatic works for the stage, but his popularity suffered from Lully's disfavor. (Rec. 5.80, 5.81)

Dietrich Buxtehude (1637–1707) was a famous German organist and composer. Buxtehude influenced J. S. Bach who made a two hundred-mile journey on foot in 1705 from Arnstadt to Lübeck to hear Buxtehude play. Buxtehude's works included all the current forms of organ music, much choral music, and a variety of chamber and harpsichord compositions. (Rec. 5.82)

Johann Pachelbel (1653–1706), a middle German organist and composer, wrote mainly organ works, though he also wrote for other keyboard instruments. His fugues are of utmost importance, not only because of their influence on Bach's writing, but for their intrinsic artistic value. (Rec. 5.83)

Arcangelo Corelli (1653–1713) was an Italian composer of great importance as well as a violin virtuoso. He is looked upon as the founder of modern violin technique, with its intricacies of bowing, performance of double stops, and chord effects. He was not a prolific composer. His entire output consisted of six opus numbers or collections, of which four are devoted to trio sonatas, one to violin and keyboard, and one to the concerto grosso. The latter represents a new form of composition of which Corelli is recognized as the creator. Handel was acquainted with Corelli and was undoubtedly influenced by his instrumental writing. (Rec. 5.84, 5.85)

Henry Purcell (c. 1659–1695) was England's most famous Baroque composer, and his death in 1695 brought to an end any important musical contribution from a native English composer for the next two hundred years. Despite a very short life, his works are numerous and represent all areas of composition. He was equally gifted as an instrumental and vocal composer. Among his most important works are numerous anthems and religious choral compositions, the collection of twelve trio sonatas published during his lifetime, and his one opera, *Dido and Aeneas,* a work still frequently performed. Purcell was singularly gifted in his ability to compose on a ground bass, one of which is Dido's lament, *When I am laid in earth.* (Rec. 5.86, 5.87)

Johann Kuhnau (1660–1722) was a German composer whose works for the harpsichord are the most important among his other instrumental and vocal compositions. He was J. S. Bach's immediate predecessor as cantor at St. Thomas Church in Leipzig. His most important works are his sonatas for harpsichord, especially the group of six entitled *Biblische Historien* (Biblical Sonatas). These are early examples of music in which stories are illustrated by means of musical allusion. (Rec. 5.88)

Alessandro Scarlatti (1660–1725) was known mainly for his contributions to the style of the Neapolitan opera of which he wrote over one hundred. He also added a rich literature of chamber and orchestral music as well as religious cantatas and masses to Italian music of the Baroque. Scarlatti established the da capo aria in the Neapolitan opera, a form which was generally adopted for all dramatic arias. (Rec. 5.89)

François Couperin (1668–1733), a member of a famous French family of musicians, was known as Couperin le Grand, because of his enormous skill as an organist. His religious compositions, mainly for the organ, constitute a large part of his works. His most numerous and renowned compositions, however, are those instrumental works which he wrote for the harpsichord during the last part of his life. The many ordres or suites for clavecin consist of dances that are often programmatic in nature. He also wrote *L'Art de toucher le clavecin* (The Art of Playing the Clavecin), which had wide influence. Among his best known works are the *Concerts Royaux* (Royal Concerts), the four volumes of *Pièces de clavecin* (Pieces for the Clavecin), and *Les Gouts réunis* (Gathered Tastes), the latter consisting of a number of concerted pieces written for strings and clavecin. Couperin's works are characterized by simple harmonies, generous ornamentation, and short phrases, all typical of the gallant style of his time. (Rec. 5.90, 5.91)

Antonio Vivaldi (1678–1741) was the most celebrated of all the Baroque Italian masters and probably the most musically prolific. While he wrote a large number of operas, oratorios, secular cantatas, and church music, his present fame rests on his concerti grossi and solo concerti. These number over four hundred. Vivaldi was a priest in the Roman Catholic church and for many years was in charge of the musical program of the Ospidale della Pietá in Venice, a home for orphaned and foundling girls. It was in discharge of this duty that he wrote most of his instrumental and smaller choral works which were performed by the girls in the institution. Among the most famous of the concerti grossi are the works known as *L'estro harmonico* (Harmonic Whim), *Il cimento dell' armonia e dell' inventione* (The Struggle between Harmony and Invention) and *Le quattro stagione* (The Four Seasons). J. S. Bach was especially influenced by Vivaldi's concertos and transcribed several for clavier. (Rec. 5.92, 5.93)

Georg Philipp Telemann (1681–1767) was perhaps the most prolific of German composers of the late Baroque era. His compositions were designed for every conceivable type of musical performance. Some concept of his enormous output can be gained from the fact that he wrote over forty operas, about three thousand cantatas and motets with orchestra or organ, six hundred overtures, forty-four passion settings, and equally numerous works for special occasions such as funerals, weddings, coronations, and consecrations. His fame was considerably greater during his lifetime than that of J. S. Bach. The last forty-six years of his life were spent in Hamburg where he was director of music for the city. He took this position in preference to that of cantor of St. Thomas Church in Leipzig. The latter position was then assumed by Bach who was second choice after Telemann in the eyes of the church council. Telemann remained relatively unknown during the nineteenth and early part of the twentieth centuries. However, the revival of interest in Baroque music during the past thirty years has brought his music to the fore again, particularly the orchestral and chamber music. (Rec. 5.94, 5.95)

Jean-Philippe Rameau (1683–1764) was well known in his day as a musical theorist, organist, and composer. His early career was devoted to organ playing in several of the great cathedrals of France. While serving in this capacity at Clermont-Ferand, he wrote his famous *Traité de l'harmonie* (Treatise of Harmony) in 1722. In this work he stated his system of chord building on superimposed thirds; the conception of a chord in all its inversions as one and the same entity; and the idea of a fundamental bass by which chord progressions are determined. His fame as a composer, however, is based mainly on his dramatic compositions, of which the works *Les Indes galantes* (The Gallant Indians) and *Castor et Pollux* are his masterpieces. In addition to many ballets, operas, and much incidental music for drama, Rameau wrote frequently for clavecin and chamber groups typical of the Baroque period. Rameau's dramatic works were exceptional for their expressive melodic line, originality of instrumentation, and richness of

Johann Sebastian Bach (1685–1750)
(Free Public Library of Philadelphia.)

harmonic idiom. Rameau's ideas aroused violent interest both antagonistic and favorable, first between those who favored him and those who favored Lully, and later between his adherents and the *Encyclopedists.* The latter exchange was known as the "War of the Buffoons." The perennial charges against the operatic innovator that were leveled against Monteverdi, Gluck and Wagner were leveled at Rameau. His critics found that his works lacked melody, were filled with illogical harmony, and used orchestral instruments in a noisy fashion. (Rec. 5.96, 5.97)

Johann Sebastian Bach (1685–1750) certainly was one of the greatest composers of all time. He was a member of what is, perhaps, the most interesting musical family in history. During a period encompassing several generations, over one hundred members of the Bach family in Thuringia were occupied in musical activities. Of this number some twenty were performers and composers of special significance, including both ancestors and offspring of Johann Sebastian.

At fifteen years of age Bach spent a short time of study with his brother Johann Christoph in Lüneburg. A year as violinist in the orchestra of the Duke of Saxe-Weimar was followed by his first real post as organist in Arnstadt in 1704. He left Arnstadt in 1707 to take the post of organist in Mülhausen. In 1708 he moved again, this time to Weimar where he was made court organist and chamber musician to the Duke of Weimar. In 1714 he was raised to the rank of chamber musician and remained in this post until 1717. During this time he made a reputation for himself as one of the great organists of his day as well as a composer of a wide variety of works in both secular and

Manuscript page from Bach, "B minor Mass," showing the instrumentation of the *Osanna.*

religious forms. In 1717 he accepted the post of chapelmaster and director of chamber music to the Prince of Anhalt at Cöthen. Here Bach composed most of his orchestral and chamber music. His wife Barbara died in 1720, and in 1721 Bach married Anna Magdalena Wülcken, a gifted musician whose handwriting is often found in early manuscripts of Bach's works.

In 1723 Bach succeeded Kuhnau as cantor of the Thomas School in Leipzig, a post he held until his death in 1750. As organist and director of music at the two principal churches in Leipzig, Bach composed most of his great church music during the next twenty-seven years.

Among the many visits he paid to other cities in the capacity of organist, organ installer, and composer, none was more famous than the one to the court of Frederick the Great in Potsdam. Bach's second son, Karl Philipp Emanuel, was chamber musician there. It was during this visit that Bach improvised upon a theme given him by Frederick, a theme which he later used as the basis for his work known as *Musikalisches Opfer* (Musical Offering). An unsuccessful eye operation in 1749 caused Bach to become totally blind, and in 1750 he died from a stroke. Bach represents the culmination of an era, particularly through his great emphasis on contrapuntal style. He was a master of the art of tonal counterpoint and his *Kunst der Fuge* (Art of the Fugue) is a veritable exhaustive treatise dealing with all manner of contrapuntal devices illustrated in the canons and fugues which comprise the work. His skill in handling fugal treatment is evident in all of his compositions: instrumental, vocal, secular, and religious. In his use of instruments he foreshadowed the future. He composed in every conceivable form except opera. While the preponderance of his works were written for the church, there is much of his instrumental output that is strictly secular in nature. Even the smallest works, however, demonstrate his care and attention to compositional excellence. His mastery of counterpoint within the tonal system is comparable to that of Palestrina within the modal system.

It was more than a half-century after his death before any measurable appreciation of his great contribution to the history of music was realized. Mendelssohn brought Bach to the attention of the musical world of the nineteenth century with a performance of the *Saint Matthew Passion* in Leipzig in 1829.

A great number of Bach's works were lost in manuscript; a comparatively small amount was published during his lifetime. Despite the great loss, the complete edition, begun in 1850 by the Bach Gesellschaft, contained forty-seven volumes. A second complete edition was begun in 1954. Bach's works were not given opus numbers. Today they are most commonly referred to by BWV (Bach Werk Verzeichniss) numbers. A more logical thematic catalogue is that by Wolfgang Schmieder, published in 1950 (6th edition, 1969). (In this catalogue, the numbers are preceded by "S.")

Among the great masterpieces remaining today are the following works listed under vocal and instrumental headings:

Vocal works: *Mass in b minor, The Passion According to St. Matthew, The Passion According to St. John, The Christmas Oratorio,* a *Magnificat,* approximately one hundred and ninety church cantatas, over twenty-five secular cantatas, and many other shorter works.

Instrumental Works: *Kunst der Fuge* (Art of Fugue), *Musikalishes Opfer* (The Musical Offering), the *Italian Concerto, The Goldberg Variations, Das Wohltemperierte Klavier* (The Well Tempered Clavier), suites, partitas, and inventions for harpsichord, four overtures (suites) for orchestra, six *Brandenburg Concerti,* six unaccompanied *Suites for Violoncello,* three sonatas and three partitas for solo violin, numerous works for organ, including chorale preludes, toccatas, preludes, fantasias and fugues, and concertos for harpsichord and violin as well as numerous sonatas for instrumental combinations. (Rec. 5.98–5.102)

Domenico Scarlatti (1685–1757), the greatest of the Italian composers for the keyboard, was one of the most original composers in the history of music. While he wrote works for the church and for the operatic stage, his greatest contribution was his more than five hundred compositions for the harpsichord. He was the son and pupil of Alessandro Scarlatti. After a very productive youth in Italy, he took a post with the Portuguese court in Lisbon where he became music master to the Princess Maria Barbara. It was for her that he composed the works that were to make him famous, the *Esercizi per gravicembalo* (Exercises for the Harpsichord), which are usually referred to as sonatas. When the princess married the heir to the Spanish throne, Scarlatti moved to Madrid where he spent the remainder of his life (from 1729 to 1757) as master of the salon. His sonatas are the finest example of late Baroque writing for the harpsichord. Scarlatti managed to exploit the instrument to the utmost in these works, and in so doing laid the foundation for future keyboard technique. Many of the works call for such innovations in performance as the crossing of the hands. The sonatas of Scarlatti reflect the whole gamut of moods from gay and dance-like, which often include Spanish rhythms, to lyric and romantic. (Rec. 5.103)

George Frideric Handel (1685–1759) was a compatriot of Johann Sebastian Bach, and one who shares with him the distinction of bringing the Baroque era to a close. In contrast to Bach, Handel was a cosmopolitan composer who added to his German heritage a wide study and firsthand knowledge of Italian musical style. He practiced these accomplishments during most of the last fifty years of his life, which he spent in England. Handel was something of a musical prodigy; for after instruction in organ, oboe, and harpsichord as well as counterpoint and fugue, he assumed a position as assistant organist in Halle, his native city, at the age of twelve. During this year he also composed a number of choral and instrumental works. In 1702 Handel went to Hamburg where he was associated with the opera until 1706. In the same year he went to Italy where he became successful as a composer of Italian opera and dramatic oratorios. In 1710 he returned to Germany as chapelmaster to the Elector of Hannover, a relationship that resulted in his going to England when the German prince took over the throne of England.

From this time on, Handel was occupied with a variety of activities such as teacher, director of the Royal Academy of Music (an institution whose prime purpose was the production of Italian opera in

George Frideric Handel (1685–1759)
(Free Public Library of Philadelphia.)

London) composer, opera impresario, and traveler. His main compositional area was that of opera until 1741, when he turned to the
composition and production of oratorios. It is in the latter field that
he achieved his most lasting fame.

His compositions of both secular and religious drama reveal a
spirit of grandeur, for there is always something of the pomp of the
court about his work. He wrote twenty-seven oratorios and over forty
operas as well as a great quantity of other vocal works such as anthems, cantatas, and vocal solos and ensembles. Handel was also a
prolific composer of instrumental compositions which include all the
Baroque forms: concerti grossi, harpsichord suites, organ concerti,
chamber music for strings, winds, and keyboard, and large orchestral
works. Among his numerous works, a few stand out as masterpieces:
the oratorios (*Messiah, Samson, Judas Maccabaeus, Solomon, Israel in Egypt,
Saul*), the operas (*Alcina, Giulio Cesare, Rinaldo, Xerxes*), the orchestral
music (*Water Music, Fireworks Music*), and twelve concerti grossi for
strings.

Several incomplete and often inaccurate editions of the works of
Handel have been issued from time to time. In 1955 work was begun
on a new complete edition issued by the Georg Friedrich Händel Gesellschaft of Halle. (Rec. 5.104–5.106)

Giovanni Battista Pergolesi (1710–1736), whose short life fell entirely within the eighteenth century, was, however, still a representative of the Baroque style of composition. He wrote both instrumental
and vocal music, but it was his opera buffa compositions which were
to bring him fame. Pergolesi wrote three of these works which were
performed between the acts of his serious operas. The most famous

Manuscript page from the bass aria, "Who may abide the day of coming?" (The Bettmann Archive) from Handel's "Messiah."

of these, *La Serva padrona,* which was the rival opera to Rameau's works that were the focus of the War of the Buffoons (1752), is still found in the modern opera repertoire. While a large number of trio sonatas, solo sonatas, and concertos in the Baroque style are ascribed to Pergolesi, it is now certain that many of them are not his works. A number of his religious works were published during his lifetime, the best known today is the *Stabat Mater.* (Rec. 5.107, 5.108)

ADDITIONAL COMPOSERS

    A. Austria
       Heinrich Ignaz Franz von Biber (1644–1704)
       Johann Joseph Fux (1660–1741)
    B. England
       Henry Lawes (1596–1662)
       Matthew Locke (c. 1630–1677)
       Pelham Humfrey (1647–1674)
       John Blow (c. 1648–1708)

C. France
   Robert Cambert (c. 1628–1677)
   Michel-Richard Delalande (1657–1726)
   Jean-Marie Leclair (1697–1764)
D. Germany
   Melchior Franck (c. 1579–1639)
   Franz Tunder (1614–1667)
   Johann Kaspar Kerll (1627–1693)
   Nikolaus Adam Strungk (1640–1700)
   Johann Christoph Bach (1642–1703)
   Johann Krieger (1651–1735)
   Georg Muffat (1653–1704)
   Philipp Heinrich Erlebach (1657–1714)
   Georg Böhm (1661–1733)
   Reinhard Keiser (1674–1739)
   Christoph Graupner (1683–1760)
   Johann Gottfried Walther (1684–1748)
   Johann Friedrich Fasch (1688–1758)
   Johann Adolph Hasse (1699–1783)
E. Italy
   Emilio del Cavalieri (c. 1550–1602)
   Adriano Banchieri (1568–1634)
   Salomone Rossi (1570–c. 1630)
   Stefano Landi (c. 1590–1639)
   Domenico Mazzochi (1592–1665)
   Biagio Marini (1597–1665)
   Barbara Strozzi (1619–c. 1664)
   Giovanni Legrenzi (1626–1690)
   Giovanni Battista Vitali (1632–1692)
   Alessandro Stradella (1644–1682)
   Agostino Steffani (1654–1728)
   Giuseppe Torelli (1658–1709)
   Antonio Lotti (c. 1667–1740)
   Giovanni Bononcini (1670–1747)
   Tomaso Albinoni (1671–1750)
   Evaristo Felice dall' Abaco (1675–1742)
   Francisco Durante (1684–1755)
   Nicola Porpora (1686–1768)
   Benedetto Marcello (1686–1739)
   Francesco Geminiani (1687–1762)
   Francesco Maria Veracini (1690–1768)

VII. HISTORIANS AND THEORISTS

Giovanni de' Bardi (1534–1612) was an Italian aristocrat who, because of his philosophical and literary interest, helped found the Florentine Camerata, the group whose investigations led to the first operatic composition. His writings, all in Italian, are concerned with speculations concerning the new music.

Giovanni Maria Artusi (c. 1540–1613) was an Italian writer on music. *L'Artusi, overo delle imperfettioni della moderna musica* (Artusi, concerning the imperfections of modern music) printed in Venice in 1600 is a representative critical essay. Artusi was very conservative in his musical philosophy and is remembered mainly for his criticism of the new style as represented by Monteverdi at the opening of the seventeenth century.

Michael Praetorius (1571–1621), a German musician, composer, and theorist, wrote his three-volume *Syntagma Musicum* (Musical encyclopedia) between 1615 and 1618. The first, written in Latin, deals with ancient church music and secular instruments. The second volume, in German, is an exhaustive treatise on the instruments of the Baroque period and is the most important source of information concerning instruments of the early Baroque. Forty-two woodcuts depicting the principal instruments add to its importance. The third volume contains accounts of secular music. His writings are among the most valuable treatises on music written during the Baroque period. Reprints of the second and third volumes were made in 1929 and 1916 respectively.

Marin Mersenne (1588–1648) was a French theorist. His *Traité de l' harmonie universelle* (Treatise Concerning Universal Harmony), Paris 1627, was published in an expanded form in 1936 and 1937 as *Harmonie universelle*. It includes a discourse on harmonic theory and an especially valuable description, both verbal and pictorial, of all the instruments of the seventeenth century. An English version of this work was published under the title *Harmonie Universelle: The Books on Instruments*, published in The Hague in 1957.

Christopher Simpson (c. 1610–1669), an English violist and composer, wrote *The Division Violist or an Introduction to the Playing Upon a Ground*, in 1659. It is a book of instruction for improvisation and the playing of the viol. A modern edition was published in London in 1958.

Johann Joseph Fux (1660–1741) was a German composer and theorist whose most important work was *Gradus ad Parnassum* (Steps to Parnassus), published in Vienna in 1725. It became a standard text in contrapuntal instruction and was studied by such masters as Mozart and Haydn, and used by such distinguished teachers as Cherubini and

Albrechtsberger. It was of great influence in the teaching of counter-point for well over a century. An English translation was published in 1943.

François Couperin (1668–1733) was a French composer, organist, and clavecinist. *L'Art de toucher le clavecin* (The art of playing the harpsi-chord), Paris 1716, described Couperin's manner of performance of his clavecin pieces. It is of greatest importance in its description of the manner and style of playing the keyboard literature of the seventeenth and eighteenth centuries.

Johann Mattheson (1681–1764) was a German composer and writer. His *Grundlage einer Ehren-Pforte, woran der tüchtigsten Capellmeister, Componisten, Musikgelehrten, Tonkünstler, etc., Leben, Werke, Verdienste, etc., erscheinen sollen* (Foundation for a triumphal arch on which the lives, works, and success of the greatest directors, composers, learned musicians, and artists shall be inscribed), Hamburg 1740, was a bio-graphical dictionary which is a source of historical information of the period.

Jean-Philippe Rameau (1683–1764) was a French composer and theorist. His *Traité de l'harmonie reduite a ses principes naturels* (Treatise on Harmony), Paris 1722, presented the revolutionary idea of a har-monic system in which the chords were built on thirds and were clas-sified in all their inversions as the same chord. Rameau's treatise also established the primacy of chords on I, IV, and V in a given key.

Francesco Geminiani (1687–1762) was an Italian violinist, composer, and writer. *The Art of Playing the Violin*, London 1730, was first pub-lished anonymously, and was the first method for violin instruction to be written. In 1751 it was published under Geminiani's name as *The Compleat Tutor for the Violin*. However, many scholars today be-lieve that this is an incorrect attribution. A facsimile edition was pub-lished in 1952. This work is of utmost importance in the study of principles of violin playing of the Baroque era.

Giuseppe Tartini (1692–1770), Italian violinist, composer, and theorist, wrote a number of theoretical works dealing with his dis-covery of combination tones and other theories concerning harmonic structure and the performance of agrements.

Jacques Hotteterre (1674–1763) was a French flutist. His *Principes de la flûte traversière ou flûte d'Allemagne, de la flûte à bec ou flûte douce et du hautbois* (Principles of playing the transverse or German flute, the recorder or sweet flute and oboe), Paris 1707, is the earliest work on the performance of these three woodwind instruments.

Important excerpts in English from several of the foregoing works can be found in *Source Readings in Music History* by Strunk.

*   *   *

The Mozart family in performance. An engraving showing Leopold Mozart and his children, Wolfgang and Nannerl. (Art and History Archive)

6

Chronology
of the Classic

1701 Giovanni Sammartini (1701–1775)

1706 Benjamin Franklin (1706–1790)

1710 Louis XV (1710–1774)

1714 Christoph Willibald Gluck (1714–1787)
C. P. E. Bach (1714–1788)

1717 Johann Stamitz (1717–1757)
Maria Theresa, Empress of Austria (1717–1780)

1726 Charles Burney (1726–1814)

1732 Franz Joseph Haydn (1732–1809)

1735 Johann Christian Bach (1735–1782)

1738 George III of England (1738–1820)

1739 Karl von Dittersdorf (1739–1799)

1743 Luigi Boccherini (1743–1805)

1749 Johann Wolfgang Goethe (1749–1832)

1755 Marie Antoinette, Queen of France (1755–1793)

1756 Wolfgang Amadeus Mozart (1756–1791)

1760 Luigi Cherubini (1760–1842)

1769 Napoleon Bonaparte (1769–1821)

1770 Ludwig van Beethoven (1770–1827)
First New York performance of Messiah

1776 Burney's History of Music published

1789 Beginning of the French revolution

1790 Haydn's first trip to London

1794 Haydn's second trip to London

1795 Paris Conservatory founded

1799 Beethoven's First Symphony completed

6
Classic
(1725-1800)

I. SOCIOCULTURAL INFLUENCES ON MUSIC

The term *Classic* is used here to designate the music of the eighteenth century. This term has also been used by historians to describe all the arts that are concerned mainly with problems of form, logic, balance, and restrained expression, and that were also based on models of Greek and Roman art. Unfortunately, there are no such models for Classic music to emulate. Consequently the term, as applied to music, refers to the works of those eighteenth century composers whose music gives the impression of clarity, repose, balance, lyricism, and restraint of emotional expression. In the opinions of many, the Classic period is one of the high points of music history and was nourished by a number of important developments in the patronage and function of music during this time.

An important feature of the eighteenth century, affecting all areas of society—theology, philosophy, science, morality, politics, and the arts—was the movement called the Enlightenment. Among its chief characteristics was a shift from traditional Christian theology to a morality based on social equality, and a shift from absolutes in governmental authority to greater independence and freedom of thought and behavior. Among the Enlightenment's effects on music were changes in the nature of patronage, particularly regarding the church and the courts of the aristocracy.

Austria and Germany became centers of vital musical activity. In these countries there were numerous courts that were able to maintain their independence. This was in contrast to France and England, where almost all aristocratic life had come under the influence of a central power. In Austria and Germany, however, these small courts gave up much of their political and economic independence, but maintained their artistic and social status. There was even greater rivalry among them in artistic and social matters. Moreover, a long tradition of instrumental music, an abundance of talent, a natural love of music among all classes, great artistic ambition combined with great wealth—together these made the perfect conditions for an enthusiastic patronage.

Composers depended upon the patronage of a court or aristocratic society that was very discriminating in its tastes. This society was not only sophisticated and elegant, but disclaimed any affinity for being profound, or showing its emotion. The Age of Reason and Enlightenment had placed a premium on intellectual pursuits and looked with a good deal of suspicion on any reliance upon feelings.

The concert hall and opera house became established institutions. This made it possible for all classes to enjoy the fruits of creative activity, whether aristocratic or not.

Publishing houses became well established and exerted a strong influence on both composers and the public. They not only made performances of musical works more widespread, but publishers were in a position to champion certain composers, often at the expense of others.

There was a general decline in the patronage of the church toward serious music. While there were certain reform movements in both Protestantism and Catholicism during the eighteenth century, none of them provided a suitable climate for a continuous growth of religious music. Certainly, the rather shallow attitude of aristocratic society did little to maintain the religious music at the level of the Baroque.

II. FUNCTION OF MUSIC

Music in the Classic era served a highly sophisticated and aristocratic society. Its most common function was to provide delightful entertainment for guests in exclusive salons. Unlike Baroque music which often had a descriptive character, Classic music was more abstract and tended to avoid representation. (See *Empfindsamer Stil.*) However, one movement in this period, *Sturm und Drang* (named after a literary movement), belies to a degree this assertion with its emphasis on dynamic power and high emotions.

A larger but still discriminating audience patronized public concerts of orchestral music and the elegant spectacle of opera.

Music also served an important function in the home, for this was an era of amateur musical performances, both vocal and instrumental. Many serious composers were called upon to write chamber music as well as vocal solos and ensembles for amateur consumption. Naturally, music for dancing was in popular demand for a society that loved gaiety and entertainment. While the church was not a major patron of serious music, it still demanded that composers write sacred music for its services in the spirit of secularism that prevailed.

III. STYLE AND PERFORMANCE PRACTICE

The following characteristics of style applied to some extent to all vocal and instrumental forms in the Classic era.

Formal Organization

Classical compositions were typically constructed around one melody contrasted homophonically with a second melody, leading to A B A form. This was partly in protest against the complications of polyphony and partly an effort to create a form that could be grasped and enjoyed by all, aristocrat and bourgeois alike. Classic music was characterized by a symmetry of form that was precise and clear, with sections clearly marked off by cadences. Musical periods tended to be balanced, often in units of four-measure phrases.

Folk music in all its forms and idioms was gradually introduced into serious music, including chamber and symphonic writing as well as opera and song. This was especialy true in the works of Haydn, who used Croatian melodies and rhythms among others in his music. No doubt the use of folk music was due to the great diversity of the Classic audience.

Melody

There was an emphasis on lyricism with smooth melodic contours. Melodies were extended to the double phrase and more, in contrast to the generally short, cryptic melodic devices of earlier music. Ornaments (often written out) became a lyric part of the melody, and sequential patterns were formalized to the extent of being cliché. These characteristics, together with dramatic dynamic changes and expressive chromaticisms are important characteristics of the *Empfindsamer Stil.*

Chordal structure was often the basis for melodic configuration. In fast tempos ascending chordal patterns were often referred to as *rocket figures* (Ex. 28).

Rhythm. Classic composers most often wrote simple and constant rhythmic patterns that were clearly punctuated by rhythmic cadences. There is a tendency toward uniformity among these rhythmic patterns. Polyrhythms were no longer used as in earlier music. An

Example 28. *Symphony in G major* including "rocket" themes

Stamitz

Example 29. Alberti bass

important formal device of rhythm in the Classic era was the *Alberti bass*, which breaks up the triad into its components, creating broken chord figures in a repeated rhythmic pattern (Ex. 29).

Silence became an expressive rhythmic factor in the Classic era. For example, strong cadences are sometimes followed by a measure of silence in order to heighten the effect of the cadence. The tempo of a movement, or section, remained constant from beginning to end.

Harmony. In music of this period harmony is relatively simple, utilizing primary chords, their inversions, and various seventh chords (Ex. 30). It is tonal, with a harmonic rhythm that moves slowly and is subordinate to the melody. This results in a predominately homophonic style (Ex. 30). Because the bass no longer served a melodic

Example 30. *Piano Sonata*, K570 illustrating simple harmonies

W. A. Mozart

function, the Baroque polarity between soprano and bass disappeared. Consequently, the practice of the basso continuo was discontinued.

There is a formal key relationship among themes and among movements of forms. These key relationships serves to provide contrast and interest without introducing new material. In the exposition of sonata form the first theme is in the tonic. The second theme is in the dominant of the original, or the relative major if the first is in a minor key. The development usually contains a number of modulations away from either the tonic or dominant with a return to the tonic. In the recapitulation the second theme is in the tonic, thus reconciling the key relationships and enabling the movement to end with a tonic cadence. The key relations among movements are less varied. In general all movements are in the same key with the exception of the second movement, which is in the subdominant, dominant, or relative minor. If the first movement is in minor, the last movement is sometimes in the parallel major.

The most commonly used cadence was the IV, V, I with the final tonic on a strong beat (Ex. 31).

The feminine cadence was also frequently employed. This is the normal authentic cadence, but with the final tonic on a weak beat (Ex. 32).

Example 31. An authentic cadence (masculine)

IV   V   I

Example 32. An authentic cadence (feminine)

IV   V   I

Texture

The texture of Classic music is essentially homophonic, with lyric melody predominating. Even when polyphonic texture is present, there is great clarity and transparency of line. In orchestral music this clarity of texture is emphasized by means of contrasting tonal coloring.

Instrumentation and Tone Color

The most popular means of musical expression was instrumental —the orchestra, chamber music (both strings and winds), and music for solo instruments.

The orchestra in the Classic period usually consisted of two flutes, two oboes (two clarinets), two bassoons, two horns, two trumpets, two tympani, and a complement of strings that numbered about twenty-five. The orchestra was divided into four major groups—strings, woodwinds, brass, and percussion. With the exception of the percussion, each group became a complete choir in itself. Though the harpsichord was still frequently used for the bass line and to supply harmonic texture, in general its use for this purpose diminished significantly toward the end of the eighteenth century.

Haydn's "Creation" in performance in a palatial hall early in the nineteenth century. (Historical Pictures Service, Chicago)

While the lute and harpsichord had been the household instruments during the Renaissance and the Baroque, they were superceded by the piano as a chamber instrument during the late eighteenth century. Instrumental chamber music became very popular. The large number of amateur performers and the intimacy of aristocratic society supplied a suitable climate for its development. Some of the finest of all Classic music can be found in the literature of the string quartet, piano quintets, trios, or sonatas.

(Appendix 1 includes further information on instruments.)

Apart from opera, vocal music was of minor importance, but remained in the form of religious music, folk songs, and the Lied. Opera was in great demand. Testimony of this can be seen in the large number of operas composed by both major and minor composers.

In the printed scores of the Classic period dynamic markings became commonplace. This was an important means of achieving contrast, but instead of changing the sonority as in the Baroque tutti and concertino, the Classic composer employed crescendo and diminuendo as well as sudden, dramatic, dynamic changes. Composers gave explicit directions in dynamics, tempi, phrasing, and all other interpretive matters, leaving little for the performer's discretion.

While ornaments were not always written out, there was a precise formula for the designation of each figure. It is in this area that Classic composers depended upon tradition and consequently the correct interpretation of ornaments is a serious problem for today's performer.

In the Classic period composers wrote for specific instruments and combinations of instruments such as the string quartet or woodwind ensemble. Composers designated the instrumentation to be used, in contrast to the Baroque practice of permitting the performers to choose suitable instruments.

Among the important composer performers of the Classic period, Mozart stands out as a virtuoso pianist with numerous performances as both pianist and conductor. While Haydn was not a virtuoso performer, he was a formidable conductor, scoring great success both at the Court of Esterházy and, in his later years, in London with his Salomon symphonies. Boccherini was also a notable cellist.

IV. MUSIC FOR VOICES

Single Movement Forms and Compositional Devices
Recitative

This is not a form, but a method of composition carried over from the Baroque period. Recitativo secco involved minimal accompaniment from the continuo forces. Both recitativo secco and recitativo accompagnato had considerable musical interest, apart from carrying the narrative portions of the drama. The accompaniment itself was often highly suggestive of the atmosphere of the text. (Rec. 6.1)

Aria

The aria in the Classic operas of Gluck and Mozart most often avoided the spectacular virtuosity of Baroque opera. While the principle of the da capo aria still prevailed, it was a much more expressive musical realization of the text. As in the recitative, the orchestra created the proper mood by means of lyric melody and tone color. (Rec. 6.2)

Choruses and Ensembles

The chorus is an effective part of the drama in the operas of Gluck and Mozart. Ensembles, especially in Mozart, marvelously present subtle musical dramatization. In contrast to the homophonic texture of arias, these choruses and ensembles are usually polyphonic. Each member of the ensemble is often declaiming elements of counterplots and intrigue along with the main story. In essence, this is both musical and dramatic counterpoint. (Rec. 6.3)

Vocal Polyphony

While homophony was the basic texture of Classic vocal as well as instrumental music, polyphony as a compositional device still prevailed in some forms. This was especially true in operatic ensembles and in the chorus sections of masses and oratorios. Examples can be found in the ensembles of *Le Nozze di Figaro* and *Don Giovanni* by Mozart. Haydn's *Die Schöpfung* (The Creation) and Mozart's *Requiem Mass* include examples of polyphonic texture in religious vocal music. Polyphonic forms such as the canon and the motet were still composed. Both Haydn and Mozart wrote in these forms. (Rec. 6.4, 6.5)

Lied

The Classic Lied replaced the ornamented pathos of seventeenth century arias and songs. The Lied was characterized by simple folklike melodies and was usually strophic (the same melody and harmonic substance for each stanza of the poem). Some of the finest strophic songs were written in the late eighteenth century by Mozart and Haydn to the poems of Goethe. (Rec. 6.6, 6.7)

Composite Forms

Opera

In the eighteenth century opera underwent considerable reform, moving away from the stereotypical practices of the Neapolitan school. These reforms were realized in the works of Gluck, who thought of himself as a reformer of opera, and by Mozart. In general, it can be said that the structure of opera in the late eighteenth century became much more fluent and subtle than that of the Baroque. The relation between music and drama was somewhat restored. No longer were singers left to their own devices in improvising dazzling vocal effects that had little to do with the story, nor was the stage mechanic more important than the composer. There was a strong emphasis upon skillful characterization of the protagonists, together with greater dramatic force. The principle of sonata structure was applied with great success to operatic scenes and arias. Each became a closed form, complete in itself. In addition to *opera seria* there was further development of comic opera in the eighteenth century: *opera buffa* in Italy, *opèra comique* in France, *ballad opera* in England, and *Singspiel* in Germany. Each represented a national style and all were characterized by spoken dialogue along with recitative and aria. (Rec. 6.8–6.10)

Oratorio

The Oratorio was continued in the tradition of the Baroque, but with emphasis on classic characteristics of style. The most well known Classic oratorios are by Haydn. *Die Schöpfung* (the Creation) was based on a text from the Book of Genesis and Milton's *Paradise Lost*. *Die Jahreszeiten* (the Seasons), is a secular work on poetry by the Scottish poet, James Thomson, and translated into German. Both of these works have become successful concert pieces. (Rec. 6.11, 6.12)

Mass

Despite the substantial contributions to mass literature, there was a general decline in the quality of religious music composed during the Classic era. Much of what was composed was written for liturgical use, but was also appropriate for the concert hall. The Mass was the favorite of these forms and consisted of the setting of the Ordinary of the Mass with soloists, chorus, and orchestra, and was symphonic in nature. (Rec. 6.13, 6.14)

IV. MUSIC FOR INSTRUMENTS

Single Movement Forms and Structural Devices

Sonata Form

The sonata form is by far the most representative single movement form. It is almost always used as the first movement of a composite sonata or symphony, but may also be used as a slow movement or the final movement. It was also used as the design for some single movement compositions. Its organization consists of three parts: 1. the presentation of two contrasting harmonic sections, each of which may have the same or contrasting themes or theme groups (the exposition or statement); 2. the development of these themes through harmonic and motivic exploration and transformation (development section); and 3. their reconciliation harmonically, melodically, and rhythmically (the restatement or recapitulation section).

The following is the plan of the Classic sonata form: (In the diagram, Th. I represents the first theme; trans. indicates transition; Th. II represents the second theme; and C1. Th. indicates the closing theme. The second line is the pattern when the movement is cast in a minor key.)

Exposition
    ‖:Th. I. (maj.) trans. Th. II. Dom. trans. C1. Th.:‖
    ‖:Th. I. (min.) trans. Th. II. Rel. trans. C1. Th.:‖
Development
    Varied treatment of material of the exposition in distant keys
       followed by a cadence.
Recapitulation
    Th. I. (maj.) trans. Th. II. tonic trans.
    Th. I. tonic min. trans. Th. II. tonic min. trans.

        C1. Th. tonic, Coda
        C1. Th. tonic min., Coda

Sonata form sometimes began with a slow introduction, a carryover from the French overture. This served as a musical device to quiet the audience and gain attention. There was usually no connection between the musical material of the introduction and the thematic material of the sonata movement. This introductory section was most often used in the first movement of the symphony.

Many large movements in sonata form added a coda to the recapitulation. This was a section in the tonic key which strengthened the finality of the closing cadence. (Rec. 6.15, 6.16, 6.17)

(Because a large number of scores and recordings by numerous publishers and recording companies exist for almost all music from the classic era to the present day, references to specific editions and recordings will be omitted from this point on. Scores may be found in the anthologies suggested in the Introduction.)

Rondo

The rondo is also based on the principle of repetition after digression. It differs from sonata form in that it has no development section and that the principal theme is always repeated in the tonic. The typical form is as follows: A B A C A B A. In major keys, Section B is usually in the key of the dominant. If Section A is in a minor key, B is in the relative major. C, which is in the tonic, is usually a melodic idea of minor significance or merely an episode between the repetitions of A. Late eighteenth-century composers frequently combined aspects of the sonata and rondo forms, resulting in an expansion of the middle section (C) through use of development techniques. This modification is often referred to as the "sonata-rondo form." (Rec. 6.18, 6.19)

Variation Form

In the Classic period the variation was still popular, as the second movement of keyboard sonatas and also in some quartets and symphonies. In the Classic period, the variation form was primarily homophonic. Variations were both harmonic and melodic, using contrasting tempi and rhythmic patterns as well as changes in tone color. (Rec. 6.20–6.22)

Three-Part Song Form

The three-part song form is in reality an instrumental form based on lyric melodies. It was often used as the second movement of a sonata. (Rec. 6.23, 6.24)

Minuet and Trio, and Other Dance Forms

While there were numerous single dance forms written specifically for ballroom dancing, the minuet is practically the only one which succeeded in achieving a place in the art music of the Classic period. In general the dance forms retained their two-part form of the Baroque, but with the addition of the trio the minuet became a three-part form in its Classic guise. Its plan is as follows (note that each of the sections is a three-part form):

Minuet ||: A :||: BA :||
Trio ||: C :||: DC :||
Minuet || A || BA ||
(Rec. 6.25, 6.26)

Overture

The eighteenth century overture was usually a sonata structure. It was associated almost exclusively with the opera and was used as an expression of mood preparatory to the first scene. In the late eighteenth-century composers began to incorporate material from the main body of the opera into the overture. (Rec. 6.27, 6.28)

Polyphonic Instrumental Forms

The polyphonic forms of the Baroque were not completely discarded during the Classic period. They were, however, most often used as musical devices rather than complete forms. For example, the first theme in sonata form was sometimes cast as a *fugato* (fugal passage). Fugal passages were also often used in the development sections of the sonata form. Both Haydn and Mozart made extensive use of the fugue in this manner and used polyphonic forms both as single works and as complete movements in some of their later works. In contrast to the Baroque fugue, however, their subjects were usually longer and more lyrical. (Rec. 6.29, 6.30)

Composite Forms

Sonata

The most important composite form of the Classic era is the sonata, an abstract instrumental form of large dimensions in three or four separate movements. It was developed from the seventeenth century dance suite and trio sonata. It was also influenced by the Italian operatic overture. A Classic sonata usually consists of (1) a fast movement in sonata form; (2) a slow movement in three-part song form, variation, or sonata form; (3) a minuet and trio; and (4) a very fast movement in rondo or sonata form. On occasion this last movement may be a set of variations, but it is always in a fast tempo. If there are only three movements, the minuet is omitted. A sonata is the name used for this composite form when written for one or two instruments. When written for more than two instruments, it takes the name of the particular ensemble, such as a symphony, or trio. There is a potential universality about the sonata. It is the only form that is divorced from religion, drama, and the dance. It also has more universal appeal than the polyphonic forms such as the fugue because it is less complicated intellectually. C. P. E. Bach is the composer who was mainly responsible for the classic sonata, although he cannot be credited with its invention. (Rec. 6.31, 6.32, 6.33)

Symphony

The symphony is a sonata for orchestra and is normally in four movements, the first of which was often preceded by a slow introduction. The use of a larger group of instruments called for a much more extended composition. The varied tonal possibilities of the orchestra made it possible to have a greater variety of style, more extended climaxes, and a more complex development section.

There were two important "schools" of Classic symphony composers: the Mannheim school with Stamitz as its most important composer and the Viennese school of Haydn, Mozart, and Beethoven. (Rec. 6.34, 6.35, 6.36)

Concerto

The concerto is a work for solo instrument (more rarely for two or more solo instruments) and orchestra in the pattern of the sonata. The concerto generally omits the minuet and trio thus making it a three-movement composition. In the first movement the orchestra presents an abbreviated exposition in the tonic, followed by the solo instruments direct statement of the thematic material, a compositional practice known as the double exposition. The development follows with the solo instrument pitted against the orchestra. Following the recapitulation, there is usually a brilliant cadenza—a free improvisation on the themes by the performer, although this was sometimes written out by the composer. The second and third movements follow the forms of second and third movements of the sonata with optional cadenzas. (Rec. 6.37, 6.38, 6.39)

Chamber Music

All kinds of small instrumental ensembles, using the forms of the sonata come under this heading. These forms were called Trios, Quartets, Quintets, and Sextets and were for various combinations of string and wind instruments. However, the String Quartet was the most common. When the piano was used in combination with string instruments, the form was designated as a Piano Trio, Piano Quartet, or Piano Quintet. (Rec. 6.40, 6.41, 6.42)

Serenades, Divertimenti, Cassations, Notturni

These works constituted a rather large body of literature usually written for specific occasions. They were related to the earlier suites and sinfonie of the Baroque, but were now based on the Classic characteristics of form and style. They were written for any number of instruments from small chamber groups to the full orchestra and in many instances consisted of a large number of separate movements. (Rec. 6.43, 6.44)

VII. IMPORTANT COMPOSERS

Giovanni Sammartini (1701-1775) was a pioneer in the development of the Classic sonata. He is also known for his chamber music in the Classic style. He was Gluck's teacher. His principal works that survive today are sonatas for chamber ensemble, especially the string quartet, and symphonies.

Christoph Willibald Gluck (1714-1787) was an opera composer who initiated many reforms that laid the foundations for later opera composers. However, his reforms had little immediate effect on the composers of his time. Gluck, after writing in the traditional Italian style, finally came to the conclusion that the dramatic force of the libretto must be the most important aspect of opera. To achieve this he made the following innovations: (1) he eliminated virtuosity, substituting lyric simplicity; (2) he strove to create musical portraits of his characters and their feelings; (3) he returned to the use of plots taken from mythology—plots that avoid the complex counterplots and minor intrigues of Neapolitan opera; (4) he made the recitative more musically expressive; (5) he used the instruments of the orchestra as a tonal palette, creating the proper mood and atmosphere by tonal coloring; (6) he employed the chorus to create dramatic intensity; and (7) he made the overture an introduction to the mood and spirit of the opera. His most important works were *Orfeo ed Eurydice*, 1762; *Alceste*, 1767; *Armide*, 1777; and *Iphigénie en Tauride*, 1779.

Carl Phillip Emanuel Bach (1714–1788), the son of J. S. Bach and sometimes known as the Berlin Bach, was well known as a keyboard performer as well as a composer. He was very influential in establishing the form and style of Classic composition, and is often credited with being the first to write in sonata form. There is no doubt but that both Haydn and Mozart were influenced by his style. He wrote more than 200 sonatas and solo works for the piano, in addition to numerous concerti and chamber music works. His sonatas show the basic form of that genre, but there is little, if any, development of themes in his sonata-allegro movements.

Johann Wenzel Anton Stamitz (1717–1757), the founder of the Mannheim school, made a number of important contributions to both orchestral playing and writing for orchestra. The most important of these were: the first use of extensive dynamic shading in orchestral performance, the introduction of the clarinet into the orchestra, the introduction of the minuet into the symphony as the third movement, and the creation of what was known as the finest orchestra in all of Europe. He wrote about 74 symphonies, but these are seldom performed today.

Franz Joseph Haydn (1732–1809) was one of the most prolific composers of the eighteenth century. Haydn's career exemplified the patronage system functioning at its best. Born in lower Austria, he received his early training as a choirboy at St. Stephen's cathedral in Vienna. Aside from this schooling, he was largely self-taught in music, drawing heavily upon the style of such Classic composers as C. P. E. Bach. Haydn was finally given a post as assistant Kappelmeister at the Court of Prince Esterházy in 1761 and was to enjoy an ideal patronage for a period of over thirty years. His duties were to provide music requested by the prince for any and all occasions. Consequently, he was called upon to write in every conceivable musical form. A most important factor in the developmnt of his orchestral music was the fact that he had an orchestra at his disposal at all times. This enabled him to experiment with various orchestral instruments and orchestral timbres. It was Haydn who brought unity to late eighteenth century music and perfected the Classic style. Haydn wrote an enormous amount of music; much of it has been lost and the remainder is only now being published in a complete edition. His more important works

Franz Joseph Haydn (1732–1809)
(Free Public Library of Philadelphia)

are the symphonies (well over 100 of which 104 are published) and 82 string quartets. His main contributions to the Classic style consist of the use of a slow introduction to the first movement of the symphony, enlarging the development section of the sonata form and developing fragments of themes, using variation form for the slow movement of symphonies and quartets, and using a more flexible orchestration that permitted melodies to be imitated in contrasting timbres. The following works are his most representative: the London Symphonies (nos. 93–104); the later quartets, especially the *Emperor, Op. 76, no. 3* and the *Lark, Op. 65, no. 5;* two oratorios, *Die Schöpfung* (the Creation) and *Die Jahreszeiten* (the Seasons); and the piano sonatas.

Johann Christian Bach (1735–1782), also a son of J. S. Bach, is known today as the London Bach. He lived and studied in Italy for a time after his early musical preparation in Berlin with his brother, C. P. E. Bach. He later went to England where he became music master to the Queen of England. He was an important composer of the light homophonic genre and his music was an important source of the Classic style. He wrote numerous operas in addition to piano sonatas, symphonies, and various kinds of chamber music.

Karl von Dittersdorf (1739–1799) was a successful composer of Classical symphonies, church music, and opera, although he was eclipsed by both Haydn and Mozart. His opera, *Doktor and Apotheker* (the Doctor and Pharmacist), still survives, as do numerous string quartets and a few symphonies.

Luigi Boccherini (1743–1805) was a composer and cellist who was a great admirer of Haydn's music and who copied his style. He wrote a great quantity of chamber music, including 102 quartets and 125 quintets. His six cello sonatas and four cello concertos are still prominent in present-day repertory of music for cello.

Wolfgang Amadeus Mozart (1756–1791), whose creative inventiveness and lyric genius place him among the three or four giants of music, was born in Salzburg. He showed great creativity from infancy. His youth was spent in the atmosphere of the Salzburg court where his father was a violinist. His genius was recognized early and his talents as a performer and as a composer were displayed to almost all of Europe through tours to the important courts and musical centers. In spite of almost ideal conditions for a successful career and despite his superior talents, Mozart's life was one of struggle and disappointment. In contrast to Haydn, Mozart never really had a patron. He was one of the first independent composers who had to struggle for recognition and commissions without the security of a permanent post. Without patronage, Mozart was forced to write in every popular form of his day in order to interest people in his music. His death and burial in a pauper's grave came just as he was gaining some public acclaim for his opera, *Die Zauberflöte* (The Magic Flute), a recognition that might have brought him the security of a permanent position. In style, Mozart was a conformist. He refined and polished the Classic forms, but made no major innovations over those made by Haydn. Mozart knew Haydn and their friendship probably influenced Mozart's mature works. While there are many similarities between their styles, Mozart is distinctive in the following ways. In general, his melodies were more lyric, more extended, and more subtle in their lyric expressiveness. He seldom repeated phrases note for note, but made changes in ornaments, rhythm, harmonic structure, or dynamics. Mozart seldom included slow introductions to his symphonies. He indulged in melodic and harmonic chromaticism, foreshadowing the romantic style. In his chamber music especially, all parts became equal in importance.

While he did not follow the devices of Gluck's reforms, his refined classic taste and his innate feeling for and love of the theater led him to write what was perhaps the happiest solution to the problems of combining pure music and extra-musical ideas. Mozart's operas can be placed in three general classifications: (1) opera buffa, the most important of which are *Le nozze di Figaro* (Marriage of Figaro), *Così fan tutte,* and *Don Giovanni;* (2) the German operas (Singspiel)—*Die Zauberflöte* (The Magic Flute) and *Die Entführung aus dem Serail* (The Abduction from the Seraglio); and (3) the Italian style operas (Open seria)—*La Clemenza di Tito* and *Idomeneo.*

It is difficult to pick out the major works from Mozart's total output of over 600 compositions. However, there are a few that stand out from the rest as monuments to his creative genius. Mozart did not number his works chronologically by the usual opus numbers, but Ludwig von Köchel compiled a largely chronological catalog of them in the middle of the nineteenth century. This catalog was brought up to date by the late Alfred Einstein and this numbering system is used today. (Mozart's works are designated by the letter K and the appropriate number.)

From among this genius's works, the authors would especially like to direct the reader's attention to the following:

(1) the last three symphonies, *Symphony No. 39 in E flat major* (K.543), *Symphony No. 40 in g minor* (K.550), *Symphony No. 41 in C major* (K.551)

(2) the ten celebrated string quartets (Köchel numbers 387, 421, 428, 458, 464, 465, 499, 575, 589, 590)

(3) the chamber music for winds and strings (Among these are the *Clarinet Quintet in A major* (K.581), *Serenade in D major for winds and strings* (K.320), *Divertimento in D major for String quartet and 2 horns* (K.334), and the *Sextet for String Quartet and 2 Horns* (K.552).)

(4) the violin concerti, especially those in G major (K.216), D major (K.218), and A major (K.219).

(5) the twenty-five piano concertos (Those most frequently performed are in C major (K.415), B flat major (K.450), G major (K.453), and d minor (K.466).)

(6) the piano sonatas in c minor (K.467), C major (K.545), B flat major (K.570), and D major (K.576)

(7) the *Requiem Mass* (K.626), his crowning achievement in sacred music. (It was left incomplete by Mozart, and his student, Süssmayr, completed the work from Mozart's sketches.)

Luigi Cherubini (1760–1842) was the last important composer to show the classical restraint that identifies him as a Classic composer even though he lived well into the nineteenth century. He was born in Italy where he became a successful Italian opera composer. He soon made Paris his permanent home and devoted his creative life and conducting duties to the French style. His operas were influenced by Gluck's reforms, but never received any great acclaim. Perhaps his best opera is *Médée* which has been revived in recent years. Other French operas by Gluck are *Lodaiska* and *Les Deux Journées*. His two requiem masses demonstrate the high quality of his church music and its superb counterpoint.

Ludwig van Beethoven (1770–1827) must be considered both a Classicist and a Romanticist. (His work will be discussed more fully in the chapter on Romanticism.) While the greater portion of his compositions reveal the characteristics found in the Romantic style, his earlier works conform to the style of the Classic. It is generally accepted that those works written before 1802 are patterned after the traditions of Haydn and despite an occasional outburst of impatience with the harmonic and dynamic simplicity of Classicism, his acceptance of the tradition is fairly complete. The important earlier works include the piano sonatas up to Opus 53, the first three piano concerti, the string quartets of Opus 18, and the first two symphonies.

ADDITIONAL COMPOSERS

A. Austria
  F. X. Richter (1709–1789)
  Georg Christoph Wagenseil (1715–1777)
  George Matthias Monn (1717–1750)
  Michael Haydn (1737–1806)
B. England
  Thomas Arne (1710–1788)
  William Boyce (1711–1779)
C. France
  Jean-Jacques Rousseau (1712–1778)
  François-Joseph Gossec (1734–1829)
  André Grétry (1741–1813)
D. Germany
  Johann Joachim Quantz (1697–1773)
  Wilhelm Friedemann Bach (1710–1784)
  Christian Cannabich (1731–1798)
E. Italy
  Niccolò Jommeli (1714–1774)
  Niccolò Piccini (1728–1800)
  Domenico Cimarosa (1749–1801)
F. United States of America
  William Billings (1746–1800)

VII. HISTORIANS AND THEORISTS

Because Classicism was concerned mainly with form, there was little philosophizing about music. Most of the writers were seeking to formalize musical performance and consequently gave detailed instructions as to how to play instruments and also how to interpret the various devices of musical practice. A few of the more important writers and their works are listed on the following pages. In most cases the writers were also creative artists, or at least performers.

Johann Joachim Quantz (1697–1773) was a composer and flutist as well as the author of *Versuch einer Anweisung, die Flöte traversiere zu spielen* (Essay on Instruction for playing the Transverse Flute), Berlin 1752. While the title suggests a method for flute, Quantz deals with problems and questions of the performance practice of his time.

Jean-Jacques Rousseau (1712–1778) was a French writer, philosopher, and sometimes music scholar and composer. His *Dictionaire de musique* was published in 1767. This work contains many of Rousseau's articles written originally for the *Encyclopédie* to which he was a major contributor.

Christoph Willibald Gluck (1714–1787) wrote an important treatise on opera: the *Preface to Alceste* (Vienna 1769). *Alceste* was composed in 1767, but the printed score did not appear until 1769. It was in this preface that Gluck sought to establish the aesthetics of his musical theories concerning opera. He also gave an account of what he believed to be serious abuses of the true purpose of opera in the Italian school.

Carl Phillip Emanuel Bach (1714–1788) wrote *Versuch uber die wahre Art, das Klavier zu spielen* (Essay on the True Art of playing Keyboard Instruments), Berlin 1753–1762, (New York 1949). This work is still an authoritative source of information on the traditions of performance of Classic music for the keyboard. It is also very valuable in the realization of classic ornaments and embellishments.

Leopold Mozart (1719–1787) was the author of *Versuch einer gründlichen Violinschule* (Treatise on the Fundamental Principles of Violin Playing) Augsburg 1756, (London 1951). Leopold Mozart was the father of Wolfgang Amadeus and an eminent violinist and teacher. This work is one of the first written on successful methods of violin playing. Along with C. P. E. Bach and Quantz, he provided an account of the musical practice of the classic era.

Sir John Hawkins (1719–1789) was an English music historian who wrote *A General History of the Science and Practice of Music*. It was published in London in 1776 and republished in 1875. Hawkins' history, published about the same time as Burney's, is filled with reliable information, especially about the musical scene in eighteenth century London.

Charles Burney (1726–1814) was the most important English music historian of the eighteenth century. *A General History of Music* (London 1776, reprinted New York 1957) is the first important history of music in English. It contains many interesting comments on the contemporary musical trends that reveal the general attitude of both the creative musician and the public during Burney's time. Burney made extensive trips to the musical capitals of Europe and wrote two volumes concerning the musical scene on the Continent.

(Important excerpts in English from several of the foregoing works can be found in *Source Readings in Music History* by Oliver Strunk.)

*   *   *

Paris Opera House (1861–1874). There is an opulence about this structure that reflects the tastes of the newly rich of the nineteenth century Industrial Revolution. This opera house and others like it were the setting for the Romantic opera with their extravagant spectacles dealing with heroic and epic subjects, supernaturalism, mystery, and passion. (Courtesy National Monuments Record, London—Art Reference Bureau)

7
Chronology
of the Romantic

1770	Ludwig van Beethoven (1770–1827)	1813	Giuseppe Verdi (1813–1901)
1776	American revolution began		Richard Wagner (1813–1883)
1782	Niccolò Paganini (1782–1840)	1818	Charles Gounod (1818–1893)
1786	Carl Maria von Weber (1786–1826)	1819	Clara Schumann (1819–1896)
1789	French revolution began	1822	César Franck (1822–1880)
1792	Gioacchino Rossini (1792–1868)	1824	Bedřich Smetana (1824–1884)
1797	Franz Schubert (1797–1828)		Anton Bruckner (1824–1896)
	Gaetano Donizetti (1797–1848)	1833	Alexander Borodin (1833–1887)
1801	Vincenzo Bellini (1801–1835)		Johannes Brahms (1833–1897)
1803	Hector Berlioz (1803–1869)	1837	Queen Victoria's reign (1837–1901)
1804	Napoleon becomes Emperor	1838	Georges Bizet (1838–1875)
1805	Fanny Mendelssohn Hensel (1805–1847)	1839	Modeste Mussorgsky (1839–1881)
1809	Felix Mendelssohn-Bartholdy (1809–1847)	1840	Piotor Ilyitch Tchaikovsky (1840–1893)
1810	Frédéric Chopin (1810–1849)	1841	Antonin Dvořák (1841–1904)
	Robert Schumann (1810–1856)		Saxopohone invented by Adolphe Sax
1811	Franz Liszt (1811–1886)		

1843	Edvard Grieg (1843–1907)	1861	American Civil War (1861–1865)
1844	Nikolai Rimsky-Korsakov (1844–1908)	1862	Claude Debussy (1862–1918)
1845	Gabriel Fauré (1845–1924)	1864	Richard Strauss (1864–1949)
1858	Giacomo Puccini (1858–1924)	1865	Jean Sibelius (1865–1957)
1860	Hugo Wolf (1860–1903) Gustav Mahler (1860–1911)	1877	Edison invents the phonograph

7
Romantic
(1800-1910)

I. SOCIOCULTURAL INFLUENCES ON MUSIC

The early nineteenth century saw the rise of a style of music, literature, and art that we refer to as Romantic. The nineteenth century was a time of dramatic thought and action. It was also a time of strong contradictions between capitalism and socialism, freedom and oppression, logic and emotion, science and faith. The consequence of these contradictions was a change in the thinking of people, especially creative artists. An intellectual change took place in the minds of composers that was many-sided, complex, and often confused. Consequently it is impossible to say that there is a definite Romantic style. Other periods of the past had a core of accepted beliefs and practices that drew composers together with a similarity between their music. Romanticism, on the other hand, had the tendency to isolate creative personalities because their practices and beliefs were often in opposition and, like Romanticism itself, complex.

The revolutionary spirit that finally exploded in the French Revolution infused artists with the ideals of liberty and individualism. In terms of music, there were several Romantic results. There was a general impatience with the rules and restraints of Classicism. Just as the Revolution opposed the eighteenth century status quo, so music revolted against the practices of Mozart and Haydn. To be different was the goal and the Romantic period was to witness a great variety of musical experiments to achieve individualism. Moreover, to implement the ideals of liberty, composers sought to express their own personal convictions and to portray events and ideas as they understood them. The expression of emotion and the evocation of imagination became the primary goal of most Romantic music. In an effort to stimulate the imagination there arose a predilection for the strange and the remote, a fascination for the mysteries of the universe.

The Industrial Revolution caused a major change in the economic and social life of the common man and also gave rise to a wealthy, capitalistic middle class. There was a general leveling of society and, while composers did not write for the lower classes, their music was addressed to the masses to a far greater degree than before. The wealthy middle class was the potential patron for the composer who had all but lost aristocratic patronage because of the increasing decline in the power and influence of the court. Literature and the visual arts were quick to use the injustices of the Industrial Revolution, the exploitation of the workers, the low standards of living, and the social abuses of the lower classes as subjects for their works. Music, however, when presented in its absolute form, tacitly denied the existence of these pressing problems. Composers expressed the emotional extremes of the human spirit, often in ways that seem to be an escape from reality.

The development of the business of music was also an important influence on the direction composers took in their writing. In order to cultivate the patronage of a wider and unorganized public, the composer, together with his publisher and concert manager, had to sell music to the public. Publication was on a different basis than it had been. In the effort to capture audiences, a dynamic and colorful personality came to be an important asset, as can be noted in such individuals as Liszt, Berlioz, and Wagner. The concert manager, or impresario as he was often called, was also an important figure in the business of music. His opinion as to what the public would accept and be enthusiastic about was a strong motivation for many composers and performers. Another important person behind the scenes of music was the music critic. He was a sort of liaison between the public and the composer. In this role critics served not only to interpret the composer to the public, but to also set standards of musical taste. Needless to say the composer was usually in conflict with most of the critics, but the critic was still often responsible for the acceptance or rejection of a composer's works.

While the revolutionary spirit had its origin in France, it was in Germany and Austria that Romanticism had its strongest manifestation. The French almost abandoned the Romantic ideal because of their affinity for the classic. Germany and Austria, however, were younger; they had never known the kind of oppression generated by a strong central absolutism. There seemed to be a conscious emphasis on folklore and historical epics in their desire to achieve a cultural heritage equal to the older and longer established countries. Whatever the reasons, the seeds of musical romanticism were to fall upon very fertile ground, particularly in Vienna.

II. FUNCTION OF MUSIC

Romantic music still served a sophisticated and aristocratic society as had been the case with Classic music. Aristocratic patronage was considerably reduced from what it had been in the eighteenth century, and there were practically no opportunities for the kind of patronage enjoyed by Haydn. The intimacy of the exclusive salon was still an ideal setting for chamber music and solo forms. Performance was no longer by amateurs, however, for Romantic music was usually too technically demanding for unskilled performers.

Outside the patronage of the exclusive salon was a large, but unorganized and unsophisticated, concert-going public that loved music. Romantic composers were constantly striving to gain the recognition of this vast audience, and, in an effort to win acceptance, they were very sensitive to the likes and dislikes of these music lovers. These middle-class listeners searched for new excitement or relaxation from everyday life in music. The function of composers was to create music that evoked and explored human feelings. There were several types of music that appealed to these patrons—especially symphonic music and the extravagant spectacle of opera and ballet and virtuosic music of all kinds.

Performers, as well as composers, wanted to be acceptable and to dazzle audiences. Composers, like Liszt and Paganini, who were often also fine performers themselves, wrote a large number of virtuoso pieces to thrill the public with technical display. In fact, virtuoso performers and their agents, the impresarios, were central to nineteenth-century concert life.

Because Romantic composers expressed personal feelings and convictions, a lot of music was written without benefit of patronage. They expressed themselves in personal documents of art. These were often experimental and uncompromising as far as public taste was concerned. The last piano sonatas and string quartets of Beethoven and many songs by Schumann and Wolf are examples of this kind of expression.

Social dancing by all segments of society gave composers a large market for dance music. The great popularity of the waltz led to fame and fortune for composers like Johann Strauss and his son of the same name, and in addition, aroused the envy of many who may have been artistic successes, but never gained public favor.

In the Romantic period the Church was no longer a patron of music to any significant extent. The small amount of sacred music written during this time contained the personal religious feelings and convictions of the composer, expressed in music, largely for the concert hall.

The teaching of music became an established profession. Many fine conservatories and schools of music were founded for the education of the performing and creative musician. Research in music history and theory was introduced into the programs of many universities by the end of the nineteenth century. A great number of prominent composers and performers such as Liszt, Mendelssohn, Rimsky-Korsakov, and Schumann achieved wide recognition as teachers. To meet pressing needs for pedagogical material composers wrote études and other short pieces for teaching purposes. Many of these works, like the *Études* of Chopin, are of a very high level of artistry and form an important segment of the repertory for the piano.

Research at universities led to the beginning of complete editions of composers' works, including Bach, Mozart, and Beethoven, to name but three, as well as large anthologies or collected editions, such as the *Denkmäler der Tonkunst in Oesterreich*, and the *Quellenlexikon der Musiker und Musikgelehrten* of Robert Eitner.

III. STYLE AND PERFORMANCE PRACTICE

Because Romanticism is so personal and so filled with contrasting concepts of music, not all characteristics of style are present in all forms. There are contradictions in style between groups of composers and even within the works of individual composers. There were Romantic idealists or absolutists who insisted that music must exist for its own sake without extramusical associations. In contrast, the champions of program music believed that music could and should tell a story, imitate sounds of nature, or illustrate a scene aurally.

In the Romantic period there was a dualism between virtuosity and intimacy. Some Romantic composers excelled in spectacular virtuosity, which was expressed by brilliant technical performances and often by the resources of a vast number of performers. On the other hand, there were those who emphasized the intimacy of miniature forms and delicate textures expressing their personal feelings in solo songs, chamber music, and lyric piano works. Solo songs enjoyed considerable attention during the Romantic era, as composers became involved with literary forms for their texts.

There was also a contrast between nationalism and internationalism. There were composers whose aim was to extol national characteristics and evoke patriotic feelings by using folklore, folk songs, and dances. They often used realistic devices to evoke expressiveness associated with national or ethnic subjects. Nationalism became strong in such countries as Russia, Poland, and Bohemia. In Russia a group called the *Russian Five,* or *Mighty Five,* whose members were César Cui, Mily Balakirev, Modest Mussorgsky, Alexander Borodin, and Nikolai Rimsky-Korsakov, made a special effort to break away from the dominance of the Italian and German tradition. There were also Romanticists who avoided nationalistic devices in the search for a universal musical language. In general these composers were the so-called absolutists who believed that music should express itself and not be contaminated by extramusical ideas.

The concept all Romanticists had in common unifying their music was the evocation of emotion as its primary function. The concept is based on the premise that a feeling of musical tension is necessary to achieve a corresponding intensification of emotional response. All Romantic music, therefore, concerns itself with the problem of achieving this tension. Most Romanticists revolted against the restraints and formalism of the Classic era. However, some Romantics, such as Schubert, Mendelssohn, and Brahms, cast their Romantic expressions in molds of Classic forms.

Impressionism was a revolt against Romanticism by writers, painters, and composers. It emerged at the close of the nineteenth century, and was the connecting link between Romanticism and the experimentalism of the early twentieth century. It was a cult whose artistic language included suggestive colors, lines, words, melodies, and harmonies. The listener, viewer, and reader were called upon to supply the details and complete the impressions. The movement was strongly influenced by the painters Monet and Manet and by the symbolic imagery of the poets Verlaine and Mallarmé, among others. Led by Debussy, composers denied both the objectivity of programmatic composers and the pathos of the Romantic idealists. Impressionistic music was a music of coloristic effects, of vague harmonies, and loosely knit forms.

Formal Organization

Musical form continued to be based on contrasting melodies in the homophonic style, making the sonata the most important type of formal organization. Rather than two contrasting melodies, there were often contrasting theme groups and sometimes only motives pitted against each other.

In addition to the Classic forms that were still in use, there were sectional forms, such as the ballade, nocturne, or fantasy. These were most common in piano music. The free forms, however, were still based on contrasting themes, but usually without development sections. Sometimes, in the very short preludes or études, only one theme or melody might be used with changes in harmony or rhythm for contrast.

Forms were not as precise and clear as in the Classic period, but were often overlapping, vague, and without strong cadences. Sections and even movements of the longer works often merged into one another by means of subtle and mild harmonic and rhythmic cadential effects.

It was common practice, especially in the larger forms, to use some of the same thematic material in each movement as a means of maintaining a constant expressive character. This is referred to as *cyclic* construction.

Forms were not always symmetrical or balanced. Within a musical composition, phrases and periods were often of uneven lengths. Development sections in sonata forms were frequently extended, where composers could use imagination and ingenuity to best advantage.

Folk melodies, or at least folk-style melodies, were frequently included in Romantic music. This was especially true in nationalistic music, but was also a common practice in the music of the Romantic idealists. Folklore was especially popular in Romantic opera, where it was, no doubt, aimed at arousing enthusiasm among the general public.

Melody

Melody was charaterized by an intensity of personal feelings. Dynamic climaxes and frequent changes in dynamics served to build the tension necessary for its expression. Frequent chromaticism helped to create harmonic tension.

Melodic themes were of varying length and form, and were frequently fragmentary, with rhythmic interruptions and irregular phrases. They could be extremely long, with many avoided and deceptive cadences, giving a feeling of continuous "spinning out." There was also a tendency to write many rising and falling melodic curves.

The whole-tone scale was sometimes used by the Impressionists for both melodic and harmonic purposes. This scale, which does not have the perfect fourth, fifth, or leading tone, denies a sense of tonic, or center, thus permitting each tone to move without creating tension to any other tone of the scale (Ex. 33).

Example 33. *Piano Prelude: Voiles*

Debussy

Rhythm

In the early Romantic period, the element of rhythm remained much as it had in the Classic. From about the middle of the century, however, rhythm became more irregular and more interesting, often with changes in the number of beats in a measure, cross-rhythms, and syncopations (Ex. 34).

Example 34. *Nocturne in F♯ major*

Chopin

Rhythm was often complex and rhapsodic. It sometimes avoided strong stresses in order to increase the sense of tension, especially in slower movements. Tempo in Romantic music was not always constant. There were frequent changes in tempo, and many occasions for rubato, accelerando, and so forth.

Harmony

Romantic harmony was still tonal, but the sense of key center was eroded throughout the nineteenth century. Devices such as chromaticism, nonharmonic tones, altered chords, and extensive use of ninth and thirteenth chords served to build harmonic tension and weaken the sense of tonal center (Ex. 35). In fact, almost all the characteristics of harmony during this period show a gradual disintegration of the major-minor system.

Example 35. *Prelude* to *Tristan und Isolde*

Wagner

Tonality was weakened by the fusion of the major and minor modes, using chords typical of one mode in the other. Key relationships were less formalized than in Baroque and Classic music. Modulations to distant keys, including the mediant and submediant, and sudden moving in and out of keys for short periods of time also added to tension and to the weakening of a strong feeling for a particular key. Strong formal cadences sometimes were avoided with numerous deceptive cadences that give a harmonic sense of motion and tension. Modal harmonization of folk melodies, especially in nationalistic music, served to open new avenues of harmonic expressiveness.

Texture

The texture of Romantic music mixed vertical and horizontal elements. Polyphonic texture was not pervasive, and occurred more as a device than a style. An accompanied lyric line was one important stylistic feature of the Romantic era, most particularly evident in the German Lied. The texture also can be described as heavy, in contrast with the lighter and transparent quality of the Classic. Even in works for solo voice, the accompaniment provided a sonority of tonal fabric that served to blend the voice with the instrument.

In orchestral works the larger complement of instruments yielded a richer texture. In addition, the texture was made even more sonorous by more subdivisions of instruments, increasing the number of independent parts. Wagner, for example, sometimes divided the first violin section into as many as four different parts.

Instrumentation and Tone Color

The piano became the most popular instrument of the Romantic period because it could run the gamut of all ranges of sound and because it could be played by one person. It became almost a musical symbol of Romanticism. Moreover, the piano was enlarged to give it a wider range and more tonal power. The instrument reached such heights of popularity that it became the favorite household instrument with every family that could afford it.

Tone color became an integral part of the melodic and harmonic texture. Melodies were created in terms of timbre, with their musical expressiveness identified with specific instruments. Harmonic texture was also influenced by innovations in orchestration that created new and unusual combinations of instruments and the subdivision of the usual choirs of instruments.

The orchestra grew to be the favorite large ensemble of the century. It featured great size and varied color, capable of creating "Romantic expression." It had been expanded from the Classic orchestra by the addition of instruments such as the English horn and clarinet, and also by the addition of more brass and percussion instruments. Moreover, the virtuosity of the orchestra was increased by technical refinement to already existing instruments, especially brasses and woodwinds.

(Appendix 1 includes further information on instruments.)

The solo song with piano accompaniment (Piano Lied) was another favorite medium of Romantic expression. The voice was also a personalized instrument, for it combined with the literary elements of Romanticism to give an added intensity to the poetic text. Aside from the solo song and opera, vocal music was of minor importance in the period.

Opera was an important musical medium in the Romantic era. Combining, as it does, drama, poetry, and the visual experience of action, along with music, it is able to make a powerful impression on the emotions of an audience. Its popularity and importance can be realized by noting the large number of Romantic operas that are still in the repertory today.

The operetta, a light form of musical dramatic production made its appearance in the nineteenth century as a development of the forms of comic opera of the eighteenth century. With its farcical or sentimental plot and its alternation of light songs and spoken dialogue, the operetta gives expression to romanticism in popular form.

Written dynamic indications became more explicit than in the music of the Classic period. Subtle shadings of timbre and minute gradations of loudness were indicated by more specific terminology, and tempi were more accurately designated by the use of metronome markings.

Due to the fact that the orchestra was enlarged to become one of the more important vehicles of Romantic expression, the orchestral conductor emerged as a virtuoso performer. The use of the baton took the conductor from the keyboard to the podium. Von Weber, Mendelssohn, Berlioz, Liszt, Wagner, and Mahler were among the many composers who achieved fame as conductors. While they were not great composers, Hans von Bülow and Hans Richter became well known for their conducting skills.

It was an era of massive festival performances. Because of the fondness for sonority and power, an enormous number of participants were often used. Sometimes, as in the case of the works of Berlioz, the large orchestra and chorus constitute an essential part of the composer's style. At other times the usual number of performers were greatly augmented to suit the public's taste for massed effects. Large festival orchestras and choruses appeared in all countries, and are still very popular. There have been many instances in which over a thousand performers have taken part in the performance of a single work.

The middle-class love for music-making led to the establishment of choral societies. Folk music, political songs, and popular melodies provided the musical fare, but the artistic level was rather shallow. A few such societies made presentations of Handel and Haydn oratorios, but they had little effect on the Romantic quality of their own composers.

The art of improvisation was generally discarded in the practice of Romantic music, due to the complexity of its composition and the complete directions for performance. A few individuals, like Chopin and Liszt, continued to make brilliant use of it, but in concerto writing most cadenzas were written in a manner to give the effect of improvisation.

Because of the emphasis on individualism and the spectacular, it follows there would be a number of virtuoso performers during the Romantic. Beethoven, until deafness curtailed his performances, was a pianist of exceptional virtuosity. His early triumphs in Vienna were probably due to his pianistic artistry as much as to his compositions.

Franz Liszt was the most successful Romantic virtuoso pianist. His personality and theatrical effects coupled with his spectacular performance made him almost a legend in his own time. His virtuosity had a marked influence on piano performance for all time. Frédéric Chopin was another pianist whose music and performance was so personal, refined, and brilliant, that he has become almost a symbol of the Romantic spirit. In addition, Carl Czerny, Anton Rubinstein, and Robert and Clara Schumann were known both as pianists and composers.

Niccolò Paganini developed the technique of the violin to its present state. His dazzling performances of double stops, harmonics, runs, and trills are still a challenge to violinists. His fame as a performer was widespread and influenced many composers including Liszt and Berlioz. Joseph Joachim, a later Romantic violinist, had an important influence on the music of Brahms.

Because instrumental virtuosi were usually composers as well, their technical exploits were notated in their scores. This was not true, however, for operatic singers. Theirs was usually a spontantous realization of the basic ideas of the composer. It was not until the development of the recording industry that reliable examples of singers' technical skills became available.

Paganini. Caricature of the renowned violinist's playing. (Private Collection of Milo Wold)

IV. MUSIC FOR VOICES

Single Movement Forms and Structural Devices
Art Song

The solo song occupied an important place in Romantic music. Romantic poetry was set for the voice and piano in a highly personal and subjective musical manner. The two basic types of formal organization in these works were strophic and through-composed. The latter had more possibilities for the Romantic idiom because it allowed every poetic nuance to have its own musical expression. The piano created and sustained the mood of each poem and was an equal partner with the singer. German composers of *Lied* set poems by such writers as Heine, Schiller, and Goethe, poets who epitomized the Romantic spirit. Songs with related texts were often grouped into cycles. These song cycles were frequently settings of one poet, and were related by a central idea, or theme. Schubert, Schumann, Brahms, and Hugo Wolf were the most important composers of the German Lied. While the German Lied held the prominent place in song literature, both the French and the Russians also fostered an art song literature of high quality. The French especially were helped by the French Romantic poets to create songs of exceptional lyric beauty, commonly referred to as *mélodie*. (Rec. 7.1–7.4)

Choral Music

There was very little music written for liturgical purposes in the Romantic period. However, composers wrote for voices and instruments, with emphasis on the symphonic ideal rather than on vocal possibilities. These were heard most often in the concert hall, and when used in a church they served a nonliturgical purpose. (Rec. 7.5–7.7)

While there was a great wealth of secular choral music written in the nineteenth century, only a few important works have survived and most of these are for voices and orchestra. Some composers, Beethoven, Liszt, and Mahler, used the chorus as a part of the symphonic form. The part songs of Schubert, Schumann, Mendelssohn, and Brahms, to name but four, may have been conceived for one voice on each part, though today they are often treated and performed as choral works. (Rec. 7.8–7.9)

Composite Forms

Opera

Opera provided the best opportunities for all aspects of Romantic music to be combined into a single form. All Romantic operas can be described as extravagant spectacles with a tendency toward heroic and epic subjects, supernaturalism, mystery, and passion. Eighteenth-century opera was dominated by the Italian style with its multiplicity of closed forms, but in the nineteenth century, Italy, France, and Germany continued to develop their own styles with special qualities that were indigenous to each. Therefore, it becomes necessary to describe briefly the form of opera in each of these countries.

1. *Italian opera.* Early Romantic opera in Italy retained the Neapolitan style with a series of recitatives, arias, duets, and choruses with little dramatic continuity. Later in the century, mainly under the influence of Verdi, it showed greater dramatic unity, better developed characters, and more credible plots. These plots were often quasi-dramatic, but there was a general improvement in quality. The recitative and aria were still the principal closed forms with melody in the popular bel-canto style and an emphasis on virtuosity. There was also greater balance among voices and instruments, but the orchestra still served as accompaniment.

Another development in Italian Romantic opera was the style known as *verismo,* or realism. Realism was not limited to music. It was also shown in the choice of libretti that presented subjects from everyday life and depicted people in familiar situations. (Rec. 7.10–7.13)

2. *French opera.* Opera in nineteenth-century France showed some characteristics that were different from the Italian. During the early part of the century there was a marked distinction between Grand Opera and Opéra Comique, but as Romanticism matured the two styles merged into one. Opéra Comique was generally distinguished from Grand Opera by use of some spoken dialogue instead of a continuous musical texture. Generally it was simpler in musical expressiveness and used fewer characters with very little chorus. In the French lyric opera the theatrical aspect and the simpler forms of Opéra Comique were combined with the virtuosity and drama of the Grand Opera. A particular trait in all French opera was the ballet and it became even more important during the Romantic era. There was unity of dramatic action with the music that was seldom found in the Italian style. There was also less virtuosity with more emphasis on the lyric quality of melody. Moreover, French Romantic opera rarely displayed the intensity and passion of either the Italian or the German but was more conservative in its music and in its dramatic content. (Rec. 7.14–7.16)

3. *German opera.* Opera in Germany presented two significant styles: German Romantic opera and music drama, the latter conceived and developed by Richard Wagner. In German Romantic opera, like the music drama, the libretti were often based on German legends and folklore with the mystery of nature and supernatural forces serving to itensify dramatic expression. Unlike the music drama, recitatives and arias were distinct forms, and were sometimes based on folk song or melodies in folk style. *Melodrama,* instrumentally accompanied speech sometimes an independent form was used for special effects. Two other traits of the music drama were exhibited to some degree in the German Romantic opera. The orchestra became a powerful instrument in creating atmosphere, moods, and even bits of realism. There was also a prototype of the music drama's Leitmotif in which particular instruments and melodies are used to identify and characterize individuals. (Rec. 7.17)

The ideal of music-drama, or the art of the future as it was called by Wagner, was that of an art form in which all the arts were woven into one cohesive and continuous line of dramatic expression. Wagner continued the German tradition but wrote his own stories, drawing heavily upon German myths and folklore. His libretti were filled with romantic mysticism and supernaturalism, and almost all were concerned with the concept of redemption through love. There were few closed forms, such as recitative and aria. The vocal line became a continuous melody rising out of an orchestral fabric that was also continuous, without usual cadences. The Leitmotif became a unifying device in the sonorous and tension-filled musical texture. The Wagnerian Leitmotif was a musical figure that was associated with a particular idea, person, object, mood, or situation. Because Wagner used the orchestra as the main source of dramatic expression, his operas are symphonic in nature. Consequently, it has been possible to have successful concert performances of much of his music without staging or the vocal parts. (Rec. 7.18, 7.19)

4. *Nationalistic opera.* In addition to Italian, French, and German operas, there were operatic developments in those countries where nationalism was strong, especially in Russia and Bohemia. These operas were also based on folklore or upon events of national significance with nationally important personages. Composers such as Mussorgsky in Russia created works that are highly original with great dramatic power without using the closed forms of the Italian and without imitating Wagner. (Rec. 7.20, 7.21)

Oratorio

The Romantic oratorio followed the choral tradition of Handel in the works of Mendelssohn, who added the melodic, harmonic, and sonorous qualities of Romantic style. While there were very few who wrote for the Protestant church, there were many composers who set quasi-religious stories of mysticism and Catholic symbolism to music in the manner of the oratorio. These forms are not easily classified because they are neither operas, oratorios, nor cantatas. The orchestra generally plays a more important role than in earlier oratorios, with the chorus and soloists bringing texts to what were conceived largely as symphonic works. Mendelssohn, Liszt, and Berlioz wrote compositions in this fashion for performance in the concert hall. (Rec. 7.22–7.24)

V. MUSIC FOR INSTRUMENTS

Single Movement Forms and Structural Devices

Sonata Form

The Romantic sonata form was still based on the organizational principles of the Classic sonata. There was, however, a notable expansion of both the melodic and harmonic substance. Instead of two contrasting themes, composers often used groups of themes in the exposition. In such cases different theme groups were frequently presented in different, often remote keys, extending the harmonic range. In order to develop this melodic and harmonic material, the development was often much longer than in the Classic era. In order to reconcile the key changes and to reestablish the tonic, a long coda was sometimes added. (Rec. 7.25–7.27)

Two-Part and Three-Part Song Forms

Varied descriptive titles were attached to short forms which suggested moods or revealed the personal feelings of the composer. These were often referred to as *character pieces*. They were usually in two-part or three-part forms, but sometimes were short enough to have only one section. These forms bore such titles as nocturnes, preludes, caprices, serenades, bagatelles, impromptus, and so forth. Ballades were usually longer works which suggested the possible moods of stories without defining a particular sequence of events. In addition, titles suggestive of personalities, scenes, or ideas were often applied to these shorter pieces. There was no formal distinctiveness, nothing except mood and atmosphere, to differentiate one from another. (Rec. 7.28–7.31)

Variations

While the variation form was sometimes used as a movement of a sonata or symphony, it also held a high place as an independent form for both orchestra and piano solo. Variations were created on preexisting themes, or on specially composed melodies. Occasionally variations were made to suggest particular moods or ideas suggested by the theme. (Rec. 7.32–7.34)

Dance Movements

The nineteenth century saw the rise in importance of stylized dance movements for both the orchestra and solo instruments, especially the piano. Dances of a national character such as the Polonaise, Mazurka, and Jota, were set by many composers. Moreover, general national types—Hungarian, Spanish, and Slavonic—formed the basis of many works. These were usually expanded, idealized concert versions of the dances, not social dances. Sometimes dance movements which symbolized ideas or events such as *Danse Macabre* by Saint-Saëns and Liszt's *Mephisto Waltz* gave Romantic composers the opportunity to use realistic devices to intensify the mood or atmosphere. (Rec. 7.35–7.37)

Rhapsody

Rhapsody was a term often used in Romantic music to designate a free fantasy on themes of a national or epic character. It was a single movement form with the usual contrasts and Romantic tensions. It appeared in orchestral and piano literature, and sometimes for a solo instrument combined with orchestra. (Rec. 7.38–7.40)

Études

A particular form for solo instruments was the étude. Originally it was a study piece designed for the perfection of technique, but was expanded as a concert work with emphasis on a display of virtuosity. Even when it became a concert piece, however, it never lost its function as a study piece. Each étude usually emphasized some particular technical problem. They are in binary or three-part form, with the usual tension of contrast and repetition. (Rec. 7.41, 7.42)

Concert Overture

The concert overture is a symphonic work in the manner of an overture that is not associated with an opera. In general, the concert overture does not attempt to tell a story, but creates a mood that can be associated with a literary theme, a place, or an event. Many works of this nature adhere closely to the principle of the sonata form. (Rec. 7.43, 7.44)

Symphonic Poem

One of the typical forms of orchestral program music is the symphonic poem. It was the invention of Franz Liszt and was sometimes called a tone-poem, especially when it was based on a poetic idea. The form comprises one continuous movement, and is based on the principle of variations on a theme, or contrasting themes, that are inspired by a program or a literary idea. It is a transformation of themes in which they retain their identity through various stages and forms. (Rec. 7.45–7.47)

Composite Forms

Sonata and Symphony

The Romantic sonata and symphony, like the sonata form itself, was based on the Classic pattern of sonata and symphony. Some composers, such as Beethoven and Schubert, adhered rather closely to the Classic, but others, including Berlioz, Mahler, Bruckner, and Tchaikovsky, made significant departures from it. During the early years of the Romantic era the piano sonata retained its popularity, along with sonatas for violin or cello and piano. As the century progressed, however, the symphony became the most important composite instrumental form. Composers enriched its sonorities and combined it with literary ideas because of its new sonorous possibilities for realism. There was greater contrast among the themes of the Romantic symphony than in the Classic, especially contrast between a vigorous first theme or theme group and a more lyric second theme or theme group. Modulations were more varied, often without the usual preparation. Because there was less emphasis on balance and logic, a more sectional scheme of organization resulted. Unity among movements was often achieved by the cyclic principle, that is, using the same themes, or portions of them in each movement. While the emphasis in the Classic sonata or symphony was on the first movement, the Romantic symphony often placed its emphasis on the last movement. This is especially true when such works were cast in cyclic form in which the climax, or culmination of the thematic material, occurred during the last movement. A number of composers included solo and choral vocal writing in their symphonies in the desire to emphasize the climax of the last movement. The minuet was usually replaced by a scherzo, a movement quicker in tempo that provided more contrast to the second and last movements. The variation form was frequently used as either the second or last movement. Some composers used five movements in their symphonies in contrast with the usual four-movement Classic symphony. (Rec. 7.48–7.54)

Concerto

The Romantic concerto became more symphonic than its eighteenth century counterpart; technical demands made the solo parts more spectacular. To a large degree the musical development of the Romantic concerto was dependent on the orchestra rather than on the solo instrument. The double exposition of the Classic concerto was usually abandoned. The Romantic predilection for cyclic form was also apparent in the solo concerto. (Rec. 7.55–7.56)

Chamber Music

The forms of music for chamber ensembles generally followed the forms of the Romantic symphony and sonata. The instrumentation, however, remained much the same as in the Classic period. There was an increased emphasis on virtuosity which demanded a higher degree of professional skill for performance than in the chamber music of Haydn and Mozart. (Rec. 7.57–7.59)

Ballet

While the ballet had been a part of opera in the seventeenth and eighteenth centuries, it was not until the Romantic era that it achieved consideration by composers as a unified dramatic form independent of opera. Dramatic expression was achieved by the music and its corresponding dance, which was performed by soloists and ensemble, serving the same purpose as the vocal solo and chorus in opera. (Rec. 7.60, 7.61)

Symphonic Suite

The suite was revived about the middle of the nineteenth century. However, instead of the traditional scheme of dances as written during the Baroque era, it presented a free succession of contrasting movements, usually national dances or ballet movements. It was sometimes a series of extracts from a ballet, or incidental music to a play. It often suggested a series of scenes, sometimes from a story, as in a suite of symphonic poems. It was usually for orchestra, but also appeared in the literature for piano. (Rec. 7.62, 7.63)

VI. COMPOSERS

Ludwig van Beethoven (1770–1827) was named earlier among the composers of the Classic style, but it is as a Romanticist that his greatest compositions were conceived. Born in Bonn, Germany, Beethoven displayed strong musical gifts as a child. He suffered at the hands of his father who hoped he could mold the young talent into a prodigy like Mozart. The incompetence of his father as a manager finally caused Beethoven to become the sole support of his family. His gifts as a pianist, organist, violinist, and composer won him an official position at the Bonn Court where he remained until 1792 when he left for Vienna, where he was to live the rest of his life. While he was first known in Vienna as a brilliant pianist, a slowly developing deafness caused him to abandon performance for composition. He was the first composer in history to live exclusively independent of the patronage of the aristocracy, or the church, and to make a comfortable living from the sale of his compositions.

His life is generally viewed in three periods. The first during which time he was a pianist and composer, ends about 1802. Compositions from this period hold the seeds of Romanticism, but are still cast in the molds of the Classic tradition of Mozart and Haydn. The second period ends about 1814, and reveals him coming to maturity a complete Romanticist. The third and last period is somewhat enig-

Beethoven at work

matic. In it Beethoven seemed to be breaking the bounds even of Romanticism by becoming more introspective, more profoundly spiritual, more improvisational, and even recalling the contrapuntal style of the Baroque.

Beethoven was largely responsible for freeing music from the harmonic, rhythmic, and formal restraints of Classicism, and for leading the way to individualism and subjective feeling in music. He made important contributions to the literature of every musical genre, especially the symphony and the string quartet. His works became models for his contemporaries as well as later composers. Almost all of the Romanticists found justification in Beethoven for their individual styles. Beethoven's major contributions can be summarized as follows: (1) he showed a remarkable economy of material in the sonata form that led the way to the cyclic type of multiple forms; (2) his themes were often constructed from short motives that were gradually built up and expanded into full-length lyric melodies; (3) he raised the piano to a new level of importance and Romantic expression; (4) he expanded the use of polyphonic procedures in thematic development; (5) he used dissonance as a functional part of his harmonic

Manuscript page from Beethoven's, "Piano sonata in E♭" Opus 81a. (Historical Pictures Service, Chicago)

structure; (6) he achieved a new fluency in modulation that opened new possibilities of harmonic contrast and interest; and (7) he changed and expanded the traditional forms of the sonata and symphony to accommodate thematic materials and expressive purposes, rather than making the materials fit the forms.

Beethoven's compositions exerted an important influence on nearly all subsequent composers. Among his many important compositions the authors cite the following:

(1) Nine symphonies, among which *Symphony No. 3 in E flat major,* Op. 55 (Eroica); *Symphony No. 5 in c minor,* Op. 67; and *Symphony No. 9 in d minor,* Op. 125 (Choral) are the best known;

(2) instrumental concertos, include five for piano and one for violin;

(3) thirty-two piano sonatas, including the *Sonata in c minor,* Op. 13, (Pathétique) and *Sonata in f minor,* Op. 57, (Appassionata);

(4) prodigious numbers of chamber music, of which the sixteen string quartets are justly renowned;

(5) large works for voices and orchestra, including one opera, *Fidelio,* Op. 72b; an oratorio, *Christus am Oelberg,* Op. 85; and the *Missa Solemnis,* Op. 123.

Niccolò Paganini (1782–1840) was the first of the great instrumental virtuosi of the nineteenth century. An Italian violinist, he developed a spectacular technique that enabled him to dazzle his audiences. In addition, his innate showmanship gave him an almost hypnotic power over his listeners. His compositions consist mainly of virtuoso études for violin and a brilliant violin concerto. He had a profound effect on many Romantic composers, especially Schumann and Liszt, who tried to adapt Paganini's concepts of virtuosity to the piano.

Carl Maria von Weber (1786–1826) was the founder of the German Romantic school of opera. His father was an amateur musician and also the director of a traveling theatrical group. No doubt this environment helped to stimulate young Weber's imagination as a dramatic composer. He was something of a child prodigy, learning the piano and violin at an early age. His first piano works were published when he was twelve years old. His most important posts as a mature musician were as Kapellmeister at Prague and as Director of the Opera at Dresden. In addition to his fame as a composer, he was well known as a brilliant pianist and conductor, and was among the first to use a baton, which he grasped in the middle. While he composed in almost every medium, his best works are for piano or the stage. The piano works are brilliant concert pieces with emphasis on virtuosity and, with the exception of the *Invitation to the Dance,* are seldom performed today. His opera *Der Freischütz* is based on a German folk tale that dwells on supernatural phenomena, and reveals the sentimentality of the middle class. While Weber broke with the Italian operatic tradition, he still used arias in the Italian manner. It was the chorus effects, the orchestral coloring, and the stories that made the operas typically German. His music includes motifs which predate the Leitmotifs of Wagner. These motifs are associated with specific moods and ideas. For Weber the overture was a collection of the most important melodies in each opera, serving as a sort of preview of what was to come. His most important operas are *Der Freischütz, Euryanthe,* and *Oberon.* The latter was first produced in England a few months before his death in 1826.

Gioacchino Rossini (1792–1868) was one of the most brilliant of the early Italian Romantic opera composers. He exhibited a remarkable flow of melody in the bel canto tradition. This, combined with brilliant orchestration, dynamic rhythms, and clear-cut phrases, made his operas popular all through Europe. One of his notable devices of orchestration was the use of crescendo by means of numerous repetitions of a phrase, adding instruments and increasing the degree of loudness with each repetition. Rossini was at his best in opera buffa and his principal works in this form are *La gazza ladra* (The Thieving Magpie), *L'italiana in Algeri,* and *Il Barbiere di Siviglia.* The latter became his most popular opera and was produced in almost every opera house of Europe.

Franz Schubert (1797–1828) was one of the few Viennese composers to claim that city as his birthplace. His early musical training was as a member of the Vienna Court singers and as a student in the Convict, a training school for singers. Here he learned to play the violin and studied theory, as well as singing. When his voice changed he had to leave the school. For a time he held a post as an elementary school teacher, but gave it up after three years. After this brief period of teaching, Schubert's life was illustrative of a kind of Bohemianism often associated with the Romantic spirit. He was one of the few Romantic composers to live in poverty. He never held a position as a musician in either an institution or in an aristocratic household. Moreover, he did not even have the security of a benevolent patronage nor a steady income from the sale of his works. He eked out a precarious existence as a private tutor, sold a few compositions to publishers and had a few commissions for works. His early death at the age of thirty-one was unquestionably hastened by poverty. While Schubert's piano, chamber, and orchestral works are significant contributions to the literature of music, it is in the art songs that his expression of Romanticism reaches its height. Among the outstanding qualities of his music are his lyric melodies and harmonic coloring. Moreover, in his Lieder there is a musical sensitivity to the poetic expression that makes Schubert's songs among the finest in all vocal literature. His piano works, chamber music, and orchestral works are generally classic in their formal organization. The Romantic element lies in the substance of melody and harmony.

Schubert composed over 600 songs, nine symphonies, twenty-two piano sonatas, seventeen operas, six masses, about thirty-five chamber music works, and numerous occasional pieces for orchestra and solo instruments. It is only Schubert's operas that have failed to gain recognition. Some of his best songs can be found in the two song cycles, *Die Schöne Müllerin* and *Die Winterreise.* Of his symphonies the *Symphony No. 8 in b minor* (the Unfinished) and the *Symphony No. 9 in C major* are the most well known. The *String Quartet in d minor* (Death and the Maiden), the *Quintet in A major,* and the *Piano Trio in B flat major* hold a high place in the literature for chamber music. The piano sonatas in c minor and B flat major are among the finest works for this instrument.

Gaetano Donizetti (1797–1848) was one of the most prolific of the Italian opera composers. His music is notable for its remarkable melodies, with which he expressed the gamut of emotions. Actually, his harmony, rhythm, and orchestration are at times repetitive, but it is his talent for melody and stagecraft that caught the public's favor and served to keep many of his works popular to this day. While he wrote instrumental music, cantatas, and church music, his operas are all that receive frequent performances. The best of these are *Lucia di Lammermoor* and the comic operas *La Fille du régiment* (The Daughter of the Regiment) and *Don Pasquale*.

Vincenzo Bellini (1801–1835), like so many Italian opera composers, is remembered for his gift of melody. More reserved in range of expression than Donizetti, Bellini was exceedingly adept in psychological characterization. The Romantic element lies mainly in his sentimental melodies rather than in the tension of harmony and sonority. All of his operas were based on serious subjects. The more important works are *Norma*, *La sonnambula* (The Sleepwalker), and *I Puritani* (The Puritans).

Hector Berlioz (1803–1869) was one of the first recognized composers who did not come from a musical family, or at least a strong musical background. His father was a doctor, and young Berlioz was also destined for a medical career. However, his interest in music caused him to desert his medical studies in Paris in favor of composition. Berlioz never became a proficient performer on any instrument, nor was he a practicing musician in any professional sense. His only musical post was as a music librarian at the Paris Conservatory. In effect he was a free-lance composer-conductor, writing music and then arranging concerts for its performance. He wrote mainly in the larger forms of the overture, symphony, and opera, composing virtually nothing for solo instruments or chamber music.

Berlioz was a pioneer in the area of symphonic program music. He developed the *idée fixe,* a recurring melody or theme that identifies programmatic ideas and persons in a purely musical manner. His most famous programmatic symphony is the *Symphonie Fantastique*. In it, Berlioz shows his mastery of orchestration, bringing new colors and even new sounds into the orchestral fabric. He also enlarged the orchestra to almost gigantic proportions, even planning a work for an orchestra of 465 performers. His technique of orchestration and instrumentation was set forth in his *Treatise on Instrumentation and Orchestration* published in 1844, a book which served as a dictionary of

Berlioz conducting (Art and History Archive)

orchestration well into the twentieth century. Berlioz was also a musical journalist, a career that enabled him to campaign actively on behalf of the Romantic ideals in opposition to the conservatism of Classicism.

His important works, in addition to the *Symphonie Fantastique*, are *Harold in Italy*, for solo viola and orchestra; *Roméo et Juliette*, for solo voices, chorus, and orchestra; *The Damnation of Faust*, a concert opera; a *Requiem Mass*; *L'enfance du Christ* (The Childhood of Christ), for solo voices, chorus, and orchestra; and the opera *Les Troyens* (The Trojans). In addition he wrote a number of concert overtures, of which the *Roman Carnival* and *Benvenuto Cellini* are still frequently performed.

Felix Mendelssohn (1809–1847) was the son of a wealthy banker and the grandson of a famous philosopher. He was fortunate in being surrounded with the finest opportunities for becoming a musician,

Manuscript page from Mendelssohn's, "Fingal's Cave," Opus 26. (Robert V. Eckert, Jr. EKM-Nepenthe)

for he had the wealth for unlimited study and a highly cultivated cultural and social background. He became a proficient concert pianist as well as a competent composer. His most important positions were Director of the Royal Conservatory in Leipzig, which he founded, and Conductor of the Gewandhaus Orchestra, also in Leipzig. He was widely traveled and his music became very popular in many countries, especially in England. Among his other accomplishments, Mendelssohn was largely responsible for the revival of interest in the works of J. S. Bach. Mendelssohn's music is closely allied to the Classic traditions in form; the Romantic spirit appears in his melodies and imaginative orchestral coloring. His music has little of the passion and violence of Romanticism, but almost always expresses a serenity and sentimentality that achieved wide audience appeal.

Mendelssohn wrote copiously during his short life, but his fame rests largely on works for piano, orchestra, and on two oratorios, *Elijah*, Op. 70, perhaps the finest Romantic oratorio, written especially for performance in England, and *St. Paul*, Op. 36. Among the orchestral works the *Overture to a Midsummer Night's Dream*, Op. 21; the *Hebrides Overture*, Op. 26; the *Symphony No. 3 in a minor*, Op. 56 (the Scottish); and *Symphony No. 4 in A Major*, Op. 90 (the Italian) are the most often performed. His *Violin Concerto in e minor*, Op. 64 has remained a classic in violin literature. His finest large work for piano is the *Variations sérieuses in d minor*, Op. 54. However, he more characteristically wrote small piano pieces, as in the *Lieder ohne Worte* (Songs Without Words).

Frédéric Chopin (1810–1849) was born in Warsaw, Poland, but left his native land at the age of twenty and spent the rest of his short but creative life in Paris. He composed almost exclusively for the piano and was most successful in the shorter forms of occasional pieces such as the étude, nocturne, impromptu, mazurka, and polonaise. He exploited the melodic and harmonic possibilities of the piano to a greater degree than any other composer. He concentrated on melody, which he decorated with delicate and graceful, often virtuosic passages. He also made daring harmonic innovations with enharmonic modulations and new dissonances, which often prolonged harmonic tension far beyond that of his contemporaries. Moreover, Chopin enhanced the harmonic texture of piano music by skillful use of the pedal to increase the number of tones in a chord. He was also responsible for the development of the left-hand figuration based upon tenths rather than the fifth and octave of the Alberti bass.

Chopin's music is often associated with Polish nationalism. Frequent settings of the *polonaise* and *mazurka* illustrate this facet of his creative output. He generally eschewed the larger forms. Consequently, it is the twenty-four *preludes*, the *impromptus, waltzes,* and *ballades* and *études* that most often hold the interest of present-day pianists and their audiences.

Robert Schumann (1810–1856) was the son of a bookseller, a circumstance that brought him into close contact with the writings of the new Romantic movement during his formative years. After a period of law study and an unsuccessful attempt to become a concert pianist, he turned his efforts toward composition and musical journalism. He founded and became editor of the *Neue Zeitschrift für Musik,* a journal devoted to musical criticism. He also taught for a time at the Leipzig Conservatory and was Municipal Musical Director at Düsseldorf. However, organized musical activity was not congenial to his nature, and he devoted most of his time to writing, composing, and going on concert tours with his wife, Clara Wieck, who was the first prominent woman concert pianist. Schumann suffered from a mental disorder and, after attempting suicide, was confined to an asylum where he died in 1856.

Schumann, more than any other composer, became the spokesman for the revolt against Classicism and the champion for revolutionary tendencies in music. In addition, he became the ardent supporter of such men as Chopin and Brahms, and it was through his writing that much of their music became known to the concert world. While his compositional efforts cover the range of music from opera through piano works and solo song, it is in the smaller forms that he is most successful. While the symphonies, piano concerto, and some chamber works are still retained in the repertory, it is generally recognized that Schumann did not have the craftsmanship to mold the larger forms successfully. Schumann's music can be identified by its lyric melody, its vague and imaginative formal structure, and its remarkable range of expression from the most tender to the most heightened passion. He showed his interest in Bach by using contrapuntal devices within the framework of Romantic harmony. His piano music is idiomatic, making full use of the harmonic and tonal possibilities of the instrument. He had a Romantic predilection for suggesting poetic titles for many of his piano and orchestral works, but admitted that the music was always composed before the title was attached. In his Lieder, many of which were written in 1840, the year of his marriage to Clara, the piano played an almost equal role with the voice.

Clara (1819–1896) and Robert (1810–1856) Schumann both were gifted composers and performers. Only recently has Clara Schumann begun to receive the acclaim that her works and performing career deserve. (Art and History Archive)

He often used the piano to interact with the vocal melody, and to suggest and sustain the mood of the poem. In some of his Lieder the piano plays an extended prologue or epilogue. His major works include a large number of songs of which the love songs are perhaps the best. The cycle *Dichterliebe,* Op. 48, on poems by Heine represents the finest of these. The piano music includes the *Concerto in a minor,* Op. 54, *Carnival,* Op. 9, *Kreisleriana,* Op. 16, *Papillons,* Op. 2, the *Symphonic Études,* Op. 13 and many other short works. The four symphonies and numerous works of chamber music are also important.

Franz Liszt (1811–1886) was one of the most fascinating of the Romantic personalities. As a virtuoso pianist-composer he left the imprint of his virtuosity and sentimental Romanticism on almost all subsequent pianists. Born in Hungary, he studied in Vienna and then in Paris where he became known as a concert pianist. He later settled in Weimar, Germany. There he devoted the major portion of his energies to composing and teaching with only an occasional concert tour. Liszt was deeply impressed by the virtuosity of the great Italian violinist Paganini and tried to do for piano technique what Paganini had done for the violin. In addition, Liszt inaugurated the recital as a popular form of musical presentation. He was also a popularizer of music and made innumerable transcriptions for the piano of all sorts of music from Beethoven symphonies to Schubert Lieder. As a Romantic realist, Liszt was a champion of program music and was responsible for the creation of the symphonic poem. His orchestral music gives the effect of an extravagant theatrical style with a wide range of emotion from tender sentimentality to intense passion. To gain these effects he used a large orchestra and followed the lead of Berlioz in colorful orchestration.

Liszt's piano music contains brilliant technical passages, dense chromaticism, sentimental melodies, all set with a loose sense of organization. The outstanding piano works by Liszt are the *Concerto in E flat major*, the *Sonata in b minor*, *Mephisto Waltz*, the *Transcendental Études*, the Hungarian Rhapsodies, and numerous short virtuoso pieces. While Liszt's orchestral music has less appeal today than in the nineteenth century, the symphonic poems, *Les préludes* and *Mazeppa* are often programmed by present-day orchestras.

Giuseppe Verdi (1813–1901) is the greatest figure in the history of Italian opera. He was no revolutionary like Wagner, for he never departed completely from the traditions of the closed forms of recitative and aria. But he enriched the long established forms with superb melodies, dramatic scenes, and an instinctive sensitivity for the theater. Some of his earlier works were rooted in nationalism and succeeded in stirring up the patriotism of Italians who yearned for their freedom and unity as a nation. Verdi's position as a nationalist was further enhanced by a brief period as an elected member of the Italian Parliament. His operas cover a wide range of subjects from the Egyptian story of *Aida* through the dramas of Shakespeare. With the exception of the *Requiem*, his nontheatrical works are of lesser importance. Verdi's more important operas are *Macbeth, Rigoletto, Il trovatore* (The Troubadour), *La traviata, Un ballo in maschera* (A Masked Ball), *La forza del destino* (The force of Destiny), *Don Carlos, Aida, Otello*, and *Falstaff*. All of these works are still prominent in the repertory of opera companies.

Richard Wagner (1813–1883), one of the most controversial figures in music history, was the arch romanticist of the nineteenth century. Raised in a theatrical atmosphere by his stepfather who was an actor and playwright, young Wagner's musical training was rather desultory. However, his ambition to be a conductor and a theatrical composer finally brought him conducting posts with provincial orchestras. Filled with ambition, he went to Paris where he hoped to rival the success of Meyerbeer. After a disastrous three years in Paris he finally returned to Germany. The Paris years, however, saw the completion of the operas *Rienzi* and *Der fliegende Holländer* (The Flying Dutchman), both of which were finally produced in Dresden. But Wagner became embroiled in the revolutionary movements of the time and was forced to flee Germany.

He spent the next twelve years in exile during which time he wrote *Tannhäuser* and *Lohengrin.* It was during these years that he formulated his theories about the opera, writing a number of easays on aesthetics, the most important of which was *Oper und Drama.* It was in this essay that he set forth the idea that the ideal art form would be equal portions of music, drama, poetry, and stagecraft. He called this art form the music-drama, the art of the future. One of the important results of his new theories was the beginning of the *Der Ring des Nibelungen,* a gigantic saga of four operas to be given on successive nights: *Das Rheingold, Die Walkure, Siegfried,* and *Gotterdammerung.* Drawing heavily on German and Norse mythology and based on the idea of redemption through love, the "Ring" is the longest and most complicated dramatic work ever to be successfully staged. The whole cycle took more than twenty years to complete.

In 1864 Wagner was invited to Munich by the young King Ludwig II of Bavaria and it was here that *Tristan und Isolde* was first produced. Because of Wagner's expensive tastes, the drain on the Bavarian treasury was too great and he was forced to leave the country. He then moved to Lucerne, Switzerland, where he wrote *Die Meistersinger.* The "Ring" was completed in 1874. Wagner had long dreamed of a theater especially constructed for his own works, and finally in Bayreuth, northern Bavaria, such a theater was built with a revolving stage, sunken orchestra pit, and every device of stage mechanics possible at that time. In 1876 the first performance of the "Ring" took place in this theater, which has since become a mecca for lovers of Wagnerian opera. His last opera was *Parsifal,* a quasi-religious drama based on the story of the Holy Grail. Wagner died in Venice in 1883.

Critics of Wagner were usually either violently opposed to his theories and music or were ardent supporters in his struggle for recognition. As a man, he was a supreme egotist. As one writer has put it: "Wagner thought of himself as the world's greatest composer, poet, dramatist, philosopher, and politician, and remarkably, he was very nearly all of these."

Wagner's musical style reveals the Romantic ideal at its greatest intensity. A few of the most important devices he used to achieve his Romantic expressiveness are discussed here. Wagner used the Leitmotif to identify people, objects, ideas, and emotions in his music-dramas. In addition to serving as a unifying device, it also convinces the listener of the reality of his Romantic illusions. Wagner's music-dramas were through-composed rather than being a series of recitatives and arias. He carried the dissolution of tonality to the very edge of atonality by the use of chromatic harmonies and vague cadences. This tendency is especially prevalent in *Tristan und Isolde*. The orchestra carries the burden of dramatic expression, thus making his operas predominantly symphonic in nature. Consequently, he enlarged the orchestra by adding instruments and subdividing the normal sections. This resulted in range of sonorities that made it possible to reach new heights of orchestral tension.

Charles Gounod (1818–1893) was a French composer who is best known for his operas and for his Romantic sacred music in the Catholic tradition. His most famous works are the operas *Faust* and *Roméo et Juliette*. Both of these remain in the opera repertory of today. *Faust* was first composed as a lyric opera with spoken dialogue and was later reworked in its present form with sung recitatives. Gounod's music abounds in sentimental lyricism and a type of mild Romanticism that was imitated by many lesser talents of his time.

César Franck (1822–1880) was a Belgian organist and composer whose musical style is that of French Romanticism. He lived in Paris where he was an organist, choirmaster, and teacher of such composers as d'Indy and Chausson. His music reveals a polyphonic treatment of Romantic melody and a harmonic substance comparable to that of Wagner. There is an air of Romantic mysticism in almost all of his works. He was one of the few Romantics to write extensively for the organ, but his greatest religious music is the oratorio, *Les béatitudes*. He is best known for the *Symphony in d minor*, the *Violin Sonata in A major*, and a number of works for piano, including the *Symphonic Variations for Piano and Orchestra*.

Bedřich Smetana (1824–1884) is considered the father of Czech music. An ardent nationalist, he wrote a long orchestral work called *Ma vlast* (My Fatherland), consisting of six symphonic poems depicting scenes from the life and history of Bohemia. *Vltava* (The Moldau) is the most successful of this cycle. Smetana was a disciple of Liszt and his symphonic poems are modeled after those of Liszt. A *Quartet in e minor* (From my Life) and an opera, *The Bartered Bride*, are two of his most well-known works.

Anton Bruckner (1824–1896) was an Austrian composer whose symphonic style, serious and profound, permeates everything he wrote. An organist and a deeply religious man, Bruckner wrote a number of religious works for the Roman Catholic church, including a *Te Deum* and three masses. His nine symphonies make up his major works and are marked by their great length and a rather massive sonorous structure. There is also a kind of religious mysticism about all of his works, especially in the slow movements. He used songlike themes as a basis for the symphonic forms and achieved great climaxes by using the orchestra in a manner that suggests the sound of a full organ. Bruckner is regarded as a nationalist in his native Austria.

Alexander Borodin (1833–1887) was a member of the "Russian Five," a group which was dedicated to the development of an indigenous Russian style in music. Other members of the "Five" included Mily Balakirev, César Cui, Modest Mussorgsky, and Nikolai Rimsky-Korsakov. While professionally Borodin was a teacher of chemistry, his intense interest in music brought forth a number of notable compositions. His music reveals a kind of Russian orientalism that was based on Caucasian and central Asian coloring. His main works are an opera, *Prince Igor;* a symphonic poem, *In Central Asia;* three symphonies; two string quartets; songs; and numerous other small works.

Johannes Brahms (1833–1897) was born in Hamburg, Germany, and began the study of the piano at age eight. By the time he was thirteen he was playing the piano in taverns to help supplement the meager income of his family. After a period of teaching and concertizing he moved to Vienna in 1863, where he was to remain until his death in 1897. While he held minor positions as director of various choral societies, he was never interested in a permanent position, but preferred to remain as an independent free-lance composer.

It was Schumann who called attention to Brahm's genius as a composer in an essay in the *Neue Zeitschrift für Musik.* Stylistically, Brahms is Romantic in his emotional expressiveness, but more Classic in his formal organization. He is sometimes referred to as a Neoclassicist because of his devotion to the principles of the Classic sonata

Brahms playing the piano. (The Bettmann Archive)

and the polyphonic treatment of his musical materials. He was an absolutist, writing no program music in the Romantic sense of the term. Brahms often used a motif as a basis for an entire movement, or even a complete symphony. His orchestration is always full, giving a massive musical sound. Rhythmically, Brahm's music is exceedingly complex, using cross-rhythms with numerous shifting accents and metric patterns. He is best known for his four symphonies. Other important works are the *Violin Concerto in D major*, Op. 77, the *Piano Concerto in B flat major*, Op. 83, and a substantial amount of Solo piano and chamber music. His writing for voices includes *Ein Deutsches Requiem*, Op. 45; *Schicksalslied*, Op. 54 (Song of Destiny); the *Alto Rhapsody*, for alto, men's chorus, and orchestra; and over two hundred songs.

Georges Bizet (1838–1875) was one of the first French composers to be influenced by Wagner. Perhaps this influence was responsible for the failure of his earlier works, for the French generally were not sympathetic towards the Wagnerian style. Bizet's fame rests almost solely on the opera *Carmen*, which was a failure when it was first performed in 1875. In *Carmen*, Bizet introduced realism into French opera. Wagnerian influences are apparent in such devices as the "death motive," but Bizet shows originality in the vivacity of the music and the psychological characterizations. *Carmen* has become the most popular opera of all time. Bizet also achieved some success with incidental music to *L'arlésienne*, a composition for orchestra based on a play by Daudet, but most of his music gained popularity only after his death.

Modest Mussorgsky (1839–1881) was an ardent Russian nationalist and probably the most talented and important member of the "Five." He was untutored in the basic theory of music, but possessed a great genius for creative expression. Mussorgsky never held a musical post, but spent most of his life as a government clerk. His early death was probably hastened by malnutrition and excessive use of alcohol. His greatest works are in the medium of song and opera, although his orchestral suite *Pictures at an Exhibition*, originally for piano, and *A Night on Bald Mountain*, both programmatic works, have retained their popularity. His greatest gift was his ability to translate the inflection of speech into dramatic, passionate, and poetic melody. His most famous opera is *Boris Godunov* in which he created a nationalistic music-drama. Divorced from the Italian operatic tradition, yet not imitative of Wagner, *Boris Godunov* is truly an original work that had great influence on many non-Russian composers. Because Mussorgsky was unskilled as an orchestrator, his operas and orchestral music were revised and orchestrated by Nikolai Rimsky-Korsakov, and it was in this form that they were first introduced to the European audiences.

Piotor Ilyitch Tchaikovsky (1840–1893) embarked on a course of law study and entered government service, but gave it up at the age of twenty-three and turned to music. After only two years of intensive study he was appointed professor of composition at the Moscow Conservatory. While Tchaikovsky is associated with the Russian spirit in music, and emotionally was a nationalist, he was not a member of the "Five." He also wrote in the style of Schumann and Berlioz. His melodies are lyric with a tinge of the Slavic modal harmonies that identify them with Russian folk song. His music is often sentimental, but it has a directness and a range of emotional expression that has wide appeal to all audiences. He is best known for his fourth, fifth, and sixth Symphonies; the concert overture, *Romeo and Juliet*; the ballets, *Swan Lake* and *The Nutcracker*; and the *Piano Concerto No. 1 in b flat minor. Eugene Onegin*, one of two operas, is still in the operatic repertory.

Antonin Dvořák (1841–1904), a Czech nationalist, first gained recognition through his Slavonic orchestral dances. He later turned to symphonies and chamber music. His style is closer to that of Brahms, although there are suggestions of Wagnerian harmonies in his music. His best-known work is the *Symphony No. 9 in e minor*, better known as the "New World Symphony," written during a sojourn in the United States where he had come to be the Artistic Director of the National Conservatory in New York. For decades it has been claimed that the "New World" was based on themes derived from Negro and Indian folk tunes, but more recent opinion attributes the origins to his Bohemian heritage. Among his other well-known works that remain alive in music literature are the *Slavonic Dances*, Op. 46 and Op. 72, the *Concerto for Cello* Op. 104, the *String Quartet in F Major*, Op. 96, *Stabat Mater*, Op. 58, and a number of songs.

Edvard Grieg (1843–1907) was a Norwegian nationalist who wrote in the traditional style of the German Romantics. He was trained under the influence of Mendelssohn and Schumann; however, he was successful in adapting the German style to the modal melodies and harmonies of Norwegian folk song and dances. The result was music of lyricism with freshness and charm. Grieg's important large works include an orchestral suite derived from incidental music he wrote for Ibsen's drama to *Peer Gynt*, a play about a Norse folk hero, and the famous *Piano Concerto in a minor*, Op. 16. The special charm of his music, however, is found in the shorter works—songs, dances, and the many *Lyric Pieces* for the piano.

Nikolai Rimsky-Korsakov (1844–1908) was a member of the Russian "Five" and has been credited with writing the first Russian symphony. He was a naval officer and a self-taught musician. In spite of his lack of formal training he was appointed Professor of Instrumentation and Composition at the St. Petersburg Conservatory, a position which he held until his death. His music utilizes the true Russian folk idiom and oriental melodic patterns. His musical output is not large, mainly because he gave a great deal of his time to revising and orchestrating the works of his friends, especially Mussorgsky. Rimsky-Korsakov's best operas are *The Maid of Pskov, The Snow Maiden*, and *Le*

Coq d'or (The Golden Cockerel). His orchestral works include *Schéhérazade* and *Sadko*, the first Russian tone poem. Rimsky-Korsakov is also the author of a textbook on orchestration, *Foundations of Orchestration*. He also wrote an autobiography, *The Chronicle of My Musical Life*.

Gabriel Fauré (1845–1924), one of the later Romantic composers, remained outside the influence of Wagner and Brahms. He developed an almost impressionistic, melodic, and harmonic style that evolved from the use of modal scales and transient harmonies. He is best known for his *Mélodies*, but his *Requiem, Violin Sonata in A major*, and the *Piano Quintet No. 1* have remained popular.

Giacomo Puccini (1858–1924) was the most famous and successful Italian opera composer after Verdi. He was a notable representative of the "verismo" style, a style which dealt with realistic subjects from everyday life and used a kind of melodramatic recitative with less emphasis on traditional subjects and forms. He was skillful in the technique of the theater, and his operas contain a kind of Romantic sentimentality that caused them to rival Verdi's in popularity. Puccini's most successful operas are *Gianni Schicchi, La bohème, Tosca, Madame Butterfly,* and *Turandot.*

Hugo Wolf (1860–1903), an Austrian composer, represents the Wagnerian influence on the Lied. Their complex contrapuntal textures and chromatic harmonies give his songs a tension and expressiveness not unlike the music of *Tristan und Isolde.* Moreover, Wolf had the capacity for a deep insight into the poetic spirit of the text. On hearing his Lieder, one feels the text to be the dominant element, with melody and harmony subordinate. Unlike Wagner's music, his compositions are usually succinct. He used the piano to intensify the dramatic element and not as a mere accompaniment. While he also wrote an opera and some instrumental works, it is for his more than 300 Lieder that he is remembered, many of which were published posthumously.

Gustav Mahler (1860–1911), the last great composer of the Viennese Romantic style, held various positions as conductor, including the directorship of the Vienna Court Opera, the Metropolitan Opera, and the New York Philharmonic Society. Mahler's nine symphonies are dramatically conceived, colossal tone paintings. His scores call for enormous orchestral resources comparable to those of Berlioz. Mahler was also a skillful and imaginative orchestrator, devising new sounds and even special tunings for strings to achieve dramatic effects. Using song as melodic material with solo voice and choral groups, his symphonies were sometimes expanded into choral works symphonically conceived. He frequently attached programmatic notes, or poetic quotations to his scores to suggest a feeling or a mood. Mahler's most important works are *Symphony No. 1 in D major*; *Symphony no. 2 in c minor* (the "Resurrection"); *Symphony no. 8 in E flat major*, called the "Symphony of a Thousand" because of its great number of participants; *Das Lied von der Erde* (The Song of the Earth) for tenor, contralto, and orchestra; and *Des Knaben Wunderhorn* (The Youth's Magic Horn), a cycle of ten songs with orchestra.

Claude Debussy (1862–1918), a French composer, was the leading figure of the impressionistic movement in music, the most influential development of nineteenth century French music. Impressionism was an antirealistic movement that originated first in the fields of painting and poetry. In addition to being antirealistic, it was anticlassical; even its Romantic qualities were milder, and it avoided the violence and passion of the earlier Romanticists. It was concerned with vague and transitory suggestions to evoke moods and atmosphere. Debussy was one whose music was directly influenced by literature and painting; he was greatly stimulated by the poetry of Verlaine and the paintings of Monet. He tried to suggest the same kind of feeling as his colleagues in poetry and painting. Debussy sought to express the shimmering effects of light and shade in painting by tone color and chordal structure in music, sacrificing lyric melody, traditional forms, and polyphonic complexities for suggestive harmonic progressions. In order to achieve a more luminous tonal coloring he destroyed the traditional function of the successive scale steps by the use of the whole-tone scale where each note has a subtle persuasion all its own. Debussy also added to the sense of vagueness by weakening cadences with parallel chordal progressions and unresolved dissonances.

Debussy's untraditional practices aroused much controversy, even in his early works such as the *Prelude à l'Après-midi d'un faune* (An afternoon of a faun), the *Nocturnes*, and *La mer*. His opera *Pelléas et Mélisande* is almost a music drama with a restrained musical expression that creates the emotional atmosphere of Maeterlinck's drama. A string quartet and a number of pieces for piano including the *Twenty Four Preludes*, are among his works written before 1910. The very late compositions written during the last year of his life, the violin and cello sonatas, and the two books of études, place Debussy in the forefront as an innovative composer, bridging the romanticism of the nineteenth century to the twentieth.

Richard Strauss (1864–1949) was one of the last of the Romantic realists. Like a number of the late nineteenth century composers, he was also distinguished as a conductor, both in opera and in the concert hall. It is as a composer, however, that he made his greatest musical impact for he was one of the virtuosi of orchestral writing. Strauss was a disciple of Liszt, Berlioz, and Wagner, adapting their realistic methods and devices to his own uses. After a few early works in the forms of the sonata, quartet, and symphony, he turned to program music for his expression. His realism was sometimes subjective in that he attached states of feeling to melodic and harmonic ideas as in the symphonic poem, *Tod und Verklärung* (Death and Transfiguration), for which he had the poet Ritter compose a poem to illustrate the music. On the other hand he used realism in a descriptive manner by suggesting scenes, movements and actual sounds of life and nature, as in the *Alpine Symphony*, where he employs a wind machine and a thunder machine to portray a storm scene. Strauss's realism covered a wide range of subjects from the humorous to the hysteric.

His music was brilliantly orchestrated with dramatic and sweeping sonorities that are marked by strong harmonic dissonances and sharp contrasts in tonal coloring. He made use of parallel chord progressions and arbitrary dissonances that obscure tonality but do not deny it. Moreover, he used a contrapuntal fabric that ignored the traditional intervallic relationships between the moving parts that are pushed relentlessly to their climactic conclusions.

While Strauss's earlier works were mainly symphonic poems, he also made an imposing contribution to opera. His first important opera was *Salome*, based on a text by Oscar Wilde, an opera that shocked the public of the 1900s more by its subject than its music. *Elektra*, on the other hand, used sharp dissonances and strong tonal color to characterize the decadent story of hate and sordid revenge. *Der Rosenkavalier*, a comic opera written in 1911, is more Classic in its form, but is still infused with the lyric sentimentality of Romanticism. While he lived almost to the middle of the twentieth century, his period of creative greatness seemed to end with *Der Rosenkavalier*. The best of his symphonic poems are *Don Juan, Till Eulenspiegels lustige Streiche* (Till Eulenspiegel's Merry Pranks), *Tod und Verklärung* (Death and Transfiguration), *Ein Heldenleben* (A Hero's Life), *Also sprach Zarathustra* (Thus Spoke Zarathustra), and *Don Quixote* (a variation for cello and orchestra). In spite of Strauss's seeming preoccupation with the larger forms of program music, his fine songs comprise a distinct contribution to song literature.

Jean Sibelius (1865–1957) was the most important Finnish composer of the late nineteenth and early twentieth centuries. His style
remained deeply rooted in the nineteenth century Romantic tradition. He consciously carried out a program of nationalistic musical
expression, basing much of his thematic material on the Finnish folk
song idiom though never employing the folk melodies literally. Most
of his works are for orchestra. Besides seven symphonies in the romantic tradition, his orchestral compositions are typically based on
Finnish legends, history, and landscapes. Among his best known
works in this genre are the tone-poems *Finlandia*, Op. 26, No. 7; *En
Saga*, Op. 9; and *The Swan of Tuonella*, Op. 22, No. 3.

ADDITIONAL COMPOSERS

A. Austria
   Johann Hummel (1778–1837)
   Carl Czerny (1791–1857)
   Johann Strauss (Sr.) (1804–1849)
   Johann Strauss (Jr.) (1825–1899)
B. England
   John Field (1782–1837)
   Sir Arthur Sullivan (1842–1900)
   Sir Charles Hubert Hastings Parry (1848–1918)
   Sir Charles Villiers Stanford (1852–1924)
   Sir Edward Elgar (1857–1934)
   Samuel Coleridge-Taylor (1875–1912)
C. France
   François-Adrein Boieldieu (1775–1834)
   Daniel-François-Esprit Auber (1782–1871)
   Jacques Offenbach (1819–1880)
   Henri Vieuxtemps (1820–1881)
   Édouard Lalo (1823–1892)
   Camille Saint-Saëns (1835–1921)
   Léo Delibes (1836–1891)
   Emmanuel Chabrier (1841–1894)
   Jules Massenet (1842–1912)
   Vincent d'Indy (1851–1931)
   Ernest Chausson (1855–1899)
   Gustave Charpentier (1860–1956)
   Paul Dukas (1865–1935)

D. Germany
  E. T. A. Hoffman (1776–1822)
  Ludwig Spohr (1784–1859)
  Giacomo Meyerbeer (1791–1864)
  Heinrich Marschner (1795–1861)
  Carl Loewe (1796–1869)
  Albert Lortzing (1801–1851)
  Otto Nicolai (1810–1849)
  Robert Franz (1815–1892)
  Engelbert Humperdinck (1854–1921)
  Max Reger (1873–1916)
E. Italy
  Muzio Clementi (1752–1832)
  Gasparo Spontini (1774–1851)
  Arrigo Boito (1842–1918)
  Ruggiero Leoncavallo (1857–1919)
  Pietro Mascagni (1863–1945)
  Ferrucio Busoni (1866–1924)
  Ermanno Wolf-Ferrari (1876–1948)
F. Poland
  Henryk Wieniawski (1835–1880)
  Ignace Paderewski (1860–1941)
G. Russia
  Mikhail Glinka (1804–1857)
  Anton Rubinstein (1829–1894)
  César Cui (1835–1918)
  Mily Balakirev (1837–1910)
  Alexander Scriabin (1872–1915)
  Sergei Rachmaninoff (1873–1943)
H. Spain
  Isaac Albeniz (1860–1909)
I. Sweden
  Franz Berwald (1796–1868)
J. United States
  Louis Gottschalk (1829–1869)
  Arthur Foote (1853–1937)
  George Chadwick (1854–1931)
  John Knowles Paine (1839–1906)
  Edgar Stillman Kelley (1857–1944)
  Edward MacDowell (1860–1908)
  Daniel Gregory Mason (1873–1953)

IX. HISTORIANS AND THEORISTS

There was a wide variety of writings on musical subjects in the nineteenth century that can be placed in the following categories: (1) music theory, (2) criticism, (3) history and biography, and (4) aesthetics.

The teaching of music outgrew the old apprenticeship method, partly because of the large number of nonprofessionals who became interested in the processes and techniques of musical composition. Moreover, it was in conservatory and university classes that much of the music theory was taught. To meet the growing demand for a systematic approach to theory, manuals of harmony, counterpoint, form, composition, and orchestration were written.

Music criticism won the attention of many writers, including composers themselves. With less sophisticated audiences than in the eighteenth century there was an interest in, and a need for, interpretations and evaluations of musical works and their performances. Such evaluations were made not only of the contemporary composers but also of the composers of the past. In addition the rise of the virtuoso performer made performances noteworthy, and reviews of these performances had a profound effect on box-office appeal.

The most famous journals that served as sounding boards for critical writings were the *Allgemeine Musikalische Zeitung* published in Leipzig, the *Neue Zeitschrift für Musik* founded by Schumann in 1834 in Leipzig, and the *Gazette Musicale*, published in Paris.

With history moving toward becoming a science and with the romantic cult of personality, both history and biography became important areas of literary effort. The practice of musicology was systematized in the late nineteenth century, leading to authoritative editions of older composers and definitive biographies of composers and performers.

The Romantic period, as we have seen, was a time of conflicting theories and ideas about what music could and should express. Writers on aesthetics argued the pros and cons of the various opinions regarding music and its perception. This was especially true of the conflict between program and absolute music and the new theories of opera.

Ernst Theodor Amadeus Hoffmann (1776–1822) was a German writer and composer who espoused the romantic ideal of the union of the arts. He wrote poetic and romantic appraisals of such composers as Mozart and Beethoven, using the pen name of Johannes Kreisler (made famous by Schumann's *Kreisleriana*). His critical writings were published in the *Allgemeine Musikalische Zeitung*.

Francois Fétis (1784–1871) was a Belgian music theorist and historian. While he wrote a number of theoretical treatises, his most famous work is the monumental *Biographie universelle des musiciens et bibliographie générale de la musique* in eight volumes (Paris, 1833–1844). This was the first fairly complete dictionary of musicians and still serves as a prime source of information concerning some composers.

Hector Berlioz (1803–1869) wrote the first important treatise on orchestration, *Traité d'instrumentation et orchestration modernes,* published in Paris in 1844. (*Treatise on instrumentation and orchestration,* a modern edition, was published in New York in 1948.) In addition, Berlioz frequently contributed critical essays to the *Gazette Musicale,* and he published a book of essays on orchestral music, *Les Soirées de l'orchestre,* Paris 1853 (Evenings in the orchestra, New York 1956).

Charles-Edmond-Henri de Coussemaker (1805–1876) was a French music historian who wrote a number of important works on early music. His interest in ancient documents led to a number of valuable collections of early music. His major work, *Scriptorum de musica medii* (Writings of Medieval Music) was published in Paris (1864–1876).

As mentioned earlier, *Robert Schumann* (1810–1856) was the founder and editor of the *Neue Zeitschrift für Musik,* published in Leipzig. His writings were militant essays propagandizing the new Romantic ideals. In the imaginary *Davidsbündler* (Society of David) the different facets of his own romantic personality were represented by the character of Florestan and Eusebius, names he often used in signing his essays. Schumann was also the first composer to recognize the genius of Chopin and Brahms, writing enthusiastic criticisms of their music.

Franz Liszt (1811–1886) made numerous contributions to musical literature as a critic, as a commentator on the current musical scene, and as a champion of the "modern" style of his day. He wrote a series of articles *On the Position of Artists* in which he discussed the social consciousness of composers and performers. He also wrote on church music, calling for a return to the function of music as a spiritual force.

Richard Wagner (1813–1883) was the most prolific writer on the aesthetics and criticism of music among all the Romantic composers. In addition to being the author of libretti for his own operas Wagner wrote essays and pamphlets on a variety of musical subjects. Of special significance were his writings on the problems of opera. *Oper und Drama* (Leipzig, 1851) outlined his theories of the artwork of the future. His autobiography set forth his ideas on the union of the arts and his thoughts on almost everything from music to politics. He also wrote an important essay, *Religion und Kunst,* that was related to his opera *Parsifal.*

August Wilhelm Ambros (1816-1876) was an eminent German historian and musicologist. His *Geschichte der Musik* (Leipzig, 1862) was one of the first music histories that tried to draw parallels between developments in music and the developments in the visual arts.

Sir George Grove (1820-1900), an English historian and musicologist gained his claim to fame as a writer on music with the *Dictionary of Music and Musicians* (4 vols., London, 1879-1889), a work that has gone through many editions and revisions. The latest edition, titled *The New Grove Dictionary of Music and Musicians* (1980), was expanded to twenty volumes, and utilized the latest in research techniques and computer technology, allowing for frequent revisions and updating.

Herman von Helmholz (1821-1894) was a German scientist and an expert on acoustics. His *Lehre von den Tonempfindungen als physiologische Grundlage für die Theorie der Musik* (On the Sensations of Tone as a Physiological Basis for the Theory of Music, New York, 1948), was first published in Braunschweig in 1863. It laid the foundation for modern research in the physical and physiological aspects of musical sound and hearing. He based his work on experimentation, but drew heavily upon the research of Rameau and Tartini.

Eduard Hanslick (1825-1904) was the most famous of the romantic critics and aestheticians in the field of music. Born in Prague, he lived most of his life in Vienna. Hanslick was a champion of absolutism in music and his book *Vom Musikalischen Schönen: ein Beitrage zur Revision der Aesthetik der Tonkunst* (On the Beautiful in Music; a Contribution to the Revision of Musical Aesthetics, New York, 1957) was published in Leipzig in 1854. In this work Hanslick argued that the beauty of a musical composition lay wholly in the music itself, without extramusical ideas. The book's importance is demonstrated by the fact that it has been translated into many languages including English. His opposition to the new school of Romantic realism led to his criticism of Wagner, Liszt, Berlioz, and the other programmatic composers. In retaliation Wagner caricatured Hanslick in the character of Beckmesser in *Die Meistersinger,* a distinction that led to an undeserved lack of appreciation of Hanslick's writings. While he opposed the Wagnerian group, he wrote glowing accounts of Schumann and Brahms who represented the more classic facets of Romanticism.

Karl Franz Chrysander (1826-1901) was a German music historian and critic. He shared in the editing of the monumental collection of music, *Denkmäler der Tonkunst,* Leipzig 1869-1871. Subsequent additions to this collection have expanded its size considerably. Chrysander is best known, however, for his writings on the life and works of Handel. He started the *Deutsche Händelgesellschaft* (German Handel

Society) and wrote a definitive biography of Handel published in Leipzig in 1858-1867. He likewise assumed responsibility for the first collected edition of the works of Handel.

Ebenezer Prout (1835-1909) was an English theorist and teacher. He was the author of textbooks on theory including harmony counterpoint, fugue, and musical form. His text on orchestration went through many editions and has been used as a handbook of instrumentation until well into the twentieth century.

Hugo Riemann (1849-1919) systematized the discipline of musicology. He led the way in a stylistic study of types and periods of music, a specialization that has resulted in a wealth of authoritative studies by contemporary musicologists. The list of Riemann's writings is long, but most significant is the *Musik-Lexikon*, Leipzig 1882, a work that has gone through many editions, and is recognized as a standard reference in music.

Vincent d'Indy (1851-1931) was one of the few successful composers to write a text on the art of musical composition, *Cours de Composition musicales* (Course of Musical Composition), Paris 1903-1933. A student of César Franck, d'Indy also wrote an authoritative biography of the Belgian master.

*   *   *

Musical Forms, Braque (1913). A cubist painting presenting a musical theme.
Cubism evolved at the same time as serialism in music. (Philadelphia Museum
of Art: Louise and Walter Arensberg Collection)

8
Chronology
of the Early Twentieth Century

1854	Leos Janáček (1854–1928)	1883	Anton Webern (1883–1945)
1856	Sigmund Freud (1856–1939)		Edgar Varèse (1883–1965)
1857	Sir Edward Elgar (1857–1934)	1885	Alban Berg (1885–1935)
1866	Erik Satie (1866–1925)	1887	Heitor Villa-Lobos (1887–1959)
1868	Scott Joplin (1868–1917)	1887	Nadia Boulanger (1887–1979)
1872	Ralph Vaughan Williams (1872–1958)	1891	Sergei Prokofiev (1891–1953)
1873	W. C. Handy (1873–1958)	1892	Arthur Honneger (1892–1955)
1874	Winston Churchill (1874–1965)		Darius Milhaud (1892–1974)
	Arnold Schoenberg (1874–1951)	1893	Lili Boulanger (1893–1918)
	Charles Ives (1874–1954)	1895	Paul Hindemith (1895–1963)
1875	Maurice Ravel (1875–1937)	1896	Roger Sessions (1896–1985)
1876	Manuel de Falla (1876–1946)	1897	Ragtime beginning c. 1897–1915
1880	Ernest Bloch (1880–1959)	1898	George Gershwin (1898–1937)
1881	Béla Bartók (1881–1945)	1899	"Duke" Ellington (1899–1974)
1882	Igor Stravinsky (1882–1971)		

1900	Aaron Copland	1915	Panama Canal opened
	(1900–)	1917	First printed use of the
	Ernst Krenek		term "Jazz"
	(1900–)		Russian Revolution
1903	Wright brothers first	1939	Second World War begins
	airplane flight		Television developed
1906	Dmitri Shostakovitch	1945	Atomic bomb destroys
	(1906–1975)		Hiroshima and Nagasaki
1908	Oliver Messiaen		Second World War ends
	(1908–)		
1914	Beginning of the First		
	World War		

8
Early Twentieth Century

History is that branch of knowledge that relates and analyzes past events. Music history, as set forth in the many texts on the subject, deals preponderently with the description and analysis of past musical creativity, often to the utter disregard of more recent and contemporary events. This is not a criticism of historical reporting. It is rather the recognition of the fact that there is a need for perspective in assessing the importance of events, which ones deserve relating, what should be analyzed, and for what purpose.

For example, in the first half of the eighteenth century J. S. Bach was little known beyond his immediate sphere of activity, while Georg Phillip Telemann was widely recognized as an international figure. Until almost one hundred years after his death, Bach's music was practically unknown. With very few exceptions none of it was even available in published form until the nineteenth century. In the eyes (and ears) of contemporaries, Telemann was by far the more widely acclaimed. Bach was third choice, after Telemann and Graupner, for the post of cantor at St. Thomas Church in Leipzig. It was only the insight gained from historical perspective that revealed the relative importance of these composers. The importance of this historical perspective is corroborated by one of the twentieth century's most influential composers, Arnold Schoenberg, who said in *Style and Idea* (1941), "Contemporaries are not the final judges, but are generally overruled by history."

The diversity of musical styles and the frenetic artistic activity of the twentieth century make it necessary to divide the study of this century into two major historical segments. The dropping of the atomic bomb on Hiroshima, concluding the Second World War, provides a convenient watershed date for the division of the century, and for the study of its musical history. Technological developments soon after the war give such a division a certain logic. Musical evolution following these technological developments will be discussed in chapter nine. Those composers who flourished during midcentury will necessarily be mentioned in both chapters.

I. SOCIOCULTURAL INFLUENCES ON MUSIC

The transition from nineteenth-century Romanticism to twentieth-century "modernism" was as far-reaching as the transition from the ars antiqua to the ars nova, or from the Renaissance to the Baroque. As in the earlier transitions, the seeds of the new are already to be found in the dissolution of the old. While from a close perspective these changes seem almost revolutionary, historical perspective may well reveal that these changes had a logic and order as yet not immediately apparent.

Because the speed of twentieth-century attainments in so many areas has been accelerated, music, subjected to this same acceleration, has moved from one new practice to another with such rapidity that no previous era can be compared with the diversity and extremes of its expressions. The search for originality on the part of every composer led to a great variety of expression, reversion to past historical styles, neoclassicism, neoromanticism, serial composition, microtonal music, and *musique concrète*. The insistence on originality was so compelling that its end results often appear questionable.

The scientific research already begun in the nineteenth century continued in the twentieth, and led to a number of discoveries and inventions that influenced human relationships beyond all previous imagination. The invention of rapid sound communications such as the telephone and telegraph in the nineteenth century, led to the further development of sound transmission and resulted in the invention of the phonograph and radio. By the middle of the twentieth-century radio and phonograph recordings had made music available to most of the world.

Two great political movements, communism and fascism, made deep impressions on musical compositions in the first half of the twentieth century. Fascism in Italy, and its nazi counterpart in Germany were comparatively short lived. In their most virulent forms Nazism and fascism condemned all nontraditional creativity as decadent and typical of the weaknesses of western democratic society. For almost twenty years much of the creativity of Germany and Italy was carried on only by exiled composers who fled their native lands, mainly to the United States.

In the first years of the Soviet Union, following the First World War, there was a brief period in which the most advanced contemporary musical expression found performance and creative encouragement. This ended with the advent of Josef Stalin as a dominant figure, and until after his death Russia was cut off from participation in the mainstream of twentieth-century western musical creativity and performance. A strong emphasis on traditional nationalistic trends of the nineteenth century prevailed for the most part.

The other states of Europe had scarcely recovered their economic and artistic equilibrium after the First World War before the impending cataclysm of the great economic depression of the thirties and the disaster of the Second World War overtook them.

II. FUNCTION OF MUSIC

The commercial aspects of music distribution along with new means of musical communication led to great changes in the function of music. Organized concert series in large and small urban centers were a purely twentieth-century phenomenon. The availability of any and all performing artists in comparatively remote areas encouraged large audiences for a season of star performances. The composer was more and more at the mercy of a shrinking number of performers who through managerial pressure felt the necessity of emphasizing traditional works to satisfy a large but often undiscriminating audience. Such concerts had value. They undoubtedly raised the musical taste of the general public beyond that of the past century. Programs were likely to contain a preponderance of standard literature.

One twentieth-century outlet for composers was in music for motion pictures. Nowhere, however, was the effect of the mass audience more clearly discernible than in this field. The early decades of the film industry resulted in only a few film scores that were artistically distinguished. Even those films which won distinction, and for which competent composers wrote successful scores, indicate that, for the most part, writing music for films was on the periphery of the musical mainstream. Ironically, however, in one sense, the ideal of Wagner's thesis that music and drama should be a synthesis is more nearly achieved in the best motion pictures than in the musical dramas of Wagner, where music dominated. One positive aspect of this new musical genre was that film audiences were occasionally introduced to new and different musical idioms.

Beginning in the first half of the twentieth century, a great part of the world's population began to be bombarded with musical sounds from recordings and radio. These were heard in all kinds of surroundings; at home, the market, the office, the factory, the playground, and even the sports field. These venues, however, provided no outlet to the serious composer. In fact, such music serves a largely psychological function, providing an antidote for the multifarious sounds that surround humans at all times. The kind of music played has no intent to raise or lower taste. It induces the hearer to pay little or no direct attention, and thereby cultivates less discriminating listeners.

During this period the Church was not significantly involved with the music of its time. There are notable exceptions, most especially in countries where there is a state church. There, composers of stature were commissioned by the Church to write such works as Te Deums, Magnificats, anthems, and masses for their liturgies. Parish choir directors, however, found much twentieth-century religious music too difficult for their choirs to perform. Movements in the Christian church to raise the quality of the music used in the services resulted primarily in the revival of much fine music of the past, especially the sacred repertoires of the Baroque and Renaissance.

Opera continued to function as an important means of reaching a large public, its activity varied greatly from country to country. Whereas central Europe had a tremendously active opera life, opera in the United States was restricted to a few cities and to short seasons. Some of the subjects most attractive to composers of opera treated social issues. Examples of such works were Gershwin's *Porgy and Bess* (1935) and Weill's *Die Dreigroschenoper* (1928). The latter opera was imported to the United States a few years later in the translated version, *Three Penny Opera*.

III. STYLE AND PERFORMANCE PRACTICE

The break with the nineteenth century was felt as a compelling necessity by most twentieth-century composers. Musical techniques employed to achieve the realistic, impressionistic, and nationalistic ends of the previous century had been pushed about as far as possible. The composer found it necessary to explore new ways to say new things. This meant that the elements of music and compositional style had to be reassessed.

The first attempts at a new mode of composition in any age are likely to be of more academic interest than artistic. New techniques and devices must first be tried in the fires of experimental creativity until those less effective are weeded out, and a kind of consensus is established that helps to determine which musical innovations best give expression to the musical imagination of the period.

Two answers to the composers' search for new ways to say new things presented themselves: the use of more tonal material than the twelve semitones of the octave and the development of new principles of construction with the old material. The first answer gives rise to attempts at splitting the octave into smaller intervals than the twelve half steps. This device, *microtonality*, attempted by a few composers, used newly constructed instruments—quarter-tone pianos—or took advantage of those instruments which could play intervals smaller than the semitone—the violin family, the trombone, or the human voice.

The second answer, finding new principles of construction, resulted in the twelve-tone technique, as developed originally by Arnold Schoenberg. Subsequently, that technique was embraced by most of the composers of the twentieth century. Their styles placed great emphasis on timbre and rhythmic complexity, which rivaled pitch as the most important element in formal construction.

Formal Organization

The most important new means of formal organization in the twentieth century was the twelve-tone or dodecaphonic method of composition. This system, which later developed into serial composition, used the twelve chromatic tones as independent entities without reference to a tonal center. Serial composition was based on a set pattern of the twelve tones called the tone row, repeated continuously throughout the work in many varied forms. In dodecaphonic music the basic row may be subjected to the various forms of contrapuntal treatment traditionally used to secure variety in imitation: inversion, retrograde (cancrizans), retrograde inversion, augmentation, and diminution. Moreover the tone row can be transposed to any of the twelve levels of the chromatic scale. In more advanced serial composition the series might consist of less than the entire twelve tones, and might even be a rhythmic or tonal pattern. The basic device of the serial technique is, of course, nothing more than a construction of a tonal pattern (of twelve or less notes) and the continuous variation of this construction.

One of the significant characteristics of early twentieth-century formal organization was the variation principle. True repetition and contrast were used less frequently than before. Literal repetition was used for expressive purposes, not for formal organization. Repetition actually became variation.

There was a tendency toward brevity in all new musical composition. The expansive thematic structures of the Romantic gave way to motivic elements. Long, spun out themes were displaced by short epigrammatic motives. In such musical constructions all musical elements were tightly organized. The desire for brevity and economy tended to eliminate or at least shorten such formal structures as bridge passages, modulatory sections, and closing sections.

Melody

In the music of the early twentieth century the melodic line, whether for voices or instruments, is often subjected to wide intervallic leaps and a high degree of rhythmic complexity. In addition, it is often placed in extreme ranges in order to make use of varied tone qualities.

Melody of phrase and period were no longer symmetrical. There was a tendency to form melodies from short, motivic fragments. The consecutive notes of a melodic line were often sounded over several octaves, and assigned to different instruments rather than contained within the range of a single instrument. Additionally, the general tendency to write in a contrapuntal style lessened the importance of melody as a dominating vehicle in the music. Even in works for solo voices or instruments, the solo part became one of the lines of the contrapuntal fabric rather than a dominating melodic line.

Vocal melody was subjected to contours that were expressive of the text even to the extent of losing specific tonal designation as in the technique of *Sprechstimme*. This term is literally translated as "speech voice" or "speech intonation." A similar technique was apparent in the presentation of popular music where the singer did not confine the textual rendition to a well defined melody, but exaggerated and stressed the actual pitches according to the intensity of emotional expression conveyed by the words. In the following example the vocalist is instructed to avoid the absolute pitches of the notes that are designated by the crosses on the stems (Ex. 36).

Example 36. Sprechstimme from *Pierrot Lunaire*

Schoenberg

Den   Wein, den   man   mit   Au - gen   trinkt,   giebt

Rhythm

In twentieth-century music there is a continuation of the use of traditional metric units. There emerge, however, many compositions that employ irregular and asymmetrical measures and phrases. Much use is made of odd-numbered metric patterns—five, seven, eleven. Such rhythmic irregularity may be simultaneous, as in the case of polyrhythms, or more generally consecutive, as in Stravinsky's *Le Sacre du printemps*, where successive measures of 4/8, 5/18, 7/16, 4/8 yield great rhythmic energy (Ex. 37).

Example 37. Rhythmically complex excerpt from *Le Sacre du printemps*

Stravinsky

Harmony

Early twentieth-century harmony was much more dissonant than that of previous eras. Those intervals which were considered dissonant in the harmonic practice of the eighteenth and nineteenth centuries were used with great freedom in the twentieth. In music which still adhered to traditional tonality, dissonant harmonies, while much more freely used, were still recognized as dissonant and were eventually resolved, even if delayed.

Music which did not adhere to the tradition of tonality is often referred to as *atonal.* In this style, the distinction between dissonance and consonance to a large degree ceased to exist. Harmony was recognized as a relationship of all the tones to one another rather than the relationship of all the tones to a single central one. Under such circumstances all relationships were possible and usable.

The use of dissonance was extended in traditional harmony through bitonality, and eventually polytonality, the use of two or more tonal centers at the same time (Ex. 38).

Example 38. Polytonality

Ives

Sometimes traditional harmonic constructions were based on nontraditional scale patterns. Such scale patterns were derived from medieval modes, folk scales, or non-western scales.

Texture

Contrapuntal texture was frequently employed by twentieth-century composers, especially the twelve-tone composers who exploited thin, almost ephemeral, contrapuntal textures in which notated silences tended to play as important a part as the notated sounds.

Contrapuntal practice was not restricted to a counterpoint of individual melodic lines, but often extended in ensemble and orchestral works to a counterpoint of rhythms in which several rhythmic patterns were used simultaneously. Likewise, a counterpoint of timbres might have been employed in which various groupings of instruments and sound sources were pitted against one another.

With those composers who wrote in a neoromantic style the texture, both harmonic and contrapuntal, was inclined to be very thick and heavy. The full, rich, chordal structures were derived from the use of dissonance and counterpoint.

Instrumentation and Tone Color

While compositions using large forces were still written, there was a marked tendency to use small ensembles in which unusual combinations were specified. A kind of heterophony of color was achieved by the contrast of widely differing timbres in combination. In ensembles there was a tendency to combine wind instruments and string instruments in more nearly equal numbers, and wind instruments were used more often for solos and in choirs in the orchestra. The voice was often combined with instruments as an integral part of an ensemble and was exploited to give a greater variety of tonal color.

Practice and Performance

While notational and dynamic differences were often increasingly specific, there was also the opposite tendency in some compositions to leave greater freedom to the performer by calling for purely improvisational passages. Many of the directions were found in the vernacular rather than in traditional Italian, and indicated the attempt to communicate even more clearly than before.

The high standard of instrumental and vocal performance demanded by the recording industry made such technical considerations as purity of tone, accurate intonation, and technical clarity important criteria in the evaluation of musical performance. While virtuosity was no longer a leading element in the musical enjoyment of performance it was expected of all concert performers, and as such was taken for granted.

In most cases the high degree of musical specialization and competition resulted in a separation between the act of composing and that of performance. In the past composers were often virtuoso performers, whereas in the twentieth century the expectation of technical perfection in performance, both live and in recording, made demands on the performer which usually excluded creative activity. Pianists such as Ignace Paderewski, Artur Rubinstein, Vladimir Horowitz, Rudolph Serkin, Artur Schnabel, and many others became notable performers of the music of all composers from Bach to the present time. A few pianists such as Sergei Rachmaninoff, Ferruccio Busoni, and Sergei Prokofiev gained reputations both as pianists and composers. Fritz Kreisler, Jascha Heifitz, Joseph Szigeti, and Nathan Milstein were violinists who specialized in the performance of all styles of music. The list of singers who gained extraordinary reputations as performers in concert and opera is almost endless, partly because of the nature of the human voice, which limited the number of years available to them as performers. Among the great voices of the first half of the century were Feodor Chaliapin, Enrico Caruso, Lauritz Melchoir, Kirsten Flagstad, Rosa Ponselle, and Mary Garden.

Orchestral conducting demanded the same virtuoso performance as other performers. Arturo Toscanini, Leopold Stokowski, Serge Koussevitzky, Wilhelm Furtwängler, Bruno Walter, Richard Strauss, and others brought remarkable and definitive performances to millions in the concert hall, radio, and recordings.

IV. MUSIC FOR INSTRUMENTS

There is no form which is peculiar or unique to the twentieth century. As a result, composers of instrumental music returned to the classic form of the sonata as an ideal for their compositions. The sonata changed substantially in the hands of modern composers. The old symmetry of phrase, period, and sections gave way to a balance which was based on calculated psychological principles. While most composers retained the traditional terminology of the classic era, new schemes of formal organization, melody, harmony, rhythm, texture, and tone quality gave them new meaning and character.

Single Movement Forms

Overture and Symphonic Poems

The overture continued as a single-movement form quite apart from its original purpose as a prelude to a dramatic work. Most overtures in the twentieth century were short symphonic poems, often of dramatic expressive quality. Dramatic musical works rarely employed an overture in the traditional sense so that there were few overtures of this kind in the repertory of the twentieth century. (Rec. 8.1, 8.2)

Variation

Because modern composers were generally concerned with the problems of construction, the variation form regained its popularity. However, the traditional techniques of variation gave way to such devices as variations on a tone row, on tonal coloring, and on rhythmic patterns. (Rec. 8.3, 8.4)

Short Forms: Dances, Poetic Pieces

Many short works were written in modern or exotic dance forms, or in simple two-part or three-part song forms. Most of these works were written for piano, though solo instruments combined with piano and small ensembles, or even orchestral compositions were sometimes cast in these forms. (Rec. 8.5–8.7)

Composite Forms

Sonata, Chamber Music, and Symphony

These multimovement forms presented the modern composer with the principal vehicle for extended instrumental composition whether for solo, chamber ensemble (string quartet), or orchestra. In their typical contemporary style these pieces were characterized by brevity, which was achieved by reducing the recapitulation section of the sonata-form, by use of fragmentary motives rather than extended themes, by avoiding most repetition, by omitting transitions and bridge passages between motivic statements, and by reducing the instrumentation to its barest minimum. Often the whole sonata was presented in a reduced number of movements, if not in a single movement, with several related sections in differing tempos and moods. In some instances the juxtaposition of movements or of sections of the sonata were used to achieve new formal constructions.

While the strict harmonic relationship of tonic and dominant which dictated the formal structure of the classic sonata was no longer valid, this principle was still suggested in the modern sonata. This relationship or tension can be realized in a multitude of ways outside the harmonic realm, and twentieth-century composers experimented with such devices.

Those works labeled as sonatas embrace the many neoclassical instrumental works for piano as well as those for a single melodic instrument with keyboard. The idiom and style vary from composer to composer. The technical difficulties posed for the performer also vary greatly from works called *Gebrauchsmusik* to those which obviously are meant exclusively for concert performance. The former were written with the amateur and student musician in mind while the latter require proficiency of the highest order.

Due to its essential classicism, chamber music afforded the early twentieth-century composer one of the prime areas of musical expression. Outside the adoption of the general principles of contemporary music, composers of chamber music went far in using newly conceived combinations of instruments and voice in their works. The traditional string quartet was still employed as well as several other classic combinations, but there was a great amount of writing for groups of two to fifteen performers in which not only the standard instruments of all families were combined, but often rarely used instruments were incorporated. Percussion instruments of all kinds, especially those with tuned bars, were used. Instruments rarely used in recent times were reinstated in the chamber ensemble. The inclusion of the voice in small ensembles was especially characteristic of modern chamber music. The use of these instruments was more than mere exploitation of new and unusual media for the most radical composers used tone color itself as a means of formal organization.

The symphony continued to be the principal large form for instrumental composition. In the case of some writers, particularly those whose style still favored the Romantic, this form was likely to be extended with colorful orchestration and often combined voices with the orchestra. At the other extreme were those symphonic writers who collapsed the symphony to a mere shadow of its classical self. The serial composers made the most use of this treatment. A large number of composers were somewhere between these extremes and used many devices to rejuvenate the classic symphonic form. (Rec. 8.8–8.16)

Concerto

In the twentieth century the frequent return to ideas of earlier music was reflected in the revival of the concerto grosso as a prototype. Solo concertos were frequently written. The orchestral concerto in which many of the instruments act as soloists or in which groups of instruments are pitted one against the other was typical of the return to earlier forms, but utilizing twentieth-century idioms. In the solo concerto composers handled their material in much the same way as in the symphony. The solo instrument was no longer exploited only for virtuoso effects, although virtuoso techniques were required for performance. The tendency to exhibit the instrument at the expense of the orchestra was abandoned in favor of a kind of composition in which the soloist and orchestra exploited the musical material together. Cadenzas were employed only as means of developing the musical material. (Rec. 8.17–8.21)

Suite

The twentieth-century suite was usually a selection of scenes or sections from a larger work such as a ballet, incidental music to a drama or motion picture, or a series of pieces connected rather loosely by thematic relationship, mood, or extramusical idea. Only in a few instances was the suite based on the tradition of the dance suite. As a consequence it was often the product of the more romantically inclined composers due to its connection with extramusical purpose. The title "suite" was used for compositions of this character for various solo instruments and ensembles. (Rec. 8.22–8.26)

Ballet

Instrumental music written for the ballet continued into the twentieth century in a form that was much more concise than its predecessors of the nineteenth century, and in a form that was much more abstract than the set of closed dances which made up the classic ballet. Most of the ballets of the twentieth century were in one act, with one or more scenes. The music rarely consisted of set dances but was rather in the form of a highly rhythmic symphonic poem which was interpreted by the dancers in appropriate pantomime and dance gestures. The stylized figures of the dancers of the classic tradition gave way to free gestures and movements which symbolized the drama in collaboration with the musical symbolism of the orchestral score. The ballet was one of the most successful vehicles in the presentation of modern music to a receptive public. In the United States it was the most successful form of dramatic music. Ballet music constituted one of the most frequently heard forms in orchestral concert programs since the music could be presented in its entirety or in suites made up of selected scenes from the score. (Rec. 8.27–8.30)

Incidental Music for Film and Drama

While the greatest portion of the music written for film and drama in the early twentieth century was merely "background music," there was some that had artistic merit and appeared later in concert form. This was more generally the case with incidental music to the staged drama than with music for the motion picture. This music, however, when written by competent composers was so carefully integrated with the film that it could not have an independent existence. (Rec. 8.31–8.34)

V. MUSIC FOR VOICES

In general, the vocal forms used in the early twentieth century were those found in earlier periods. These earlier vocal forms, dating as far back as the Romanesque, were adapted to contemporary contrapuntal and harmonic practices. The voice in solo and choral compositions was treated more as an instrument than previously. Vocal ranges were expanded, and intervallic skips which are not technically difficult for instruments were demanded of the voice. Vocalists were confronted with technical demands of production that seemed at times insurmountable.

Single Movement Forms
Art Song

The art song continued to be a popular vehicle for composers. Texts generally tended to be more complex in structure and idea than those of the Romantic period, and avoided the sentimentality of the more typical Romantic art song. This was in keeping with the more angular melodic treatment that was given the voice and the added emphasis on the accompaniment, whether piano or chamber ensemble, which was so often used. "Accompaniment" inaccurately designates the instrumental part of most twentieth-century vocal compositions since the voice and associated instruments form a total ensemble rather than a vocal line with instrumental background. In many instances composers turned to folk melodies and set them in a modern idiom, settings that were not governed by the lush harmonic textures of Romantic music. Such works involved an instrumental chamber group instead of the piano.

A modern phenomenon of song writing has been the disintegration of the melodic line into a highly inflected declamatory part. The device known as *Sprechstimme* (literally "speech voice"), was used in combination with small instrumental groups by a number of the twelve-tone writers as well as other composers. In these cases the vocal part was almost pure declamation, without exact tonal designation, but with rhythmic notation and general inflection indicated. (Rec. 8.35–8.38)

Short Choral Works

A great demand for choral compositions developed for church, amateur, and professional choirs, and for secondary schools and universities as well. This demand gave rise to many shorter choral works, usually of one movement. These were settings of significant poems or prose texts of historical or timely interest. They were usually unaccompanied but often used the piano in support of the voices. The treatment of these texts was often contrapuntal, with independent lines and free rhythmic treatment.

One of the major areas of sociological and academic study was the collection and recording of indigenous folk songs of Europe, Australia, and North America. Composers such as Kodály, Bartók, Vaughan Williams, Holst, and Grainger created numerous and effective choral settings of these folk tunes. (Rec. 8.39–8.42)

Composite Forms
Opera

The opera tended to retain something of the symphonic character of the Wagnerian tradition; however, it became much more compact and dramatically dynamic. The general tendency toward economy of material made dramatic presentation much more concise and intense. Sometimes there was a return to set forms of aria and chorus, with composers reverting to the simplicity of Classic opera in this respect. Entire texts of dramatic works were often used as operatic librettos without any adaptation for musical setting. In some cases the operas were written in large symphonic forms in which several scenes were treated as movements or sections of abstract music such as the sonata or the variation form. Some works achieved their dramatic expression through the twelve-tone method of composition, or through highly dissonant chromaticism. Other composers reverted to the ballad opera of the seventeenth century with its simple forms such as the popular street song and folk song.

The Broadway musical came close to a revival of this later kind, with some harmonic and melodic parallels to the nineteenth-century tradition. Rhythmically it had much of the freedom of twentieth-century jazz, and the general mood of the works reflected a freedom of expression typically American. Several examples of these compositions have established themselves in the repertoires of opera houses in many countries.

Despite the variety represented in these dramatic works, an economy of treatment, realism, expressionism, dramatic intensity, some degree of dissonant harmony, and irregularity of rhythm characterized all the twentieth-century musical dramas. (Rec. 8.43–8.47)

Musical Theater

The twentieth-century musical theater was a descendant of the opera comique and the operetta but with a distinctive American flavor. It was usually romantic in nature with spoken lines, choreography, choruses, and music related to popular song and jazz. It has commanded attention in many world centers, even in the European opera houses of long established tradition. The popularity of musical theater was enhanced by many of its productions being transferred to motion pictures. (Rec. 8.48–8.51)

Oratorio/Choral Works with Orchestra

The oratorio in the twentieth century remained almost as dormant as it was in the latter half of the nineteenth century. Those that were written generally employed the traditional plan of this form, albeit in a style that was in keeping with the twentieth century. Many composers used poetic and prose texts of a less dramatic nature in works of several movements. Sometimes they were only for chorus and orchestra; sometimes soloists were added. Composers experimented with various types of instrumentation in such works in order to emphasize tone color. In most of these works the instrumental ensemble was more than a mere accompaniment, and the vocalists were something less than featured soloists. Such choral works tend to be cast in forms dictated by the texts, which were usually of the finest literary quality. (Rec. 8.52–8.55)

Liturgical Music

Early in the twentieth century there was little music written for purely liturgical purposes. Some settings of the mass for the Roman Catholic church were written using the twelve-tone system, but these were rare and their performance as liturgical music is even rarer. Likewise some able composers wrote music for the Protestant church and the Jewish synagogue. (Rec. 8.56, 8.57)

VI. COMPOSERS

It is impossible to state with any authority which of the composers of the early twentieth century will achieve a permanent position among the great composers. Lack of perspective denies to us the luxury of making such judgments. Some composers wrote predominantly in one style, but the majority, as often in the past, composed in several styles, often with equal success. Consequently, in the following, the authors have not placed the composers under stylistic headings, but rather have mentioned the important stylistic characteristics in the description of each composer.

Leos Janáček (1854–1928) was one of the renowned Czech composers. While he lived the greater portion of his life in the nineteenth
century, most of his significant works were composed very late, during
the last decade of his life. His operas, *Kat'a Kabanova* (1921) and *From
the House of the Dead* (1928); the *Glagolitic Mass* (1926); the *Sinfonietta*
(1926); and the *Concertino for Piano and Chamber Orchestra* (1925), are
examples of his late production. His musical expression was terse and
economical, based on motivic construction which was derived from
a study of speech inflection. While he wrote chamber music and orchestral works, it was his operas which first brought him worldwide
recognition and which are finding special favor again, more than fifty
years after his death.

Sir Edward Elgar (1857–1934) was probably the greatest English
composer since Henry Purcell, and the first of a line of outstanding
modern English composers. His birth, religion, and education placed
him somewhat outside the mainstream of English music. Around the
turn of the century his oratorio, *The Dream of Gerontius*, and the *Enigma
Variations* firmly established his position in the English musical scene.
He is best known for his *Pomp and Circumstance* marches, the first of
which has long been associated with English royalty.

Erik Satie (1866–1925) was a French composer whose importance
lies more in the personal influence he had on his contemporaries than
in his few compositions. He was the counselor, before the First World
War, of the group of young composers in France who came to be
known as *Les Six*, a group which comprised Darius Milhaud, Arthur
Honneger, Francis Poulenc, Georges Auric, Germaine Tailleferre, and
Louis Durey.

Satie's style can be characterized as one of complete simplicity.
He used the simplest harmonies, melodies, polyphonic texture, and
formal structures. There was no attempt to be profound. This trend
toward simplicity was the forerunner of the break with Romanticism
and impressionism and the gradual turn toward neoclassicism. His
utter distain for the sentimental and pretentious was reflected in the
titles which he attached to many of his works. These include *Cold
Pieces, Airs to Make One Flee, Three Pieces in the Shape of a Pear*. These,
and *Gymnopédies* and *Gnosiennes*, are among the best known of his
works.

Ralph Vaughan Williams (1872–1958), an English composer, very
consciously and ardently allied himself with the great English folk
song revival centered around Cecil Sharp. For a number of years he
participated actively in the search for, and study of, folk songs of the
English people. While he seldom quoted folk songs in his works and
rarely used actual folk melodies as thematic material, his whole output

Arnold Schoenberg (1874–1951) (The Bettmann Archive)

is infused with the spirit of the English folk song. He never developed a style that was at the same time national and twentieth century, but the idiom of English folk song scarcely allowed such a combination. While his works are characterized by modal polyphonic treatment, he was essentially a melodist and used chromaticism and dissonance very sparingly. He wrote in virtually all the musical genres, though his symphonic works and vocal compositions are the more frequently performed. Among the nine symphonies, *A London Symphony* (No. 2); the *Pastoral Symphony* (No. 3); and the *Symphony in f minor* (No. 4) are the best known. *On Wenlock Edge* for tenor, string quartet, and piano, and a number of sacred compositions including the *Mass in g minor* were both written in the first quarter of this century. Vaughan Williams is also remembered as a Professor of Music at the Royal College of Music, and as the editor of *The English Hymnal* and the *Oxford Book of Carols*.

Arnold Schoenberg (1874–1951) was an Austrian composer most widely known as the founder of the twelve-tone compositional technique. Schoenberg's earliest compositions were in the romantic tradition of Wagner. However, his later preoccupation with sonorities that avoided functional harmony placed him in the forefront of those radical composers often referred to as expressionists. Exploitation of new relationships among pitch materials began as early as 1914, and continued in the *Five Piano Pieces,* Op. 23.

The *Suite for Piano,* Op. 25, by Schoenberg was the first composition to be built exclusively on the principle of twelve-tone composition. Schoenberg contended that his new system was not revolutionary, but evolutionary, a natural outcome of the tradition of western European music. A group of disciples who had already gathered about him in the early years of the century adopted his techniques, and, along with Schoenberg himself, laid the foundations of the twelve-tone style.

Schoenberg's influence as a practicing teacher continued throughout his long life, from his early years in Vienna where he was later engaged as a professor of composition at the Vienna Academy, through a professorship at the Prussian Academy of Arts in Berlin, which had to be relinquished with the advent of the Nazi regime in 1933. From 1933 until his death he resided in the United States, where he was a member of the faculties of the University of Southern California and the University of California, Los Angeles.

Schoenberg was influential in the stylistic development of a large number of pupils and followers. Among the most important of these are Berg, Webern, Krenek, Dallapiccola, Skalkottas, Kirchner, and others who adopted some or all of the principles of their teacher. Even Igor Stravinsky in his seventies began to use serial techniques, showing the influence of Schoenberg.

Among the most widely heard works of Schoenberg are those of his early romantic period, *Verklärte Nacht* (Transfigured Night), originally a string sextet and later transcribed for string orchestra; the *Gurre-Lieder,* for chorus, soloists, and orchestra; a number of chamber music works such as the string quartets nos. 1 and 2, *Pierrot Lunaire,* and a large number of songs. The most outstanding of the works in the twelve-tone system are the *Piano Concerto, Violin Concerto,* Op. 36, string quartets nos. 3 and 4, as well as chamber music for unusual instrumental combinations. An incomplete opera, *Moses and Aron,* first performed posthumously, has enjoyed some success.

Charles Edward Ives (1874–1954) was one of the most unusual American composers. Trained as a musician, he hesitated to subject his creative talents to the demands of others, knowing that he would be dependent on their musical tastes for his livelihood. As a consequence he entered the business world and became a very successful insurance broker, leaving his composition free from all remunerative

Charles Ives (1874–1954) (Art and History Archive)

considerations. This double life led to a physical breakdown in 1918 that ended his compositional career. The result of his early decision was that almost all of his works were written in the years between 1896 and 1918.

In some respects he foreshadowed many of the practices of later twentieth-century composers such as Schoenberg and Stravinsky. His use of polytonality, polyrhythms, and the contrapuntal methods are also part of the serial composers' technique. Inversion, retrograde, augmentation, and diminution, are all characteristic of Ives's music. While his works are always constructed on a tonal basis, he achieved a considerable degree of dissonance, in some cases almost a feeling of atonality with these devices. Despite all the characteristics of modern music, Ives' musical ideas were deeply rooted in the folk and religious music of New England with themes from folk songs and New England hymns. Strangely enough, almost none of his compositions were performed until the 1940s. The *Symphony No. 3*, which received a Pulitzer Prize, was performed in 1947, almost forty years after it was written. *Symphony No. 2* was given its first performance exactly fifty years after it was written. Their influence on American composers was not felt until a few years before Ives' death. His output

was devoted mainly to orchestral, chamber, piano, and song literature. Among his most important compositions are the four symphonies; several symphonic poems, including *Three Places in New
England, Central Park in the Dark*, and *The Unanswered Question;* over 100
songs, among which *General Booth Enters Heaven* is representative; and
many piano pieces, including the *Concord Sonata* and some choral
works.

Maurice Ravel (1875–1937) was a French composer whose mixture
of impressionistic style with classic clarity would best label him as a
post-impressionist. He was not a pupil of Debussy but stood in close
relation to him. He extended the practice of unresolved dissonances
but rarely came to the point of atonality. In many respects he remained closer to the romanticists than to those who came to be considered the radical twentieth-century composers. Ravel's love of the
exotic in music was revealed not only in his use of rhythms and scale
constructions derived from his Basque heritage, but also in his predilection for expression in other exotic idioms. His settings of *Deux
Mélodies Hébraiques* (Two Hebrew Melodies), *Cinq Mélodies populaires
grecques* (Five Popular Greek Melodies), and the *Chansons madécasses*
(Songs of Madagascar), as well as his occupation with oriental themes
in a number of compositions such as *Schéhérazade* demonstrate this
affinity. Likewise, he was influenced by medieval as well as unusual
folk tonal systems. His *Rapsodie espagnole, Pavane pour une Infante dé-
funte* (Pavane for a Dead Infant), and *Tsigane* represent these interests.
Even in those compositions in which he exhibited a decided neoclassic tendency, the harmonic idiom, as well as the instrumentation,
reflected Ravel's deep interest in old and unusual systems and tone
colors. Among his neoclassic works are *Le Tombeau de Couperin;* the
Ma Mère l'Oye (Mother Goose Suite), *String Quartet in F major;* the *Two
Piano Concertos;* and a number of piano works, an area in which Ravel
was outstanding—*Gaspard de la nuit, Jeux d'eau* (Fountains), and *Son-
atine*. Ravel also wrote a few stage works, among them the operas
L'Heure espagnole, L'Enfant et les Sortilèges (The Boy and the Sorceries),
and the ballets *Daphnis and Chloe, La Valse*, and *Bolero*. A careful listening to any of the above compositions will confirm Ravel as the
prime orchestrator among twentieth-century French composers.

Manuel de Falla (1876–1946) was the most important Spanish composer since the Renaissance. While his style was essentially that of
the French impressionists, he combined impressionism with a very
conscious Spanish nationalism, in *Nights in the Gardens of Spain*. He
was aware, however, of twentieth-century stylistic advances, and he
combined these with a musical expression that has a genuine Spanish
authenticity. He left Spain when it fell to the anti-Republicans, and

Béla Bartók (1881–1945)
(The New York Public Library)

he lived his last years in Argentina. His most successful works were ballets, among which are *El Amor Brujo* (Love, the Magician) and *El Sombrero de Tres Picos* (The Three Cornered Hat). A *Concerto for Harpsichord, Flute, Oboe, Clarinet, Violin, and Cello* is representative of his interest in abstract forms as well.

Ernest Bloch (1880–1959) was a Swiss composer who lived a large portion of his productive life as composer, conductor, and teacher in the United States. Bloch was an intensely expressive writer, first in a neoromantic style and later in a somewhat more neoclassic style. His influence as a teacher of twentieth-century American composers was widespread, with such men as Roger Sessions, George Antheil, and Leon Kirchner, among others, as his students. His major works include a number of symphonic poems of which *Schelomo, Trois poèmes juifs* (Three Jewish Poems), and *America* are representative examples. His neoclassicism is expressed in the *Concerti Grossi Nos. 1 and 2.* He wrote much chamber music including five string quartets, some piano music with orchestra, and solo works for various instruments. His *Sacred Service* has been very successful, and the opera *Macbeth* has gained some attention.

Béla Bartók (1881–1945) was the most distinguished Hungarian composer of the twentieth century. While his harmonic idiom was not based on any preconceived theory, Bartók's music reflected the twentieth-century character of freely combined sonorities. His music is essentially tonal, but he made extensive use of nonharmonic tones. His harmonic, rhythmic, and melodic styles were derived from an intense love and study of primitive folk music. The use of exotic scales derived from this source gave rise to melodic and harmonic practices which conformed generally to the twentieth-century breakdown of the tonal tradition. Bartók also made extensive use of polytonality, a device which resulted in a kind of controlled dissonance.

Folk music for Bartók was not a means of romantic nationalistic expression, but rather a source of expressive material, universally applicable. His scholarly interest in folk music extended beyond his own national culture and included the music of all the Balkan peoples and even that of North Africa. His music not only reflects an interest in the rhythmic, melodic, and harmonic aspects of primitive folk music, but it applied the impulse of the primitive to instruments, in particular to the piano, which is treated as a percussive instrument.

In his earliest works Bartók was obviously influenced by the impressionism of Debussy. This influence never completely disappeared from his compositions and is to be found in many of the slow movements of later works. The most distinctive design employed by Bartók is the arch form, a symmetrical balance of movements within the composite form of the sonata.

His compositions, which succeeded in finding wide performance and acceptance only after his death in New York in 1945, have since become extremely popular. Among the most distinguished are the three *Piano Concertos;* the *Violin Concerto;* six *String Quartets;* and the ballet *The Miraculous Mandarin;* the opera *Duke Bluebeard's Castle;* the *Mikrokosmos,* a series of instructional pieces for piano in modern idiom; the *Concerto for Orchestra,* and many songs.

Igor Stravinsky (1882–1971), a Russian by birth, lived most of his creative life in Paris and Hollywood. While his style was one of the principal influences on other composers in the twentieth century, particularly the French and those schooled in France, he was never attached to any institution or academy and only occasionally lectured on the general aesthetics of music. He had no pupils as such. With the composition of his ballet *Le Sacre du printemps* (The Rite of Spring) in 1913, Stravinsky adopted a dissonant harmonic technique which was not based on any preconceived plan or theory. His earlier compositions showed dissonant tendencies through the use of such devices as bitonality. Further adoption of polytonality and use of free dissonances and nonharmonic tones showed an expansion of the complex chromaticism of the nineteenth century, though never to the point of complete denial of tonal center.

Stravinsky's style was characterized not only by its harmonic innovations but perhaps even more by its primitive and brutal rhythmic patterns. The resulting complexities included the consecutive use of widely varying metric patterns and a kind of polyphony of widely differing rhythmic strata. The improvisatory freedom of jazz rhythms was often employed. In many instances rhythm constitutes the single most important element in Stravinsky's musical fabric.

Stravinsky rehearsing "Le Sacre du printemps." (Historical Pictures Service, Chicago)

Stravinsky also exploited tone color to its utmost in both large and small instrumental combinations. Unusual scoring such as the elimination of all the violins, violas and clarinets in the orchestra of the *Symphony of Psalms,* or the accompaniment of four pianos and percussion in *Les Noces* (The Wedding), are typical examples.

Few other twentieth-century composers exhibited so many diverse styles as Stravinsky, who was a prolific composer for over a period of fifty years. His rich output, dating from 1908 when he was studying with Rimsky-Korsakov, never abated, and the list of well-known and often-heard works made him the one twentieth-century composer whose recognition was comparatively immediate and universal. This was probably due in part to the great number of stage works, principally ballets, which made the introduction of his music to the general public somewhat easier than if his compositions had been more predominantly in the form of abstract orchestral or chamber music.

Stravinsky was at various times a postromantic, a primitivist, a neoclassicist, a neoromantic, an abstractionist, an expressionist, and a constructionist, though throughout he maintained a certain personal idiom that marks all of his compositions.

Some of his important works written before World War II include the ballets—*The Firebird, Petrouchka, Rite of Spring, Histoire du Soldat,* and *Jeux de cartes* (Game of Cards); works for orchestra including several suites taken from the ballets *Fireworks, Concerto for Piano and Wind Instruments, Symphony in C,* and *Concerto "Dumbarton Oaks";* chamber music including *Octet for Wind Instruments;* choral works including *Symphony of Psalms;* and works for piano including *Capriccio for Piano and Orchestra* and *Sonata for Two Pianos.*

Alban Berg (1885–1935) was an Austrian composer, pupil of Schoenberg, recognized as one of the most expressive composers in the twelve-tone technique. As with Schoenberg, his early compositions showed a marked influence of Wagner and Mahler. In his masterpiece, the opera *Wozzeck,* Berg organized the musical dramatic material into abstract forms such as rhapsody, suite, and theme and variations (passacaglia). The opera caused great protest when first performed in the 1920s but has since established itself as one of the great repertoire pieces of the twentieth century. Another partially finished opera, *Lulu,* a number of songs, as well as some orchestral and chamber music, represent his short productive life. Among the instrumental works that are frequently played are a *String Quartet, A Lyric Suite,* the *Violin Concerto,* and the *Chamber Concerto for Piano, Violin, and Thirteen Wind Instruments.*

Anton Webern (1883–1945), with Alban Berg and several other Viennese composers, was a pupil and disciple of Arnold Schoenberg. Webern adapted the twelve-tone method to his *pointillistic* technique, which resulted in an extremely economical use of musical material. In it, every phase of musical expression was reduced to its barest minimum, with thematic material often replaced by motives that seem to be compressed. The polyphonic texture was varied by placing successive notes of the contrapuntal line in different octaves and by changing the tone quality of each successive note by using different instruments. The compositions were of extreme brevity, an entire symphony lasting only a few minutes. The ensemble consisted of very few instruments, and they were used only sparingly.

Such techniques gave rise to the term pointillistic to describe the writing of Webern. He wrote a large number of works but their brevity reduces his total output to something less than three or four hours in performance, a remarkable fact when compared with the total output of other composers. His influence among the serial and electronic composers later in the century is especially significant. His most important works are the *Symphony,* Op. 21, the *String Quartet,* Op. 28, and the *Cantatas,* Op. 29 and 31.

Edgar Varèse (1883–1965), a French composer who lived most of his productive life in America, was among the greatest innovators of the twentieth century. His attitude toward music was one of an experimenter. His better-known works exhibited an engagement with sounds for the sheer sake of tonal masses, a characteristic that finally led him to the exploration of electronic sounds. Although he started his musical career as a romantic or an impressionist, all traces of these characteristics, as well as the compositions dating from these periods, have disappeared. In his search for timbral richness he exploited the tone qualities of all kinds of unusual instruments and instrumental combinations, particularly percussion instruments and percussive effects that can be generated by more conventional instruments. The works which have been most frequently performed are *Hyperprism*, scored for two woodwinds, seven brass, and sixteen percussion instruments; *Ionisation* written for thirteen performers on thirty different percussion and friction instruments; *Octandre*, a chamber work for eight performers; and *Density 21.5*, for solo flute.

Heitor Villa-Lobos (1887–1959), one of the foremost South American composers, was a native of Brazil where he was eventually engaged as superintendent of musical and artistic education in Rio de Janeiro. Villa-Lobos's idiom was highly influenced by the folk music of Brazil and sometimes was actually based on folk song themes. He was interested in fusing the peculiarities of Brazilian music with the tradition of western Europe. An example of this style is *Bachianas Brasileiras*, a set of nine suites in which the Brazilian folk music idiom was combined with Bachian counterpoint. A more typically original Brazilian form was *Choros*. In a series of fourteen of these works, Villa-Lobos combined the many elements of Brazilian folk, popular, and Indian music into compositions which used quite unusual instrumental and vocal forces. The most popular among these two groups of compositions are the *Bachianas Brasileiras Nos. 1* and *5*, and the *Choros Nos. 1* and *7*.

Sergei Prokofiev (1891–1953) was one of Russia's outstanding composers of the twentieth century. He himself listed the following as the four elements of his style: (1) classicism (neoclassicism); (2) innovation, which at first was represented in an individual harmonic style, later as an expression of strong emotions; (3) the motoric element; and (4) lyricism. He regarded another element, the grotesque, as an outgrowth of the others. Much of his music is flavored by a certain puckishness or humorous quality.

Prokofiev was widely known as a concert pianist in his early years. He lived in Paris until 1933, when he returned to Russia. His connection with the modern compositional practices of western Europe often brought him criticism at home, and in some instances caused him to adopt the official Soviet aesthetic doctrine, Socialist Realism. Nonetheless, he remained a highly revered composer and undoubtedly influenced the younger composers of the Soviet Union.

His musical output was extensive. The total number of his works which eventually found concert performance was, perhaps, second only to Stravinsky among modern composers. His compositions extended into every field with the exception of sacred music. Among the best known are his *Seven Symphonies*, written between 1916 and 1951; the *Third Piano Concerto;* the *Two Violin Concertos;* the symphonic poem, *Peter and the Wolf;* the orchestral suite, *Lieutenant Kije;* ten *Piano Sonatas;* and a great many short piano works, including *Sarcasms.*

Arthur Honneger (1892–1955), a Swiss composer, was closely allied with the French trends of the twentieth century by his inclusion in the group known as *Les Six.* While his early descriptive tone poem, *Pacific 231,* was looked upon as representative of the new machine age, Honneger turned from realistic writing to a neoclassic style. His dramatic oratorios, *Jeanne d'Arc au bûcher* (Joan of Arc at the Stake) and *Le roi David,* are two of the great choral works of the twentieth century. Among a large number of orchestral compositions his five *Symphonies* stand out as worthy of note, but a more significant achievement was the large number of film scores he wrote between 1923 and 1951. Honneger also wrote music for piano, voice, and chamber ensemble.

Darius Milhaud (1892–1974) was one of the leading French composers who pioneered the modern idiom in the early part of the twentieth century. He was a prolific composer, with works in every genre. He was active as a teacher for many years in the United States. His many experiments included use of jazz, polytonality, and eventually electronic devices. He did not subscribe to any form of atonality, though his use of dissonance in combination with a lively melodic line gave his work a distinct and individual style. His ballets, *La Création du monde* (The Creation of the World) and *Le Boeuf sur le toit* (The Cow on the Roof), are representative of his concern with jazz. Other works illustrate his preoccupation with the melodies of his native Provence, such as the *Suite Provençale.* Concertos, sonatas, symphonies, and many pieces of chamber music are among the large list of compositions which date from the first half of the century.

Carl Orff (1895–1982), whose stage works have won him international recognition, was perhaps one of the most conservative of twentieth-century composers. Despite this he represents a number of trends which were typical of the first half of the century. In contrast to nineteenth-century musicians, who regarded harmony as the principal shaping force, Orff, typical of the twentieth century placed rhythm in this role. His rhythmic force was drawn from word rhythms, especially from ancient and folk speech, folk dances, and folk songs. He treated these rhythms with a kind of repetitious primitiveness that makes for intense dramatic feeling. Structurally his music is very simple. He avoids contrapuntal practice for the most part, resorting to simple, harmonized melodic lines, with rather rare instances of clashing dissonances resulting from the use of nonharmonic tones. Percussion instruments appear abundantly in all his orchestrations. His best-known works are the dramatic cantatas *Carmina Burana* and *Catulli Carmina,* along with several operas, among which *Der Mond* (The Moon), *Die Kluge* (The Wise Woman), and *Antigonae* are the most popular. In addition, Orff wrote a series of five books called *Music for Children,* which has done much to revolutionize music education.

Paul Hindemith (1895–1963), composer, performer, conductor, and teacher, was a significant musical force in the twentieth century. He employed several styles of composition. In his early works he was openly rebellious toward all tradition. His music reflected a free contrapuntal character which made much use of dissonance. Hindemith was also occupied with the idea of general music education in his production of *Gebrauchsmusik* (music for use). Later he preferred to call this music "Sing-und Spielmusik." This music, vocal and instrumental, was intended to introduce the young and the amateur to the idiom of modern times through school and home performance. A neoclassic turn is evident in much of Hindemith's music of the 1930s. Further study of early music led Hindemith to polyphonic writing, which, while modern in harmonic idiom, is reminiscent of thirteenth to sixteenth-century practices. Even the lack of bar lines and metric signs, a characteristic of music before 1600, was imitated.

Hindemith was a prolific composer, who wrote in every conceivable field of musical composition. While he wrote solo works for almost every instrument, he was not as interested in the exploitation of tone color as were his contemporaries. Construction rather than emotional expression characterizes his works.

Among his important works are a song cycle, *Das Marienleben* (The Life of Mary); an opera, *Mathis der Maler* (Mathis, the Painter); *Wir Bauen eine Stadt* (We Build a City) for children performers; *Ludis Tonalis* for piano; *Symphonic Metamorphosis on Themes of Weber;* and *The Four Temperaments,* for piano and strings.

Roger Sessions (1896–1985) is one of America's foremost composers. A pupil of Ernest Bloch, his early works tended toward the Romantic. He soon turned, however, toward a very complex counterpoint which contained much dissonance. He eventually came under

George Gershwin (1898–1937) (The Bettmann Archive)

the influence of Schoenberg and wrote much music which approached the twelve-tone system and its atonal results, but he has never adopted this style of composition. Sessions defies any label such as neoromantic, neoclassic, or expressionistic though he partakes of each of these in some degree. He has not been a prolific composer and has made his greatest contribution in orchestral, chamber, and piano music. Among the four symphonies the *First Symphony* represents his early neoclassic style. Other important works are the *Piano Sonata No. 2*, the *Second String Quartet*, and *The Black Maskers*, an early work for orchestra, written as incidental music to a play.

George Gershwin (1898–1937) was America's first and most successful composer to incorporate the popular jazz rhythms of the 1920s in classical forms. His success as a composer of popular songs and musicals was already well established when he turned to other types of expression. In these his melodic gift and rhythmic genius gained for him success as a composer. In addition to numerous Broadway hits such as *Of Thee I Sing, Let 'em Eat Cake,* and *Girl Crazy,* other popular works are *Rhapsody in Blue, An American in Paris, Piano Concerto in F major,* and the opera, *Porgy and Bess.*

Manuscript page from Gershwin's, "Porgy and Bess." (Art and History Archive)

Ernst Krenek (1900–   ) was born in Vienna, but spent a large part of his creative life in the United States. His music shows the influence of almost all the stylistic experiments of the early twentieth century. An early opera (1927), *Jonny spielt auf!* utilized jazz idioms and had great success both in Europe and America. After many experiments, Krenek finally embraced a modified twelve-tone style. A prolific composer, he has composed eleven operas, three ballets, incidental music for seven plays, a large number of choral works, five symphonies, four piano concertos, six piano sonatas, and eight string quartets. He is also the author of several books including *Music, Here and Now.*

Aaron Copland (1900–   ) was a pupil of Nadia Boulanger and is, perhaps, the most widely-known of American composers. He has adopted numerous styles and techniques; jazz, neoclassic constructivism, and modified twelve-tone. His most successful works have reflected the American scene through symphonic poems, ballets, and operas, as well as a large number of works for radio and motion picture, some of which have been performed as concert music. Copland has also written a large quantity of music of a more abstract nature; symphonies, chamber music, and piano music. Among his best known compositions are the ballets, *Appalachian Spring, Billy the Kid, Rodeo;* the orchestral works, *El Salon Mexico, Outdoor Overture, Lincoln Portrait, Third Symphony;* and the piano works, *Passacaglia, Piano Variations,* and *Piano Sonata.*

Dmitri Shostakovitch (1906–1975) was a leading composer of mid-century Russia. His *First Symphony,* written as a graduation piece when he was eighteen years of age, brought him immediate fame. He was under severe official criticism for incorporating the techniques of Modern western European music with its dissonant qualities into his music, as in such works as the opera *Lady Macbeth of Mtzensk.* Obediently he turned to the traditional forms and styles of the Classic and Romantic periods, with tremendous success within Soviet Russia. Six of his fifteen string quartets and a *Piano Quintet* are his best known chamber music. He wrote fifteen symphonies, of which the fifth has been the most popular. Several ballets and operas, including a well-known opera, *The Nose,* and many film compositions are numbered among his compositions.

ADDITIONAL COMPOSERS

A. Austria
   J. M. Hauer (1883–1959)
   Egon Wellesz (1885–1974)
   Ernst Toch (1887–1964)
   Paul Pisk (1893–   )
B. Belgium
   Marcel Poot (1901–   )
C. Canada
   Claude Champagne (1891–1965)
   Sir Ernest Campbell MacMillan (1893–1973)
D. Chile
   Domingo Santa Cruz (1899–   )
E. Czechoslovakia
   Bohuslav Martinů (1890–1959)
   Alois Habá (1893–1975)
F. Denmark
   Carl Nielsen (1865–1931)
G. England
   Frederick Delius (1862–1934)
   Gustav Theodore Holst (1874–1934)
   Havergail Brian (1876–1972)
   John Ireland (1879–1962)
   Sir Arnold Bax (1883–1953)
   Gerald Finzi (1901–1956)
   Sir William Walton (1902–1983)
   Constant Lambert (1905–1951)
H. France
   Charles Koechlin (1876–1950)
   Albert Roussel (1869–1937)
   Florent Schmitt (1870–1958)
   Nadia Boulanger (1887–1979) reknowned teacher of
   composers
   Louis Durey (1888–1979)
   Jacques Ibert (1890–1962)
   Germaine Tailleferre (1892–1983)
   Lili Boulanger (1893–1918)
   Georges Auric (1899–1983)
   Francis Poulenc (1899–1963)

   I. Germany
      Hans Pfitzner (1869–1949)
      Max Reger (1873–1916)
      Hans Eisler (1898–1962)
      Kurt Weill (1900–1950)
      Gunther Bialas (1907–   )
      Hugo Distler (1908–1942)
      Bernd Alois Zimmerman (1918–1970)
   J. Greece
      Nikos Skalkottas (1904–1949)
   K. Hungary
      Ernst von Dohnányi (1877–1961)
      Zoltán Kodály (1882–1967)
   L. Italy
      Ferruccio Benvenuto Busoni (1866–1924)
      Ottorino Respighi (1879–1936)
      Ildebrando Pizzetti (1880–1968)
      Gian Francesco Malipiero (1882–1973)
      Alfredo Casella (1883–1947)
      Riccardo Zandonai (1883–1944)
      Mario Castelnuovo-Tedesco (1895–1968)
      Goffredo Petrassi (1904–   )
  M. Japan
      Yoritsune Matsudaira (1907–   )
  N. Mexico
      Julian Carrillo (1875–1965)
      Carlo Chávez (1899–1978)
      Silvestre Revueltas (1899–1940)
  O. Netherlands
      Daniel Ruyneman (1886–1963)
      Willem Pijper (1894–1947)
   P. Norway
      Fartein Valen (1887–1952)
   Q. Poland
      Karol Szymanowski (1882–1937)
      Grazyna Bacewicz (1913–1969)
   R. Russia
      Nikolai Miaskovsky (1881–1950)
      Aram Khachaturian (1903–1978)
      Dmitri Kabelevsky (1904–   )
   S. Spain
      Joaquin Turina (1882–1949)

T. Switzerland
  Othmar Schoeck (1886–1957)
  Frank Martin (1890–1974)
  Willy Burkhard (1900–1955)
  Rolf Liebermann (1910–   )
U. United States of America
  Charles Martin Loeffler (1861–1935)
  Carl Ruggles (1876–1971)
  Charles Tomlinson Griffes (1884–1920)
  Wallingford Riegger (1885–1961)
  Marion Bauer (1887–1955)
  Douglas Moore (1893–1969)
  Walter Piston (1894–1976)
  Leo Sowerby (1895–1968)
  William Grant Still (1895–1978)
  Howard Hanson (1896–1981)
  Virgil Thomson (1896–   )
  Henry Cowell (1897–1965)
  Quincy Porter (1897–1966)
  George Antheil (1900–1959)

VII. HISTORIANS AND THEORISTS

The growth of musicological research in European and American universities during the first half of the century resulted in the publication of a large number of books by eminent scholars dealing with all phases of music. Many of these books, however, dealt not with the twentieth century but with the historical past. The authors discussed below are those who have contributed to the understanding of music in the twentieth century. Titles of scholarly works dealing with musicological research in the past are readily available, and the most important of these in the English language have been listed in the Introduction.

Guido Adler (1855–1941), Austrian musicologist, was the leader in the development of the science of musical research. Among his many publications is the *Denkmäler der Tonkunst in Oesterreich* (Monuments of Austrian Composition), which reached eighty-three volumes from its inception in 1894 to its completion in 1938 near the time of his death. Many volumes have been added to this series more recently. It served as a scientific research model for many subsequent collections and anthologies of music history.

Heinrich Schenker (1868–1935) was an Austrian theorist whose system of analysis has been influential in theory and composition. While Schenker himself was concerned principally with compositions of the eighteenth and nineteenth centuries, his disciples, such as Felix Salzer, have extended his theories to twentieth-century styles. His works, all published in German, cover a period from 1906 to 1935. *Structural Hearing* (1952), by Salzer is one of a number of English publications dealing with Schenker's theories.

Ferruccio Benvenuto Busoni (1866–1924), an Italian composer and piano virtuoso, championed new music at the turn of the twentieth century. His book, *Entwurf einer neuen Aesthetik der Tonkunst,* Trieste 1907 (Sketch of a New Aesthetic of Composition, translated by Dr. Theodore Baker, New York, 1911) was a general encouragement for the "modern" composer of that time. Another important work, available in an English translation by Rosamond Ley, is *The Essence of Music and Other Papers,* (London 1957).

Ernst Toch (1887–1964) was a Viennese by birth who lived in the United States from 1935 until his death. He was active as a teacher during much of his career in Europe and America. His *Melodielehre* (Berlin 1923), was one of the few books dealing with the nature of melody. An English book, *The Shaping Forces in Music* (New York 1948), dealt with general theory and aesthetics of music both past and present.

Joseph Yasser (1893–   ) of Polish birth fled Russia in the 1920s and has lived in the United States since that time. His most important work, among many others, is *A Theory of Evolving Tonality.* In this work he offered a hypothesis not only for the origin of the pentatonic and heptatonic scales but for a future scale which he envisaged as being implied in the work of the twelve-tone composers.

Paul Hindemith (1895–1963) always interested himself in the teaching of music. His compositions in the 1920s which he called *Gebrauchsmusik* or music for use were evidence of this interest at an early age. From 1940 to 1949 he held the post of professor of the theory of music at Yale University in the United States. Among a large number of books that he wrote, two stand out as particularly pertinent to twentieth-century theory and composition, *The Craft of Musial Composition* (New York revised, 1945) and *A Composer's World: Horizons and Limitations,* (Cambridge 1952). They state the individual theory of Hindemith's composing technique as well as his aesthetic concepts concerning music of the twentieth century.

Ernst Krenek (1900–   ) was active as a teacher and writer as well as a composer. In his book, *Music Here and Now* (New York 1939) he wrote about the contemporary scene, about which he had extensive personal knowledge.

Aaron Copland (1900–   ) is known as a writer and teacher as well as a composer. Three books dealing with music in general, but of great importance to the understanding of modern music, have come from his pen. *What to Listen for in Music* (New York 1939), *Our New Music* (New York 1941), and *Music and Imagination* (Cambridge 1952) constitute a valuable addition to the writings on contemporary music.

Portrait of Sergei Prokofiev (1934) by P. P. Konchalovsky. (Art and History
Archives, Berlin)

9
Chronology
of Music Since World War II

1895	Carl Orff	1918	Leonard Bernstein
	(1895–1982)		(1918–)
1899	Duke Ellington		George Rochberg
	(1899–1974)		(1918–)
1900	Aaron Copland	1919	Leon Kirchner
	(1900–)		(1919–)
	Louis Armstrong	1922	Iannis Xenakis
	(1900–1971)		(1922–)
1904	Luigi Dallapiccola	1923	György Ligeti
	(1904–1975)		(1923–)
1905	Michael Tippett	1925	Luciano Berio
	(1905–)		(1925–)
1906	Dmitri Shostakovitch		Pierre Boulez
	(1906–1975)		(1925–)
	Elisabeth Lutyens		Gunther Schuller
	(1906–)		(1925–)
1908	Elliot Carter	1926	Hans Werner Henze
	(1908–)		(1926–)
1909	Benny Goodman	1928	Karlheinz Stockhausen
	(1909–1986)		(1928–)
1910	Samuel Barber		Thea Musgrave
	(1910–1981)		(1928–)
1911	Gian Carlo Menotti	1929	George Crumb
	(1911–)		(1929–)
1912	John Cage	1933	Krzysztof Penderecki
	(1912–)		(1933–)
1913	Benjamin Britten		Morton Subotnick
	(1913–1976)		(1933–)
	Witold Lutoslawski	1934	Peter Maxwell Davies
	(1913–)		(1934–)
	Lou Harrison		

1935   Terry Riley
       (1935–   )
1936   Steve Reich
       (1936–   )
1937   Phillip Glass
       (1937–   )
1939   World War II begins.
1945   Atomic bomb destroys
       Hiroshima and Nagasaki.

1952   Columbia University
       Electronic Studio founded.
1957   First satellite (sputnik)
       launched by Russia.
1960   Rock and roll (c. 1960)
1969   United States lands first
       man on the moon.
1973   Vietnam War ends.

9

Music Since World War II

I. SOCIOCULTURAL INFLUENCES ON MUSIC

History reveals countless discrepancies between the views of past scholars and the public concerning their musical contemporaries and the views of later scholars and the public who view the past with the added advantage of perspective. Any discussion of music since World War II lacks such perspective. That does not mean that the assessment of recent music is necessarily invalid, but what may have looked important and permanent at one time may soon diminish in importance. Furthermore, in the modern world, the speed of communication and the rapidity of change are so great that students of music need to make a special effort to be informed about the musical activities of the present, while recognizing that their judgments regarding that music may later need to be revised.

In addition to the general sociocultural influences of the first part of the twentieth century, the application of technological and scientific discoveries is one of the greatest influences on musical creativity and production today. Some of those technological developments have resulted in a world that is not only much more thoroughly informed about events elsewhere, but is also developing similarities of taste that are more uniform than ever before. This might be illustrated by the influence of Indian music on the Beatles, or the influence of the Beatles, an English group, on American popular music.

After the war, scientific developments were turned to commercial and social uses with great vigor. Not only was the speed of communication in all its aspects increased, but all phases of communication were made universally available. Some of the post-1950 developments include television, solid-state physics (transistors), rocket propulsion (space satellites, interstellar exploration) laser beams, computers, and microchips. Each of these contributes in important ways to the musical scene of the late twentieth century.

The development of long-playing records and tapes enabled recordings of large works with minimal interruption. The transistor radio, cassette recorder, compact disc, and other relatively inexpensive and readily available instruments now make music accessible at any location, and at any time. For the first time in history, music from the banal to the most esoteric and from all historical periods became easily accessible through sound recordings. In the past, such a plethora of music was never at the disposal of even the wealthiest patron, secular or religious.

Since 1950 electronic instruments of many kinds have engaged a number of composers in experimentation with an entirely new field of sound. Rhythmic complexities beyond the possibility of human realization are comparatively easy to achieve on electronic instruments. Sound generators and synthesizers are commonly used electronic devices in musical composition. They have opened entirely new vistas of tone color and pitch manipulation. In addition to the manipulation of these instruments directly by composers is the use of electronic computers for automatic musical composition. Programmed computers are used with some frequency to compose music. Recent technology has also made available a standardized Musical Instrument Digital Interface (MIDI), to connect microcomputers to various synthesizers. This enables both the professional composer and the layman to play and write music with the computer much more easily than was possible before. Finally, the urge to achieve uniqueness has led to multimedia experiments with music, dance, lights, and other effects, especially in the commercially produced popular mixed-media entertainment for television such as Music Television (MTV).

A subtle environmental factor of the twentieth century has also made its influence felt on musical composition. We live in an environment which is much more acoustically disturbing than at any time in the past. The noise of modern life has increased enormously with sounds of the mechanized world. This heightened sound level has affected music as well. Orchestras and ensembles are not necessarily larger, but the decibel level of individual instruments, and the quality of tone called for, often tends to be strident and piercing. This is especially true in rock music, where a high decibel level is an essential part of the music.

Composers today recognize that it is through recorded music that they have the greatest opportunity of reaching the largest audience. Consequently, they compose with recordings in mind. This leads to the manipulation of the recording devices which control and change the original sound as part of the compositional process.

To many people, listening to recorded music is more satisfying than listening to live concerts. For these same people, listening to recorded music is more convenient than going to live concerts or operas. As a result there are many avid music lovers who rarely hear live music. Moreover, recordings are capable of almost perfect technical performance since all mistakes can be erased and repaired through editing, cutting, and splicing of the original tape. This undoubtedly allows composers to expect a perfect recorded performance, which has doubtless had a salutory effect on the expectations of live performances. The high degree of technical proficiency by performing artists is a consequence of these expectations. Performance skill has reached such a high level that composers have no hesitation in writing music demanding extreme virtuosity.

Following World War II, those countries that became part of the Communist bloc, such as Poland, Czechoslovakia, Hungary, Bulgaria, Rumania, and East Germany, were cut off from the leading musical trends of the second half of the century. This continued until the death of Stalin, after which some of the restrictions on artistic creativity were removed. The music of Western Europe, avant-garde and popular, has not only been introduced to Eastern Europe, but it is also being widely performed by east European artists. The composers of these countries, notably Poland, Rumania, and Czechoslovakia, are as representative of late twentieth-century western music as are the composers of Western Europe.

Another political change that has had an effect on music has been the dissolution of great overseas empires, especially those of the British, Dutch, and French. As new nations acquired their own national identity, they began to cultivate their indigenous music and art. One outcome of this has been that the music of Africa and Asia has spread worldwide, and has been a renewed influence on composers in many parts of the world.

The new interest in diverse musical cultures resulted in a revival of many exotic musical practices, and a resurgence of interest in heretofore obsolete musical instruments, especially those of the Renaissance and Eastern cultures.

One final sociological development affecting music is the worldwide emphasis on teaching music in public schools and institutions of higher education. Creative and performing musicians have been appointed to the faculties of music schools and universities where students and highly competent performing colleagues have made the study and performance of diverse musical practices possible. Such institutions have in a way offered the creative artist and performer the patronage which musicians in the seventeenth and eighteenth centuries received from the Church and the aristocracy. Among the composer-teachers of this period whose students in turn became noteworthy composers are the following. (The teachers' names are followed by their students' names in parenthesis.)

Arnold Schoenberg (Alban Berg, Anton Webern)
Paul Hindemith (Norman Dello Joio, Ulysses Kay, Lukas Foss)
Olivier Messiaen (Pierre Boulez)
Nadia Boulanger (Louise Talma, Walter Piston, Elliot Carter, Aaron Copland, Virgil Thomson)
Ernst Bloch (Roger Sessions, Quincy Porter, Leon Kirchner)

II. FUNCTION OF MUSIC

Since the middle of the century there has been a particular emphasis on the employment of composers and performers as teachers in colleges and universities in all countries. This tradition has grown exponentially in the last half of this century. In addition, "Composers in Residence," whose responsibilities are exclusively to compose music, occupy positions in schools parallel to those composers who served in Renaissance and Baroque courts. The function of the composer in these situations is twofold: to provide instruction through precept and example to those who wish to engage in the creative effort, and to provide musical fare whereby the general university community can experience the music of contemporary composers.

Because many colleges and universities have the resources in both teaching and performance, they have become fertile ground for the experimental and avant-garde composer. In fact, some of the most elaborate resources for electronic music are to be found in educational institutions. However, in Europe, the broadcasting studios have also been in the vanguard of this movement. Moreover, educational institutions can also supply audiences that are eager to experience new sounds and techniques of composing and performance.

Special festivals and concert series organized for the purpose of presenting works of contemporary composers, especially the avant-garde, have multiplied since the middle of the century. Such festivals occur in many countries. In addition, there are a number of festivals devoted to non-western music, old and new. Some receive the sponsorship of universities and schools of music, governments, foundations, or individuals who give support to the composition and performance of music of the twentieth century. Important festivals are held in Edinburgh, Scotland; Spoleto, Italy; Salzburg, Austria; and Aspen, Colorado. Central to the festival season in some cities is the production of opera. These include Bayreuth and Munich, West Germany, and Santa Fe, New Mexico.

In recent years, the number of cities in the United States that have developed opera companies has increased dramatically from two or three centers to almost every metropolitan area. Many of these opera houses produce far more historical operas than contemporary or experimental works. On the other hand, many European opera houses commit a portion of their repertoire to contemporary works. University workshops and opera studios provide some opportunity for contemporary opera in America.

During the second half of the twentieth century the musical play has experienced some decline despite the significant contributions of such composers as Stephen Sondheim and Andrew Lloyd Webber. In the same period, ballet has achieved a position of high importance in Europe and North America, where in addition to traditional classical movements, such a variety of expressive gestures and positions has developed that it is often called Modern Dance. The techniques developed by Martha Graham, Merce Cunningham, George Balanchine, Glen Tetley, John Cranko, and Jerome Robbins, all outstanding choreographers, have led to the composition of ballet music by contemporary composers.

In the field of television there has not yet been an artistically satisfying union of music and media. European television and public television in the United States, however, broadcast numerous concerts and operatic performances that include contemporary works. These broadcasts are for the most part adaptations of stage or concert presentations for television. Television offers a completely new avenue of communication to the imaginative composer of the twentieth century, which has not as yet been completely realized.

III. STYLE AND PERFORMANCE PRACTICE

Following midcentury, experiments with twelve-tone technique and other forms of atonality continued, but by the 1980s there was a slackening of interest in serial technique. Experimentalism flourished in the post-war atmosphere as imaginations ran rampant, employing unusual sound effects, unorthodox instruments, and new principles of construction. Advances in electronic tone production led to the development of very sophisticated synthesizers used to create sounds of infinitely small pitch differential and tone color. As a reaction to these experiments there has also been an increased interest in a kind of new romanticism (neoromanticism) among some composers.

Formal Organization

Complete serial composition describes works by a small group of composers including Messiaen, who treated all the elements of music in serial fashion. Their compositions are no longer formally organized around a tone row, but rather around the serial arrangement of all the musical elements.

A unique development in the second half of the twentieth century has been chance music, often referred to as *aleatoric* or *indeterminate* music. In its written appearance it takes various forms, which necessarily affect the sound outcome in performance. In some instances a prose description of what is intended is all that is presented. In other instances graphic or representational symbols suggest matters of pitch, timbre, or time. Sometimes actual musical passages are written, with the order of their presentation left to the performers. Some composers choose to control the temporal element and allow the performers to control the pitches. Other composers may choose a different pattern of freedom and control. Karlheinz Stockhausen's *Klavierstück XI* uses a type of indeterminacy by presenting 19 musical fragments on a large piece of cardboard. The pianist is to play whatever fragment his eyes fall on, while following a few rules that suggest appropriate tempos and articulations. The piece is concluded when a fragment is played more than twice.

Minimalism is a musical development of the 1960s which has achieved broader acceptance in more recent decades. The origins of musical minimalism are found both in the music of Satie and Cage and in the visual art of such painters as Ad Reinhardt and the sculptor David Smith. Minimalist music employs such techniques as drones, static harmonies, and ostinatos, all repetitious devices. The composers most readily associated in America with minimalism are Terry Riley, Steve Reich, and Philip Glass. Instrumental ensembles lend themselves well to the stylistic conventions of minimalism, and in the 1980s composers such as the Canadian R. Murray Schaffer have written minimalist music for choir. Minimalist music from the world of opera includes Philip Glass's trilogy *Satyagraha* (based on the life of Gandhi), *Akhnaten* (based on the life of an Egyptian Pharaoh), and *Einstein on the Beach*. More recently, John Adams's, *Nixon in China* has met with success.

Melody

Strictly speaking, in the more radical compositions since World War II, melody, as previously expressed, has all but disappeared. Many of the contemporary compositions are devoted to displays of tone color and rhythmic complexity. This is true not only for electronic music, but for many works for traditional instruments as well.

Rhythm

The rhythmic complexities cultivated in the music of African, Oriental, and other non-western cultures has been influential in recent music. The rhythmic freedom of popular music has also had a significant influence on the art music of the twentieth century. Music composed electronically makes possible intricate rhythmic patterns and complexities that defy human performance. Such music exists primarily in recorded form.

Rhythm is sometimes emphasized to the extent that a total composition, or parts of a work, are made up of rhythmically enhanced sonorities which are lacking melodic significance and harmonic purpose. Free rhythms, such as were found in medieval and Renaissance music, are once more used. Bar lines are often omitted. Nontraditional meter signatures often indicate only the unit of measure—quarter note, eighth note, half note—without designating the number of notes comprising a unit. In some more recent music, traditional metric units are no longer viable. Time is often measured by a stopwatch, or even left to the discretion of the performer. In minimalism the rhythms are highly repetitive, creating an hypnotic effect. Departures from these rhythmic ostinati can be so subtle as to become almost imperceptible.

Harmony

Traditional harmony is completely denied in some works, particularly those of electronic origin. The combination of different pitches is no longer based on the principle of function within a tonal system but rather on independent patterns of tonal movement and the effect of massed harmonic colors. Hence, tones of different pitches are combined in clusters or constellations and not by any principle of tension set up by consonance and dissonance.

Texture

Sound blocks, clusters, or constellations replace voice leading. Such clusters can be transparent or thick and opaque in texture, depending on the pitches selected and the number of tones in the cluster. In contrast to imitative counterpoint of earlier periods, a new kind of counterpoint persists in which each of several independent groups engage in a simultaneous presentation of individual material.

Instrumentation and Tone Color

Contemporary experiments with timbre have led to a revival of instruments which have long been obsolete or infrequently used in art music. Such instruments as the harpsichord, the guitar, the mandolin, and a great list of percussion instruments such as the xylophone and tuned drums are often used. In fact, percussion instruments

The Fairlight computer musical instrument CMI, a digital synthesizer. (Fairlight Instruments, Los Angeles, CA)

receive greater attention, and their number and variety are greatly increased. Exotic instruments, especially those of India and Indonesia, have intrigued contemporary composers providing them with new sources of tone color.

Perhaps the greatest addition to the timbral resources of contemporary composers has been provided by electronic sound synthesizers. These instruments can be used independently or can be used with more traditional instruments, sometimes even substituting for existing instruments.

Electronic instruments are capable of producing sounds of definite pitch rich in overtones, pure tones which are completely devoid of overtones, and white sounds. White sounds contain the entire spectrum of audible frequencies just as white light contains all colors of the spectrum. By being able to filter out selected overtones, a variety of sound coloring is possible. Through such electronic manipulation normal tone qualities of traditional instruments are distorted to create totally fresh sound experiences. This has been commonly employed in jazz and popular music. Variation in speed of recording is another means of achieving new tone colors. A tuba, for example, can be pitched at the level of a piccolo by accelerating the recording speed. Such new tone colors are only achievable through electrical or electronic means.

Practice and Performance

Notation of much modern music is expressed in terms of graphs, charts, and symbols, which are specifically defined for particular compositions. This practice of developing new notational symbols for specific compositions has become widespread. It has even led to the publication of books devoted to the topic of *devised notation*. To date there is no more than a very modest movement toward the standardization of these symbols.

The rise of jazz as a vehicle for creative expression is an important phenomenon which had a strong influence on composers in the twentieth century. Its influence has been felt rhythmically, harmonically, and through its improvisatory nature.

There has been a marked revival of interest in performance on early instruments such as harpsichord, recorder, krummhorn, viol, lute, and guitar. This interest has been widely stimulated through amateur performance and music instruction in schools and colleges. *Early Music*, a scholarly journal published in England, is a response to the serious interest of amateur and professional musicians in pre-classic music and its correct performance.

Many of the outstanding performers and conductors who were active during the time of the Second World War continue to flourish. The following list includes some of these people as well as the younger generation, who are widely known through their concerts, recordings, television, and radio appearances.

Among the pianists are Sviatoslav Richter, Glenn Gould (d. 1982), André Watts, Vladimir Aschkenazy, Radu Lupu, Marta Argerich, Alfred Brendel, Murray Perahia, and Alicia DeLarrocha. Leonard Bernstein and Sergei Prokofiev (d. 1953) both gained fame as pianists and composers. Prominent violinists include David Oistrakh (d. 1974), Yehudi Menuhin, Isaac Stern, Itzhak Perlmann, Pinchas Zukerman, and Anne-Sophie Mutter. Several cellists have international reputations as well: Lynn Harrell, Yo Yo Ma, Janos Starker, and Mstislav Rostroprovitch, who for years directed the National Symphony Orchestra. Jean-Pierre Rampal and James Galway are flutists who are universally known. The most outstanding singers of our generation include Joan Sutherland and Elly Ameling, sopranos; Janet Baker, mezzo-soprano; Luciano Pavarotti, Placido Domingo, and Peter Schreier, tenors; and Dietrich Fischer-Dieskau and Sherill Milnes, baritones. The list of conductors includes several people who have also had careers as solo performers. Leonard Bernstein and André Previn head this list. Other conductors include Otto Klemperer (d.

1973), Eugene Ormandy (d. 1985), Herbert von Karajan, Zubin Mehta, Seiji Ozawa, and Sir George Solti. The list of the fine younger generation of conductors should include Christoph von Dohnányi, James Conlon, Michael Tilson Thomas, and Simon Rattle.

IV. MUSIC FOR INSTRUMENTS

To this point in the book the authors have followed the evolution of numerous set forms which continued from one period to another. In some degree this is possible with contemporary music, but not nearly to the extent possible in earlier chapters. For this reason we are abandoning the previous outline which treated these forms individually in favor of a more general discussion of contemporary musical structures. Still, some composers use the traditional titles of the past, even when the music stretches their terminology in unexpected ways.

Traditional Genre

Among the forms and genres that continue to interest composers are the concerto, symphony, theme and variation, and ballet. The concerto principle has always been the exploration and contrast of unequal sound sources. That principle applies particularly well to the sound aspirations of contemporary composers and has resulted in numerous concertos in recent years. The terms symphony and sonata have always carried a certain ambiguity which has allowed composers great latitude in adapting them to their needs. Nowhere is this more evident than today, when the term "symphony" has come to designate little more than a composition for a large number of musicians on stage. Another attractive genre is theme and variation, which continues to give composers opportunities to state something musically, and then explore the various mutations and transformations possible with that musical idea. Ballet and modern dance have prospered in this century, and ballet music has prospered as well. As dance movements have changed, composers for the dance have explored a wide-ranging variety of appropriate musical sounds. (Rec. 9.1–9.12)

Nontraditional Musical Forms Using Traditional Instruments

During the last 300 years the art of instrument making has given composers instruments of great versatility. These instruments are being used in new and unconventional ways, producing sounds that were never heard before. Such performance techniques as prepared

A computer and sound synthesizer laboratory. (The Bettmann Archive)

piano and multiphonics are the result of such experimentation. Concomitant with the experimental treatment of instruments is the experimental treatment of musical forms in which these sounds are presented free of historical antecedents. (Rec. 9.13–9.18)

Electronic Music

The first electronic compositions were created through the manipulation of sounds of concrete objects or musical instruments. The invention of the electronic synthesizers made it possible to create completely unique sounds, entirely independent of preexisting sources such as musical instruments, machines, and voices. In many works, traditional instruments and/or voices are combined with taped recordings of electronically produced sounds or with live sounds generated by synthesizers. Musical compositions have also been created through the use of computers. One of the stranger effects of the use of computers for composition is that humans can be programmed out of the compositional process. This is done by giving the computer the capacity to produce numerous musical events, and then giving it the added capacity to determine the sequence of events without intervention.

Television frequently employs electronically generated sound as background for dramatic performances, the presentation of station signatures, and advertising. More often than not this use of electronic music seeks anonymity by using these techniques in an almost conventional way. (Rec. 9.19–9.23)

V. MUSIC FOR VOICES

The vocal music of the Baroque is sometimes mildly criticized for its instrumental character. In the twentieth century certain writing for voices is similarly criticized, but for somewhat different reasons. Successions of intervals that could be easily negotiated by instruments, often outside any tonal scheme, are being demanded of singers. Compositions based on twelve-tone and aleatoric principles deprive singers of the orientation to a tonal center which for many singers is almost essential for performance. During this time, in solo and choral works, the voice is often freed from verbal considerations. Shouts, screams, and grunts are used. An entirely new and separate school of vocal production has evolved surrounding "extended vocal techniques," and music is being written to utilize the new possibilities of sound derived from these.

There continues to be vocal music written using the pitch conventions of the twelve-tone and the aleatoric, but a noticable return to the more comfortable tonality of neoromanticism has also occurred. This return to the harmonic vocabulary of the Romantic is broadly based and reveals itself in a surprising variety of compositional styles.

Art Song

The art song, in individual and cyclic settings, continues to be a medium of choice for numbers of composers. These composers wed the voice to a varied array of traditional and electronic instruments, and more often than not, to poetry of high quality.

While the second half of this century has been favored with what must be a number of the finest song singers of all time, the song recital has regrettably declined in popular favor. Despite this, a substantial amount of recent song repertoire has become available to the public through recordings. (Rec. 9.24–9.32)

Short Choral Works

Choral writing during the second half of the century has been cast in virtually all the experimental and the traditional forms the period inherited. Writing for the Church, especially in England and Germany, and schools has occupied some of the composers' time, and concert music has also been in some demand. (Rec. 9.33–9.41)

Opera and Musical Theater

Opera continues to be a medium that allows for the examination of historic (*The Rake's Progress*, Stravinsky) and current (*La cubana*, Henze) themes. In the United States there has been a growing need for chamber operas capable of being launched with small forces and modest expenditures. The harmonic and timbral resources available to all composers in this century find their way into opera. There are also many works that have multimedia characteristics that almost fit into this category; works of an experimental nature that involve action, words, and other elements commonly associated with the theater. One prosperous form of musical theater is the musical play, which flourished in the 1950s and 60s in the United States, and has shown a resurgence of vitality, especially in England in the 1970s and 80s. The musical play is characterized by substantial spoken dialogue in the vernacular, music in the popular style of the day, and plots that vary from the historical to the contemporary and from the serious to the farcical. As the century has progressed the rather artificial distinction between opera and musical play has become eroded further. European opera houses have for years offered musical plays in the same season with operas. (Rec. 9.42–9.58)

Oratorio and Liturgical Music

The spirit of experimentation continues, even in sacred music, which has traditionally lagged behind the developments in other areas of musical composition. Few of the large works of religious subject matter are appropriate for liturgical services. Of the liturgical music, a considerable amount uses a style that might be called neo-Baroque, an adaptation of contrapuntal style to the dissonant idioms of the twentieth century. (Rec. 9.59–9.67)

VI. COMPOSERS

As acknowledged in several places above, the roots of virtually every movement since World War II are plainly discernible in the first half of the century. For example, many of the characteristics of electronic music (new tone color, terse themes, extreme pitch ranges, microtonal pitches, and total serial construction) on which much emphasis has been placed since 1950, were already present in the works of Varèse, Webern, Habá, Stravinsky, Cage, Partch, and many others.

(Any of the following composers whose names are identified by an asterisk (*) have already been discussed to some degree in the preceding chapter.)

*Ralph Vaughan Williams** continued writing in his typically English style, adding three symphonies and an opera, *The Pilgrim's Progress.*

*Igor Stravinsky** adopted the serial technique only after 1950. One such work is his music for the ballet, *Agon.* Another is *In Memoriom—Dylan Thomas,* for tenor, string quartet, and trombone quartet, based on a five-note tone row. His opera of 1951, *The Rake's Progress* is based on a libretto by Auden and Kallman, whose inspiration was Hogarth's engravings of the same name.

*Edgar Varèse** moved strongly into electronic music with his *Deserts,* which is for fourteen winds, pianoforte, five percussion instruments and two-track tape. Its dates are 1950–1954, and it was revised at least three times. Another composition, *Poème electronique,* (1957–1958) is for three-track tape.

*Sergei Prokofiev** continued to write prolifically after the war although he was severely censured by the Soviet government. As a result he remained sufficiently conservative in his compositions to accomodate the tastes of the Soviet government. One such orchestral composition is *The Meeting of the Volga with the Don River,* written in 1952.

*Darius Milhaud** is remembered not only as a composer, but as a teacher of composition as well, teaching both in Europe and in the United States. Like Stravinsky and others he wrote a composition commemorating the assassination of John F. Kennedy, *Murder of a Great Chief of State* (1963).

*Paul Hindemith** became an American citizen in 1946, and thereafter conducted and taught in the United States and abroad. His *Symphony in B flat for Concert Band* was premiered in 1951. The *Concerto for Organ and Orchestra* is one of his last compositions.

*Roger Sessions** made a strong contribution through his compositions, his essays, and his teaching. His cantata, *When Lilacs Last in the Dooryard Bloom'd* was written between 1967 and 1970. He wrote eight symphonies, seven of which were premiered after 1947.

*Ernst Krenek** continues to write experimentally in his later years. *Aulokithara,* for oboe, harp, and tape, Op. 213a (1971), *Spätlese,* Op. 218, a song cycle written in 1973, and *They Knew What They Wanted,* for narrator, oboe, piano, and percussion, Op. 227 (1976–77) are representative works.

Aaron Copland, conducting. (The Bettmann Archive)

Aaron Copland* is recognized today as the Dean of American composers. One of his early postwar works is the song collection *Twelve Poems of Emily Dickinson* (1948–50). More recently he has written *Connotations* (1962) in the twelve-tone technique and another orchestral work, *Inscape*, in 1967.

Luigi Dallapiccola (1904–1975) was the foremost of the modern Italian composers. He combined the dodecaphonic technique with the Italian tradition of vocal line in a very expressive fashion. His masterful adaptation of the twelve-tone system to lyrical expression is well illustrated in his *Canti di Liberazione* (Songs of Liberty, 1951–55), a set of choral songs, and in his opera *Il Prigioniero* (The Prisoner). A number of chamber music works employing voice and instruments of various kinds are also noteworthy.

Michael Tippett (1905–   ) is an English composer whose music with text shows a deep interest in social issues. His compositional style is characterized by a continuing emphasis on vigorous rhythms and luminous textures, with harmonies that go beyond the late nineteenth and early twentieth centuries without embracing serialism. The oratorio, *A Child of our Time* (1944), based on American Negro spirituals, is his most popular work in this country. His opera, *The Midsummer Marriage* (1952), continues to be performed thirty years after its premiere at Covent Garden.

Dmitri Shostakovitch* excelled in instrumental music, but very often included vocal solos and choruses in his large symphonic works, including several of his last symphonies.

Louise Talma (1906–   ), French by birth and American by adoption, was educated in both countries. Her early compositions are based on neoclassical principles, but after 1950 twelve-tone techniques began to appear in her compositions, albeit primarily in a loosely defined tonal context. The *Piano Sonata No. 2* (1944–55) shows her stylistic movement in this direction. *Let's Touch the Sky* (1952), a work for choir and woodwind trio, is full of the freshness and energy of the poem by e. e. cummings. In 1974 she was selected to become a member of the American Academy and Institute of Arts and Letters, the first woman composer to be so honored.

Olivier Messiaen (1908–   ) is a French composer, theoretician, and organist who pioneered in the area of *total serialism*, a serial organization of sounds, durations, dynamics, and articulations. In his efforts to find new effects he makes use of exotic percussion instruments, generators, and bird calls, of which he was particularly fond. His importance as a theoretician can be noted through the works of his students such as Boulez, Stockhausen, and Nono. Among his important compositions are *Réveil des Oiseaux*, (1953), *Oiseaux Exotique* (1955–56) and *Catalogue d'Oiseaux* (1956–58).

Elliott Carter (1908–   ) is an American composer whose music is essentially twentieth century in its contrapuntal texture and its occupation with rhythm and meter as form-building elements. Carter's works are infused with modal counterpoint though he has made use of a personal type of twelve-tone technique. In some works he employed a system of *Metric Modulation* whereby he has been able to modulate from one speed to another by changing the rhythmic values of the basic units. Carter is not a prolific composer, but his works are refined. His *Variations for Orchestra* (1955), *String Quartet*, No. 2 (1959), the *Double Concerto for Harpsichord*, and *Piano and Two Chamber Orchestras* (1961) are typical of his output. More recent works include *In Sleep, In Thunder*, six poems by Robert Lowell (1981) and *Changes, for Solo Guitar* (1983).

John Cage (1912–   ) is an American composer whose radical tendencies in composition have expressed themselves in the derivation of new tone colors in preparing the piano by placing on the strings of the instrument such objects as metal, erasers, and screws. For such a *prepared piano* Cage has written *Sixteen Sonatas* and *Four Interludes.* He has also experimented in the area of chance or random composition. The latter is accomplished by chance selection of pitch, note values, dynamics, and/or instrumentation, either from notated suggestions or from pure chance as in the case of one of Cage's own works, *Imaginary Landscape No. 4* (1951). In this work, twelve radios, dialed according to predetermined wavelengths, give forth whatever is presently being programmed.

Benjamin Britten (1913–1976) was perhaps the most eminent of the twentieth century British composers. While he wrote for many musical genres, it was through his operas and choral works that he achieved worldwide recognition. Britten's style was essentially vocal. He was clearly a classicist in his approach to musical composition and consequently was not interested in the Wagnerian idea of endless melody, but rather espoused the principle of closed forms in operatic writing. He was not an adherent of any set method or technique of composition, but was influenced by a number of widely varying composers in whose individual styles he found certain elements of interest. His operas include *The Rape of Lucretia* (1946), *Peter Grimes* (1945), *Albert Herring* (1947), *Billy Budd* (1951), and *Midsummer Night's Dream* (1960). Two of his well-known choral works were written aboard ship during World War II. They are *A Ceremony of Carols* (1942) and *Hymn to St. Cecilia* (1942). A more dramatic work involving far greater forces in performance is the *War Requiem* (1962), which combines texts from the Latin requiem with poems by Wilfred Owen, who was killed during World War I. His song cycles are among the most important contributions to twentieth-century vocal music. These include the *Canticles* (various dates) and *Phaedra* (1970), one of his last vocal works. Not least illustrative of his love for the variation form is the very popular *The Young Person's Guide to the Orchestra.*

Witold Lutoslawski (1913–   ) is a composer whose early concern with twelve-tone technique has given way to ultra modern practices including electronic composition. He has been widely recognized as one of the most significant of the modern Polish compposers. He has composed principally for orchestra and chamber music ensembles. Among his best known works are his First and Second Symphonies (1941–47, 1966–67), and *Paroles Tissées* (1965) for tenor and chamber orchestra. The daring of his music can be seen in *Trois Poèmes d'Henri Michaux* for choir, wind instruments, percussion, two pianos, and harp (1963), which requires two separate conductors using different scores.

Milton Babbitt (1916–   ) is a composer whose mathematical genius contributed to his exploration of the relationships between music and mathematics, even to the point of adapting mathematical vocabulary to music. His music is characterized by a strict adherence to serial technique, and he has a long-term interest in sound synthesizers and computer music. Much of his music is cerebral and nearly inaccessible to the average listener.

George Rochberg (1918–   ) is an American composer who combines twelve-tone influences with a logical harmonic style into a singularly personal idiom. For a decade he wrote extensively using the serial technique, concluding that period with the *Piano Trio* (1963). His compositions cover a wide range of instrumental and vocal forms. He has also published a number of articles dealing with the problems of twelve-tone composition. Rochberg teaches at the University of Pennsylvania. A number of his works employ quotations from other composers from the sixteenth to the twentieth century, such as Schütz, Bach, Mahler, Ives, Boulez, and Varèse. Among his works are five symphonies, a violin concerto, seven string quartets, and a recent opera, *The Confidence Man* (1982).

Leon Kirchner (1919–   ) is an American composer, teacher, and brilliant pianist who came under the influence of Schoenberg in his early musical studies. Later he studied with Ernest Bloch. These men influenced him greatly, but he never adopted a system from either of them. His music fluctuates between a very highly chromatic idiom and an atonal one. Most characteristic is its motoric drive whether the medium is the orchestra, the piano, or the string quartet. Kirchner's music is imbued with an intensity of expression that is almost exhausting in its demands on the listener. His importance in the mid-century musical scene of America is demonstrated by the large number of awards and commissions he has received. His major awards have included the New York Music Critics' Circle Award, the Naumburg Award, and a Pulitzer Prize for his third string quartet, written in 1967. His *Concerto for Piano and Orchestra* (1953), *Sinfonia* (1951), and *String Quartet No. 1* (1949) are representative of his finest style. His vocal music in the last decade has included a song cycle and an opera.

Lukas Foss (1922–   ) began his compositional career as a neoclassicist. After approximately 1960 his interest in improvisation led him to explore various aspects of indeterminancy. *Time Cycle* (1960), for soprano and orchestra, has been recorded and enjoyed considerable success. His *Baroque Variations* (1967) plays on compositions by Handel, Scarlatti and Bach.

Iannis Xenakis (1922–   ) was born in Greece, but now lives in the United States. He was a student of Messiaen and was also associated with the architect, Le Corbusier. His music is structured on the principles of mathematical probability (stochastic principles) in terms of traditional instruments and traditional notation. His interest in the aesthetics of music and mathematics led him to establish Centers for Musical Mathematics and Automation, first in Paris and then in Bloomington, Indiana, where he taught for a time. His important works include *Pithoprakta* for fifty instruments (1955–56), *Achoripsis* (1956–57), *Stratégie* for two small orchestras (1959–62), and *Metastasis* (1953–1954) for orchestra; and *Eonta* (1963–64) for piano and brass. A sizeable list of works for tape, and still others, for which a computer is helpful in performance, are also included among his compositions.

György Ligeti (1923–   ) was born in Hungary but presently lives in Germany where he is professor of composition at the Hamburg Academy of Music. His activities have taken him into almost all European countries as well as the United States. He has been associated with the Studio for Electronic Music in Cologne and is one of the leaders of the International Courses for New Music in Darmstadt. His early works, published in eastern Europe prior to his departure from Hungary in 1956, are mostly simple, folk-derived works. His later works are characterized by an emphasis on color and masses of sound. To achieve this he employs all varieties of noise makers as well as electronically generated sounds. His compositions, however, have exploited all musical media from the organ and string quartet to the symphony orchestra as well as small and large vocal ensembles. Among his works are *Volumina*, for organ (1961–62); *Requiem*, for solo voices, chorus, and orchestra (1963–65); and *Lux Aeterna*, for 16 solo voices (1966). In several compositions Ligeti has made critical comments about contemporary compositions. One such composition is his *Poème Symphonique*, for 100 metronomes all operating at different speeds (1962).

Luciano Berio (1925–   ), composer of the avant-garde, developed an interest in electronic music after his first visit to the United States. He has frequently combined performances with electronic tapes. His most significant works show a deep concern with music combined with gesture and dramatic action. *Circles* (1960), a setting of poems by e. e. cummings for voice, harp, and percussion instruments, is designed for visual and spatial realization. Berio's further involvement with music and dramatic action as well as the relation between words and music is illustrated in his opera, *Passaggio* (1961–62), and the composition *Visages* (1961), a taped composition using both electronic and vocal sounds. Many of these compositions were written for his wife, Kathy Berberian. *Recital I (for Kathy)* (1962) includes a tour de force catalogue of vocal and dramatic styles.

Pierre Boulez (1925–   ), one of the more controversial of the twentieth-century composers, has developed a very complex style of serial composition in which, like Messiaen, his teacher, he employs serialization of pitches and durations (totally controlled music). He has also explored electronic music. The best-known work of Boulez is *Le marteau sans maître* (The Hammer Without a Master), written for contralto and a group of six instruments in 1952–54 and revised in 1957. The unusual instrumentation of flute in G, viola, guitar, vibraphone, and percussion is indicative of his concern with tone color, particularly with that created by percussion instruments. As a conductor Boulez has been one of the most active participants in festivals of contemporary music. As a composer and conductor he continues to champion serial music.

Hans Werner Henze (1926–   ) is a composer active in all fields of composition. His early works showed a complete mastery of the twelve-tone technique which he later utilized in a manner that appealed more readily to the larger audience. He has been particularly successful in operatic composition. Many of his operas are intended to convey a strong social and sometimes Marxist message. Such works as *Der Junge Lord* (1965), and *Der Prinz von Homburg* (1960) have had great success. A year spent in Cuba, teaching and writing, has influenced the social focus of his writing.

Thea Musgrave (1928–   ) studied composition with Nadia Boulanger following her matriculation at Edinburgh University. Her compositional style mixes serial writing with more conservative practices. Attention was first drawn to her in the United States through her operatic works, most recently *Mary, Queen of Scots*. She has written concerti for a number of instruments, and her film scores are numerous.

Karlheinz Stockhausen (1928–   ) is a German composer who has given most of his attention to the field of electronic music, although he started his career as a disciple of Webern using conventional instruments. *Kontra-Punkte* (1952, rev. 1953), for ten solo instruments, is a representative work of this period. Another phase is represented by *Klavierstücke XI* (1956), a work constructed on the basis of random selection and improvisatory treatment of nineteen notated fragments. The best known of his electronic compositions is *Gesang der Jünglinge* (Song of the Youths, 1955–56, revised for four-track tape in

1956), which is written for human voice and electronic sound generator. The notation of such music in graphs and geometric figures precludes any performances by other than those persons tutored in reading such notation. Much of his work embraces "open" form, leaving many decisions to the performers, as in *Mixtur* (1964). The electronic equipment employed by Stockhausen, and those associated with him at the Northwest German Radio Studio in Cologne, in no way attempts to imitate the sound qualities of conventional instruments. The sounds produced by the signal generators and the electronic synthesizers are exploited for their intrinsic value as new sounds. Much of Stockhausen's music includes a theatrical element, utilizing space and movement, as in *Momente,* written in 1961 and revised several times.

George Crumb (1929–   ) is an American composer who combined study at American Universities with study in Berlin. His compositions reflect a certain tendency to relate traditional formalities with very extreme demands on technical resources. Exceptional combining of electronic instruments and conventional instruments as well as electrically amplified instruments result in extraordinary tonal effects. This interest in unusual sound qualities is demanding of his vocal forces in the singing of microtonal intervals, the use of shrieks, hisses, whisperings, and other unusual vocal sounds. Works such as *Night of the Four Moons,* for alto flute, banjo, electric cello, and percussion (1969); *Songs, Drones and Refrains of Death,* for baritone, electric guitar, electric double bass, electric piano, and percussion (1968); and *Lux Aeterna for Five Masked Musicians,* for soprano, bass flute, sitar, and two percussion players (1971) are representative of Crumb's interest in such sound effects. In addition to his writing for groups of instruments with vocalists, he has written extensively for piano. Crumb is on the faculty of the University of Pennsylvania.

Krzysztof Penderecki (1933–   ), whose compositions are represented by various instrumental and vocal combinations, is perhaps the most widely known of today's Polish composers. He has developed a style that is quite original and independent of any of the fixed systems of the twentieth century. His works allow a certain amount of freedom to improvise for the performer, which is only governed by specific time limits. He has achieved novel tonal effects in the use of traditional orchestral instruments in his very well known *Threnody to the Victims of Hiroshima* (1960). The *Passion According to St. Luke* (1963–65) is one of the most impressive choral works of the twentieth century. Likewise, the opera *The Devils of Loudon* (1969) is a powerfully dramatic work. His best-known recent work is the *Polish Requiem* premiered in 1984.

R. Murray Schafer (1933–   ) is a Canadian composer and peda-
gogue occupied with the exploration of physical sounds. His compositions range from chamber music of unusual instrumentaton to
operatic and symphonic pieces employing electronic music as well as
aleatoric devices. Among his many compositions are a *String Quartet*
(1970); *North/White*, for orchestra (1973); and *Apocolypsis*, for 500 performers (1976). A composer with a sense of humor, his *Son of Heldenleben* (1968) quotes and manipulates the music of Richard Strauss. A
more serious side of the composer is revealed in *Threnody* (1966), which
uses the words of Japanese children who survived the bombing of
Hiroshima. With a grant from the Donner Foundation he studied the
relationship of people worldwide and the sounds that surround them.
Shafer has a compelling interest in language, and its use and misuse
in communication is a source of his musical inspiration.

Peter Maxwell Davies (1934–   ) is an English composer whose
works are characterized by controlled improvisation and by an abundance of various styles and idioms from Renaissance polyphony to
extreme serialism. Some of his important works are the *Saint Michael
Sonata* (1957), *Eight Songs for a Mad King* (1969), and the *Second Fantasia
on Taverner's "In Nomine,"* (1964). Since 1970, Davies has lived in the
Orkney Islands, where he has written many works based on Scottish
and English themes. Like Shafer, he has been interested in, and
written, music for children.

Philip Glass (1937–   ), American minimalist, has studied with
many of the important teachers in the United States and France. His
travels in India, as well as his work with Ravi Shankar have certainly
influenced his movement in the direction of minimalism. He is probably best-known in this country for his film score for *Koyaanisqatsi*
(1981). This work is illustrative of his collaborative artistic efforts with
filmmakers and visual artists of all kinds, as is *Einstein on the Beach*
(1976).

Judith Zaimont (1945–   ) enjoys increasing importance, especially for her solo vocal and choral music. Recognition of her abilities
in the setting of texts has been acknowledged through the commissions of such professional choral ensembles as the Gregg Smith Singers
and the Western Wind. Additionally, she has written successfully for
various chamber ensembles, and for the piano.

ADDITIONAL COMPOSERS

A. Argentina
   Alberto Ginastera (1916–1983)
   Mauricio Kagel (1931–   )
   Mario Davidovsky (1934–   )
B. Austria
   Johann N. David (1895–1977)
   Hans E. Apostel (1901–1972)
   Hans Jelinek (1901–1969)
   Karl Schiske (1916–1969)
   Gottfried von Einem (1918–   )
   Dieter Kaufmann (1941–   )
   Klaus Ager (1946–   )
C. Belgium
   Henri Pousseur (1929–   )
D. Bulgaria
   Dimiter Christoff (1933–   )
E. Canada
   Harry Somers (1925–   )
   Serge Garant (1929–   )
F. Cuba
   Leo Brower (1939–   )
G. Czechoslovakia
   Vaclav Dobias (1909–1978)
   Jan Cikker (1911–   )
   Karel Husa (1921–   )
   Jindřich Feld (1925–   )
   Oldřich Flossman, (1925–   )
   Zdenek Lukas (1928–   )
H. Denmark
   Vagn Holmboe (1909–   )
   Niels Viggo Bentzon (1919–   )
I. England
   Sir Arthur Bliss (1891–1975)
   Elisabeth Maconchy (1907–   )
   Elizabeth Lutyens (1909–   )
   George Lloyd (1913–   )
   Peter Racine Fricker (1920–   )
   Harrison Birtwistle (1934–   )
   Oliver Knussen (1952–   )
   Dominic Muldowney (1952–   )
   Robert Saxton (1953–   )

J. Finland
   Joonas Kokonen (1920–   )
   Einojuhani Rautavaara (1928–   )
K. France
   Jean Martinon (1920–1976)
   Jean Françaix (1912–   )
L. Germany
   Werner Egk (1901–1983)
   Boris Blacher (1903–1975)
   Wolfgang Fortner (1907–1979)
   Bernd Alois Zimmerman (1918–1970)
   Hans Christian Dadelsen (1948–   )
   Detlev Müller-Siemens (1957–   )
   Wolfgang von Schweinitz (1953–   )
   Hans-Jürgen von Bose (1953–   )
M. Greece
   Yannis Papaioannau (1910–   )
   Dimitris Terzaki (1930–   )
N. Hungary
   Matyas Seiber (1905–1960)
O. Italy
   Mario Peragallo (1910–   )
   Bruno Maderna (1920–1973)
   Luigi Nono (1924–   )
   Sylvano Bussotti (1931–   )
P. Japan
   Ysushi Akutagawa (1925–   )
   Toshiro Mayuzumi (1929–   )
   Toru Takemitsu (1930–   )
   Yori-Aki Matsudaira (1931–   )
Q. Mexico
   Blas Galindo (1910–   )
R. Netherlands
   Henk Badings (1907–   )
   Hans Henkemans (1913–   )
   Luctor Ponse (1914–   )
   Ton de Leeuw (1926–   )
   Peter Schat (1935–   )
S. Norway
   Klaus Egge (1906–1979)
   Gunnar Sonstevold (1912–   )
   Finn Mortensen (1922–   )
   Arne Nordheim (1931–   )

T. Poland
   Kazimierz Serocki (1922–   )
   Tadeusz Baird (1928–   )
   Boguslaw Schaeffer (1929–   )
   Henryk Gorecki (1933–   )
U. Russia
   Tikhon Khrennikov (1913–   )
   Edison Denisov (1929–   )
   Andrei Volkonsky (1933–   )
   Leonid Grabovsky (1935–   )
   Valentin Silvestrov (1937–   )
V. Spain
   Carlos Surinach (1915–   )
W. Switzerland
   Rolf Liebermann (1910–   )
X. Sweden
   Lars-Erik Larsson (1908–   )
   Karl-Birger Blomdahl (1916–1968)
   Ingvar Lindholm (1921–   )
   Bo Nilsson (1937–   )
   Jan W. Morthenson (1940–   )
   Sven-David Sandstrom (1942–   )
   Michael Edlun (1950–   )
Y. United States of America
   Roy Harris (1898–1979)
   Randall Thompson (1899–1984)
   Otto Luening (1900–   )
   Ruth Crawford-Seeger (1901–1953)
   Harry Partch (1901–1974)
   Richard Rodgers (1902–1979)
   Vittorio Giannini (1903–1966)
   Marc Blitzstein (1905–1964)
   Norman Lockwood (1906–   )
   Halsey Stevens (1908–   )
   Samuel Barber (1910–1981)
   William Schuman (1910–   )
   Alan Hovhaness (1911–   )
   Gian Carlo Menotti (1911–   )
   Vladimir Ussachevsky (1911–   )
   Ingolf Dahl (1912–1971)
   Hugo Weisgall (1912–   )
   Norman Dello Joio (1913–   )

Irving Fine (1914–1962)
David Diamond (1915–   )
George Perle (1915–   )
Vincent Persichetti (1915–1987)
Milton Babbitt (1916–   )
Lou Harrison (1917–   )
Ulysses Kay (1917–   )
Leonard Bernstein (1918–   )
William Bergsma (1921–   )
Lukas Foss (1922–   )
Peter Mennin (1923–1983)
Daniel Pinkham (1923–   )
Ned Rorem (1923–   )
William Kraft (1923–   )
Gunther Schuller (1925–   )
Seymour Shifrin (1926–1979)
Earle Brown (1926–   )
Barney Childs (1926–   )
Emma Lou Diemer (1927–   )
Donald Erb (1927–   )
Dominick Argento (1927–   )
Pauline Oliveras (1932–   )
Morton Subotnik (1933–   )
Roger Reynolds (1934–   )
Terry Riley (1935–   )
Steve Reich (1936–   )
David Del Tredici (1937–   )
William Bolcom (1938–   )
John Corigliano (1938–   )
Charles Wuorinen (1938–   )
Barbara Kolb (1939–   )
Ellen Zwilich (1939–   )
Doris Hays (1941–   )
Beth Anderson (1950–   )

Z. Yugoslavia
   Milko Keleman (1924–   )

VII. HISTORIANS AND THEORISTS

Arnold Schoenberg (1874–1951) was known as a teacher and theorist as well as a composer. His most important work, *Harmonielehre* (1911), appeared in English as *Theory of Harmony*, (New York, 1948). In this work, as well as in subsequent English volumes, Schoenberg discusses his theory and aesthetics of music. *Style and Idea* (New York, 1950) and *Structural Functions of Harmony* (New York, 1954) are two volumes among a large number of articles and monographs by Schoenberg.

Igor Stravinsky (1882–1971), while not a teacher, delivered a series of lectures at Harvard. These were subsequently published under the title of *Poetics of Music* (Cambridge, 1947). In them he discussed his own musical aesthetics as well as the musical aesthetics of a number of other composers both past and present. A later series of six volumes under the title of *Conversations with Igor Stravinsky* were written in collaboration with Robert Craft, and discuss all matter of musical questions particularly those concerning modern music.

Rudolf Reti (1885–1957), a Serbian by birth, lived most of his life in the United States and wrote several books, the most important of which was published after his death, *Tonality-Atonality-Pantonality* (New York 1958).

Roger Sessions (1896–1985) has been actively engaged in university teaching for the greater part of his life. His very keen and analytical mind has prompted him to write several books which are the result of his long years of experience as composer and teacher. *The Musical Experience of Composer, Performer, Listener* (Princeton, 1950) and *Reflections on the Music Life in the United States* (1956) are two important works dealing with then current problems in music.

Howard Hanson (1896–1981) was a composer, conductor, and teacher. His influence on the musical life of the United States has been very great, especially because of his position at Eastman School of Music. His book *The Harmonic Materials of Modern Music* (New York, 1960), gives a midcentury view of music theory.

Theodor Wiesengrund Adorno (1903–1969) was a German philosopher, musicologist, and composer. Adorno championed the new composers of the twentieth century, particularly those of the Schoenberg school, and wrote profusely concerning the relation of music and society. Among his many works are *Einleitung in der Musiksoziologie* (Frankfurt, 1949) and the *Philosophie der Neuen Musik* (Tübingen, 1949).

The latter, his most important contribution, an excursion into dialectic, shows how the antagonism of the social condition along with ruling consciousness hinders composers from achieving self-expression.

Felix Salzer (1904–   ), an Austrian-born musical theorist, has been active in America since 1940. His two-volume work, *Structural Hearing, Tonal Coherence in Music* (New York, 1952; an unabridged and corrected edition by Dover Publications, New York, appeared in 1962) is based on Heinrich Schenker's conception of tonality and musical coherence.

Milton Babbitt (1916–   ) was attracted throughout his career to the second Viennese school and its descendents. His writings combine his interests in mathematics and twelve-tone technique, based on vocabulary borrowed from other disciplines. Among them are *The Function of Set Structure in the Twelve-tone System* (1946), *Twelve-tone Invariants as Compositional Determinants* (1960), and *Twelve-tone Rhythmic Structure and the Electronic Medium* (1962).

Leonard B. Meyer (1918–   ) is an American musicologist and aesthetician. A student of the humanities and musical composition, he has written many articles and several books on aesthetic questions. Among his books are *Emotion and Meaning in Music* (Chicago, 1956) and *Music, the Arts and Ideas* (Chicago, 1967). He also collaborated with Grosvenor Cooper on a volume *The Rhythmic Structure of Music* (Chicago, 1960).

George Rochberg (1918–   ), a teacher and composer, has written extensively about music in the twentieth century, especially about twelve-tone or serial music. Many of his essays first appeared in the *Journal of Music Theory* and *Perspectives of New Music*. In 1955 *The Hexachord and its Relation to the Twelve-tone Row* appeared in print. *The Aesthetics of Survival: a Composer's View of Twentieth-century Music* (1984) is a collection of his essays, edited by the composer, William Bolcom.

Iannis Xenakis (1922–   ) has always been interested in the connection between mathematics and music, as reflected in his writings as *Wahrscheinlichkeitstheorie und Musik* (1956), and *Elements of Stochastic Music* (1960–61).

Pierre Boulez (1925–   ) has written on a wide variety of musical topics with an emphasis on twentieth-century music. Most of these essays have appeared in such journals as *The Listener* (England), *Darmstadter Beitrage zur neuen Musik* (Germany), and *Nouvel observateur* (France). In 1978 Boulez became the director of IRCAM, an institute in Paris which specializes in the study of electronic and computer music, and electronic instrument building.

Andrew Porter (1928–   ) is the music critic for the *New Yorker* magazine. As such, his critical reviews are of major consequence, both to contemporary performers and composers. Many of his critical essays have been published in book form.

Paul Klee, "Twittering Machine 1922, Watercolor, pen, and ink, 16 1/4 × 12" Klee's wildly stylized mechanical birds jest with the modern mechanical world in a playful way much as do the composers of experimental and popular music of the twentieth century. This painting, along with others by Klee, prompted Gunther Schuller to write a composition by the same name as part of a larger work, *Seven Studies on Themes of Paul Klee* (1959). (Collection, The Museum of Modern Art, New York, Purchase.)

10
Chronology
of Popular Music of the Twentieth Century

1868 Scott Joplin (1868–1917)

1873 W. C. Handy (1873–1958)

1885 Ferdinand "Jelly Roll" Morton (1885–1941)
Jerome Kern (1885–1945)
Joe "King" Oliver (1885–1938)

1886 Ma Rainey (1886–1939)

1888 Irving Berlin (1888–   )

1892 Cole Porter (1892–1964)

1893 Walter Donaldson (1893–1947)

1894 Bessie Smith (1894–1937)

1898 George Gershwin (1898–1937)

1899 Hoagy Carmichael (1899–1981)
Edward Kennedy "Duke" Ellington (1899–1974)

1900 Louis "Satchmo" Armstrong (1900–1971)

1901 Frederick Loewe (1901–   )

1902 Richard Rodgers (1902–1979)

1903 Earl "Fatha" Hines (1903–   )

1904 Thomas "Fats" Waller (1904–1943)
Glenn Miller (1904–1944)
William "Count" Basie (1904–   )

1905 Tommy Dorsey (1905–1956)

1909 Johnny Mercer (1909–   )
Benjamin "Benny" Goodman (1909–1986)

1915 Billie Holiday (1915–1959)

1916 Harry James (1916–1983)

1917 John "Dizzy" Gillespie (1917–   )
Thelonious Sphere Monk (1917–   )

1918 Allen Jay Lerner (1918–   )

1925 Bill Haley (1925–1981)

1926 Chuck Berry (1926–   )

1928 Burt Bacharach (1928–   )

1940 John Lennon
(1940–1980)
1941 Neil Diamond
(1941–   )
Bob Dylan (1941–   )
Paul Simon (1941–   )
1944 Marvin Hamlisch
(1944–   )
1948 Andrew Lloyd Webber
(1948–   )
1950 Lionel Richie
(1950–   )

10
Popular Music of the Twentieth Century

I. SOCIOCULTURAL INFLUENCES ON POPULAR MUSIC

The first nine chapters of the *Outline History of Music* have dealt with an historical account of the development of the art music of the western world. Besides the countless musical examples which constitute the evidence of such a history, there has always been a comparably vast amount of what, for want of a better term, can be called popular music. Any attempt to define popular music in a strict sense will fail since the border between popular and art music is often indistinguishable. The term "popular" is used here to denote that music which is more immediate in its perception and appreciation, while art music normally demands more study and reflection. Popular music and art music both can evoke responses from the simple and immediate to the complex and analytical. Under no circumstance is the difference between art and popular music to be construed as a difference in quality. At best popular and art designations are only attempts at describing differences of compositional style, performance practice, and function.

Popular music was almost entirely a unnotated music until the nineteenth century. Its record is very fragmentary, depending on two sources; the oral tradition and incorporation in notated art music. Illustrations and accounts of folk song and dance give evidence of the existence of popular music from the earliest times, but it was not until the nineteenth century that any real attempt was made to collect and notate such music.

By the end of the nineteenth century popular folk music was being collected and published, and songs and dances were being written and published for the general public by such composers as Stephen Foster. While unnamed composers continued to create folk music, the establishment of copyright laws to protect composers, along with increased production of sheet music, began to flood the market with quantities of popular tunes. The twentieth century saw the widespread dissemination of popular music through mass printing and the commercial electronic media.

The social and political upheavals resulting from the two world wars, and concomitant technological developments spread popular culture, including music, throughout the world. A tremendous increase in the scope of popular music since 1950 can be attributed to the following: (1) the dissemination of popular music by means of the electronic media; (2) the attractive possibility of business profits generated by the copyright laws; (3) the development of sound recordings of all kinds; (4) the development of television, radio, and motion pictures; and (5) the discovery by business entrepreneurs, of a substantial disposable income controlled by many youth of the world. All of this has resulted in the production of popular music in quantities the world has never before seen.

Without attempting to reconstruct the many details of its development, an account of the popular music of the twentieth century seems justifiable because of its widespread acceptance, sociological significance, and musical implications. It appears that the spread of twentieth-century popular music is of a size and speed that has never before been experienced.

II. FUNCTION OF MUSIC

Many of the functions of popular music are the same as they have been throughout history: to entertain, to be danced to, and to promote love. Some functions, however, are now either greatly intensified or are peculiar to the present day. The first widespread surge of popular music in the twentieth century was that of music for dancing, and the bands that performed this music were known first as dance bands. Today their sounds are referred to as "big band sounds." As the waltz and polka craze in the nineteenth century swept all of the western world, so the foxtrot, the samba, the Charleston, and more recently the twist, the monkey, and disco had their period of ascendency.

After World War II the interest in popular music turned from its dance function to that of entertainment in a concert setting. It was in some ways related to the rebellion of youth. This was represented in songs of protest and ultimately in the emphasis on an escape from reality. This was especially true of some rock music, which employed loud volume, throbbing rhythms, and psychedelic lighting effects. An unfortunate adjunct was the use of drugs, both by performers and audience, to further the escape.

Adulation of performers, as in so many periods of history, became an important element in the success of individual musicians and groups. The adulation of such stars and groups as Frank Sinatra, Elvis Presley, The Beatles, The Grateful Dead, Stevie Wonder, Elton John, and Bruce Springsteen has exceeded that accorded military and political heroes of the past, and has often resulted in mass hysteria.

The use of sound in motion pictures and television, and the more recent development of satellite communications has given music the possibility of reaching a worldwide audience. The universal use of radio, tape, and cassette recordings has made possible the almost constant use of music in all places of work and business. Miniature radio and tape recorders have made music, and especially popular music, an easily portable and nearly constant part of daily life, especially among youth.

III. STYLE AND PERFORMANCE PRACTICE

Popular music of the twentieth century encompasses a great variety of music including folk, gospel, jazz, country and western, rock music, and all their permutations.

It is generally accepted that jazz originated in the late nineteenth and early twentieth century in New Orleans. This occurred because of the mixture of African black along with French and Spanish influences stemming from the Creole and French portions of what had been the Louisiana Purchase. These people treasured their own music and wanted to keep alive the sounds of their origins. This strange amalgamation of cultural differences, which also included the influence of Christian revival music and the use of instruments common to Civil War military bands, resulted in an exotically romantic popular music.

Blues

The term "blues" is difficult in the extreme to define with precision. In the broadest sense it represents a kind of popular music that originated among the black people of the south as an outgrowth of their sorrow songs. The blues have both the ingredients of pain and humor; pain at the many indignities of life one must suffer and sufficient humor to make that pain bearable. They have a common poetic

Scott Joplin (1868–1917), is America's most famous composer of ragtime. The 1974 film, *The Sting,* brought a renewed interest in ragtime as a musical style. Joplin's rag, *The Entertainer,* was one of the biggest popular hits of 1974. In 1972, the first complete performance of his opera *Treemonisha* took place in Atlanta. (The Bettmann Archive)

form, a distinctive scale, and an harmonic progression that are widely but not consistently used. There are times when the only thing that identifies these songs as "blues" is the title, as in "St. Louis Blues." The blues normally utilized a regular twelve-bar pattern with a free interpolation of both words and music. Performers suggested their own personal woes by flatting various pitches of the scale, most often the third, fifth, and seventh.

Blues have existed for so long that they are frequently cited as one of the forerunners of jazz. Although they have gone through several modifications, they remain a vital part of popular music today, particularly under the heading "rhythm and blues."

Ragtime

Ragtime, one of the earliest forms of black popular music, is performed almost exclusively on the piano. The first published "rag" appeared in 1897, from which time it developed concurrently with New Orleans jazz. Unlike many forms of popular music, it has from the beginning been precisely notated, eliminating an essential characteristic of much jazz, namely, improvisation. Its early dissemination was promoted through piano rolls and itinerant musicians. It was frequently in duple meter and in moderate tempos, and the form was rather predictable. Ragtime was characterized by a feeling of strong syncopation, making the weak beat strong or a strong beat weak over a regular rhythmic beat of the percussion. The greatest composer of ragtime was Scott Joplin.

Louis Armstrong (1900–1971) is America's best known jazz musician. His combo, the "Hot Five" was one of the most successful bands of the late 1920s. In his later years he became known as America's Musical Ambassador. One of his great vocal hits was *Hello Dolly* in 1964. (The Bettmann Archive)

New Orleans Jazz

The city of New Orleans is frequently identified as the birthplace of jazz, although it was in reality emerging in other localities as well. Early New Orleans jazz was characterized by a type of free counterpoint most often played by three instruments: clarinet, trombone, and trumpet, with the trumpet as the dominant or "lead" instrument. These instruments were supported by a rhythm section of drums, string bass, and piano or banjo. The music was more or less improvisatory with the trumpet being accompanied by the other instruments in their own variations of the melody.

Dixieland

While earlier jazz was largely the province of blacks and creoles, white bands came on the scene with what is generally known as Dixieland jazz. It was through this movement that jazz went north to Chicago and New York. Dixieland became popular about the time of World War I. It was in 1917 that the first recordings were made of Dixieland jazz. Stimulated by the Dixieland style, young white high school and college students developed what was known as the Chicago style of jazz, usually called two-beat jazz.

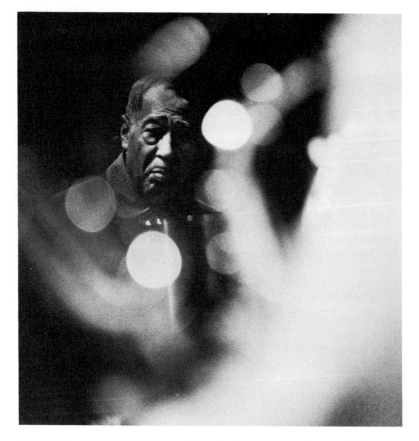

"Duke" Ellington (1899–1974) began his musical career as a ragtime musician. In the 1940s he became a proponent of the swing movement, continuing to conduct a big band. He performed on virtually every continent, and in 1969 he received the Presidential Medal of Freedom. (© Bob Coyle)

Swing

Swing came on the scene in the early thirties, making jazz legitimate for the first time. It introduced a substantially larger band and a four-beat style with more even emphasis on all four beats of the measure. Most of the music was heavily arranged. Benny Goodman, Count Basie, "Duke" Ellington, and Louis Armstrong were among the most prominent practitioners of swing. Included in the big bands were also a number of soloists: Gene Krupa, Fats Waller, and others. The orchestra and soloists, many of them trained instrumentalists, combined to produce the big sounds that typify the style. It is a style that pits the lighter texture of solo instruments against the larger ensemble in much the same manner as the concerto grosso of the seventeenth century.

Bebop

By the end of the thirties swing had become a big business in popular music. As so often happens, there was soon a movement to turn away from the established style which had with time become cliché-ridden. The new style, called "bebop," originated in Kansas City. As a reaction to swing it rejected the set format of the large band, and sought for an outlet for the musicians' personal creativity in small combos. One distinguishing musical characteristic was the use of the flatted fifth. This interval prevailed not only in harmonic structure, but also in the melodic line. This was also known as another "bluenote." The general concept of the music of bebop was that of an excited, improvisatory style with melodic fragments—not a sustained melodic line—and active rhythms.

Cool Jazz

During the fifties, jazz entered a period of calm and melodious understatement in reaction to the intricacies of bebop which immediately preceded it. The new style was referred to as "cool jazz." While there was still a good deal of improvisation, it emphasized long, linear melodies. It was a relaxed and dreamy kind of jazz with a certain amount of advanced harmony and rhythmic writing. Dotted and disconnected rhythms were replaced by legato, predominantly even notes. The melodic rhythm lagged behind the beat rather than pushing ahead as in the bebop styles. Among the leaders of this style were Stan Getz and Miles Davis.

Free Jazz

The atonal innovations of art music encountered the freedom of jazz in the 1960s in a movement called "free jazz." Atonality appeared in concert music almost fifty years earlier. Free jazz led to the disintegration of beat, meter, and symmetry, as it explored the realm of the aleatoric. It also incorporated some aspects of non-western music from such regions as India, Africa, and the Far East. There was an intensity of sound that bordered on the ecstatic, frenetic, and even orgiastic, especially in the later performances of Ornette Coleman and John Coltrane.

The Beatles (Wide World Photos)

Rock

If there was any single revolution in twentieth-century popular music, it began with the introduction of rock and roll. Now more commonly referred to as rock, it can be generally characterized as having an amplified, hard rhythmic beat, and simple, throbbing harmonic patterns. Other sometimes identified characteristics include texts with thinly disguised, and sometimes overt references to sexual activity, social and political rebellion, and, on occasion, the drug culture. With the loud volume of the music (central to the aesthetics of rock), there was no longer any place for acoustic instruments in rock bands. Consequently they were replaced by electric guitars, electric pianos, synthesizers, and countless other electronically controlled instruments. This movement has enjoyed an extended period of success.

Its adherents have explored an unusually wide variety of sounds, some of them so extreme that the music seems to achieve its purpose only through some degree of ugliness and vulgarity.

Country and Western

Country and western music is a uniquely American expression originally based on a romantic vision of rural and western life. Some of those themes continue to be used while more modern examples deal with the vicissitudes of country life. In performance it consists, even today, of a relatively unsophisticated vocal style and simple accompaniments. The vocal line is commonly supported by violin, string bass, and guitar. Nashville, Tennessee has become the mecca of the country western style of folk music. It is possible that the dramatic increase in popularity of country and western music in the last two decades is in part a reaction to the excesses of rock.

Bluegrass

This style of country music springs from the rural areas of the south, especially Kentucky and its neighboring states. Bluegrass depends on the banjo, guitar, and the violin, played in the old-time fiddler fashion. Melodies are derived from Appalachia and adjacent regions of the south, with influence from the folk music of the British Isles.

IV. MUSICAL COMPOSITIONS

In many cases there is no real division between vocal and instrumental compositions in popular music. In many instances vocal and instrumental performances are combined. Song tunes are readily and frequently adapted to become instrumental works, and sometimes they acquire an independent life in the new form.

Popular music by its very nature is not given to large forms. The many forms employed by composers of popular music are marked by their variety. The song is the basic single-movement form and the composite form is a series of varied presentations of the single unit or a mingling of two or more different units. In the last two decades, and even before that in the works of certain composers such as Kenton, Ellington, and Brubeck, forms of longer duration have become much more prevalent.

Comprehensive lists of popular music are beyond the scope of this book. However, the following list of popular music is representative of a much longer list of music that has enriched the lives of many people.

1900–1910
Bill Bailey, Won't You Please Come Home?, Hugie Cannon (1902)
Some of These Days, Shelton Brooks (1910)
Give My Regards to Broadway, George M. Cohan (1904)
1911–1920
Alexander's Ragtime Band, Irving Berlin (1911)
St. Louis Blues, W. C. Handy (1914)
Rock-a-bye Your Baby With a Dixie Melody, Jean Schwartz, Sam Lewis, Joe Young (1918)
1921–1930
April Showers, Louis Silvers, Muddy DeSylva (1921)
Stardust, Hoagy Carmichael, Mitchell Parish (1929)
Ain't Misbehavin', Thomas "Fats" Waller, Harry Brooks, Andy Razaf (1929)
1931–1940
As Time Goes By, Herman Hupfield (1931)
Sophisticated Lady, Edward "Duke" Ellington, Mitchell Parish, Irving Mills (1933)
Over the Rainbow, Harold Arlen, E. Y. Harburg (1939)
How High the Moon, Nancy Hamilton, Morgan Lewis (1940)
1941–1950
Don't Sit Under the Apple Tree, Les Brown, Charlie Tobias, Sam H. Stept (1942)
Sentimental Journey, Bud Green, Les Brown, Ben Homer (1944)
On the Atchison, Topeka and the Santa Fe, Johnny Mercer, Harry Warren (1945)
1951–1960
I Could Have Danced All Night, Alan Jay Lerner, Frederick Loewe (1956)
Seventy-Six Trombones, Meredith Wilson (1957)
Satin Doll, Johnny Mercer, Billy Strayhorn, "Duke" Ellington (1958)
1961–1970
Yesterday, John Lennon, Paul McCartney (1965)
Hello Dolly, Jerry Herman (1963)
Raindrops Keep Fallin' on My Head, Hal David, Burt Bacharach (1969)
Bridge Over Troubled Waters, Simon & Garfunkel (1970)

Simon and Garfunkel (Wide World Photos)

1971–1980
Send in the Clowns, Stephen Sondheim (1973)
Evergreen, Barbara Streisand, Paul Williams (1976)
One, Marvin Hamlisch, Edward Kleban (1975)
Shadows in the Moonlight, Burke & Black (1979)
1981–1989
Memory, Andrew Lloyd Webber, Trevor Numm (1981)
Hello Again, Diamond & Lindgren (1980)
Missing You, Lionel Richie (1984)

Similarly, many albums are representative of the music of certain performers, composers, or styles. Some examples follow.

Swing: Carnegie Hall Concert, "Duke" Ellington (1943)
Bop: Greatest Jazz Concert Ever, Charlie Parker, "Dizzy" Gillespie, Charles Mingus, Bud Powell, Max Roach (1953)
Cool Jazz: King of Blue, Miles Davis (1959) *Take Five,* Dave Brubeck
Modern Jazz: Giant Steps, John Coltrane (1959)
Free Jazz: The Shape of Jazz to Come, Ornette Coleman (1959)
Jazz-Rock: Bitch's Brew, Miles Davis (1969)
Rock: Sgt. Pepper's Lonely Hearts Club Band, Beatles *The Magic of ABBA* (1980)

V. COMPOSERS, ARRANGERS, AND PERFORMERS

Because the majority of those included in popular music were composers, arrangers, and performers, it seems practical to list them in terms of the styles of music with which they were involved. Because of their large number, the authors make no attempt to be inclusive. Only those who seem to be most influential have been listed. A number of these people were involved in more than one style, but they appear where they have had their greatest importance.

Blues:
Huddy (Leadbelly) Ledbetter, Blind Lemon Jefferson, B.B. King, W. C. Handy, Mamie Smith, Ma Rainey, and Bessie Smith
Ragtime:
Scott Joplin, Joseph Lamb, Jelly Roll Morton, Eubie Blake, and Fats Waller
New Orleans Jazz:
W. C. Handy, Jelly Roll Morton, Sidney Bechet, Bunk Johnson, Jack Teagarden, and King Oliver
Dixieland:
Papa Laine, Louis Armstrong, Bix Beiderbecke, Fletcher Henderson, Duke Ellington, "Fatha" Hines
Swing:
Duke Ellington, Wayne King, Guy Lombardo, Woody Herman, Harry James, Tommy Dorsey, Benny Goodman, Gene Krupa, Charlie Barnet, Count Basie, Artie Shaw, and Glenn Miller
Bebop:
Dizzy Gillespie, Thelonious Monk, Lennie Tristano, Charlie Parker, Billy Eckstein, Charlie Mingus, and Art Tatum
Cool Jazz:
Gerry Mulligan, Stan Getz, Lester Young, Lennie Tristano, Miles Davis, Dave Brubeck, and the Modern Jazz Quartet
Free Jazz:
John Coltrane, Ornette Coleman, Miles Davis, John Lewis
Rock:
Bill Haley, Beatles, Jefferson Airplane, The Who, Rolling Stones, Blood Sweat and Tears, Grateful Dead, Stevie Wonder, Elvis Presley, Little Richard, Elton John, Michael Jackson

Country and Western:
Glenn Campbell, Johnny Cash, Charley Pride, Loretta Lynn, Roger Miller, Bobbie Gentry, Ann Murray, Dolly Parton, Kenny Rogers

Bluegrass:
Earl Scruggs, Lester Flatt, William "Bill" Monroe, Osborne Brothers

In addition to the aforementioned jazz and popular performers, following are a number of gifted popular songwriters: Vincent Youmans, Irving Berlin, Hoagy Carmichael, Frederick Loewe, Alan Lerner, Cole Porter, Jerome Kern, George Gershwin, Sammy Cahn, John Lennon, and Burt Bacharach.

Appendix 1
Musical Instruments

I. STRINGS

A. Bowed Strings

Rebec: A stringed instrument introduced into Europe from Arabia around the tenth century. It has a rather long neck with a small round or pear-shaped body, usually with three strings. It is played with a loosely haired bow. It has a nasal timbre. The rebec was an ancestor of modern bowed string instruments.

Viols: They are a large group of bowed string instruments in use from the Gothic through the Renaissance and Baroque periods. The viols differ from the violin family in that (a) they had deeper ribs, (b) the shoulders sloped from the neck, (c) the number of strings was generally six but might be more or less, (d) frets were placed on the fingerboard, (e) the bridge was quite flat, enabling the playing of chords, (f) the viol bow stick was convex and held palm up, and (g) the instruments were held on or between the legs of the performer. The viol tone quality was light, and somewhat nasal. Viols were made in various sizes: bass, tenor, alto, and discant (soprano). The revival of viol playing in the twentieth century has been generally concerned with the tenor instrument which was the model used for solo performance in the works of Baroque composers.

Violins: The modern bowed string instruments date from the early Baroque. The most important members of the family are the violin (soprano), the viola (alto), the violoncello (tenor), and the contrabass or bass viol, the latter taken over from the viol family and often built in that form. The most famous makers were Italians, dating from the seventeenth and eighteenth centuries. Among them were Gaspar da Salo, Amati, Stradivari, and Guarneri, who made Cremona famous as the center for violin construction.

The violin, viola and cello are all four-stringed instruments tuned in fifths. The bass viol retains the tuning in fourths of the viol family. The bow used in playing instruments of the violin family differs from the earlier bow in its curvature in relation to its hair. It is held with the palm down, except for the bass viol, for which both bow styles are still in use. The violin and viola are held on the shoulder, the cello and string bass in a modified vertical position, resting on the floor. The tone of the violin family is of a rich, sweet quality rivaling that of the human voice.

B. Plucked String Instruments

Harp: one of the oldest known instruments. It was used by the civilizations c. 3000 years B.C. It appears in various forms among all folk peoples. The modern instrument (double harp) was invented by Erard in 1810 and is capable, by use of pedals, of a complete chromatic scale of six octaves. While already called for by composers of the 16th century, the harp as a solo and orchestral instrument made its real appearance in the 19th century.

Psaltery: an ancient instrument, found throughout the world in one form or another. It has a flat soundboard over which a number of strings are stretched. The strings are plucked by both hands of the performer.

Lute and Guitar: plucked string instruments that are held in the lap. They have fretted fingerboards of varying lengths and numbers of strings. Strings are fingered with the left hand and plucked by the right. Lutes are characterized by pear-shaped bodies with fingerboards of varying lengths. The guitar is a flat instrument, the body of which in other respects is somewhat in the shape of the violin.

The lute was the most important instrument of the Renaissance. Players of virtuoso capacity encouraged a large literature to be written. The introduction of keyboard instruments resulted in the decline and eventual disappearance of the lute. The guitar, because it was more easily played, became very popular in the seventeenth century and has remained so to the present day. The lute has been revived in the twentieth century due to renewed interest in Renaissance and Baroque music.

Harpsichord: includes a large variety of instruments in which the strings are plucked by a set of plectra attached to key levers. The key levers are arranged like the keys of the modern piano, and when depressed, the plectra pluck the strings, resulting in a sound very much like that of the lute or harp. Harpsichords were built in various shapes and sizes and given various names such as clavicembalo, cembalo, clavecin, virginal, and spinet. It is well to remember that the harpsichord mechanism was not the forerunner of the piano action. It could be regarded more reasonably as a mechanized lute or harp.

C. Struck Strings

Dulcimer: includes a variety of psaltery whose strings are struck by small hammers held in the hand rather than plucked. In this manner it becomes the forerunner of the piano.

Clavichord: a small keyboard string instrument usually in the form of a rectangular box in which metal wedges attached to keys strike the individual strings. The placement of the wedges determine the length of the vibrating strings and, therefore, their individual pitches. The tone is very soft and the instrument was often used in the household for teaching and practice purposes. The clavichord might be thought of as a mechanized dulcimer.

Pianoforte: a popular instrument invented by Cristofori in 1709. It is a string instrument in which the strings are sounded by the striking of a set of felted hammers attached to keys. Improvements in the mechanical construction of the piano have been concerned with the various intricacies of the key and hammer action, the construction of the sounding board, and the frame of the instrument upon which the strings are stretched. The full name of the pianoforte was an indication that this instrument could play both loudly and softly, and indeed could sustain a tone without having to keep the keys depressed. Unlike earlier keyboard instruments, this could be accomplished because of its action and the use of sostenuto and damper pedals.

II. WIND INSTRUMENTS

A. Woodwinds

Flute: one of the oldest and most widespread of all instruments. The flute appears in a variety of shapes and sizes. Both the whistle or recorder type as well as the transverse type were known in earliest times and used simultaneously throughout music history. The transverse type consists of a tube of wood or metal closed at one end, with a side hole across which the player blows. A number of finger holes enable the performer to play the entire chromatic scale. Modern flutes are made of metal and are fitted with a refined mechanism that enables rapid technical performance and accuracy of pitch. In addition to the more common soprano flute there is the very high pitched piccolo, the alto and bass flutes.

Recorders are of the flute family and are fitted with mouthpieces into which the performer blows. They were made of wood and at one time were preferred to the transverse flute which replaced them about 1750. In the twentieth century the recorder was revived with great enthusiasm by the interest in Renaissance and Baroque music. Because of limited range, recorders are made in various sizes and designated as sopranino, soprano, alto, tenor, bass, and contrabass.

Obsolete and folk flutes: the occarina is a globular flute usually made of clay with an embouchure hole and finger holes. The syrinx or pan pipes is a set of individual closed pipes, bound together, which can be sounded by blowing over the open ends.

B. Organ

The organ is a wind instrument consisting of many individual pipes which are activated by wind from a wind chamber. By the use of keys connected to the wind chest, the performer can cause different pipes to speak. Through the various shapes, the addition of metal reeds, and the combination of pipes, tone qualities characteristic of the organ itself and of various orchestral instruments are available. Organs vary in size from the small portative (movable) organ of the Renaissance, consisting of a single set of pipes, to the large nineteenth century instruments with several thousand pipes and several manuals. Other instruments using the principle of the wind organ are the regal, bagpipe, accordion, and harmonium.

C. Reeds

Single Reeds

Clarinet: a cylindrical pipe of wood with a bell-shaped opening at the lower end and a beak-like mouthpiece at the upper end to which is attached a single reed of cane. The breath of the player activates this reed and, with the aid of holes and keys, can produce a wide range of pitches as well as distinctly varied tone colors in the several registers of the instrument. The modern clarinet dates from the early eighteenth century. The fingering mechanism was greatly improved in the nineteenth century. The clarinet is made in several sizes: E flat (very high), B flat (most common), A, E flat alto, B flat bass, and B flat contrabass.

Saxophone: a family of single reed instruments that consists of conical metal pipes. Soprano (B flat), Alto (E flat), Tenor (B flat), Baritone (E flat), and Bass (B flat) constitute the usual members of the family. They were invented by Adolphe Sax in the middle of the nineteenth century. The alto and tenor saxophones are especially used in jazz and symphonic bands. A wide variety of tone qualities is possible with all types of saxophones.

Double Reeds

Oboe: a conical pipe made of wood and fitted with a double reed at the upper end. Its timbre is reedy and nasal. The modern instrument, which made its appearance in the middle of the seventeenth century, is highly mechanized. The reed is held directly by the lips of the performer who, therefore, has considerable control over the tone quality.

English Horn: An alto oboe, longer than the oboe, fitted with a pear-shaped bell at its lower end, and the reed is attached to a bent tube. It produces a rather muffled, soft sound.

Oboe da caccia and oboe d'amore: Baroque alto oboes that have been largely replaced by the English horn. These oboes are occasionally used in the performance of Baroque music.

Shawm: a family of double reed instruments, forerunners of the oboe. Shawm were commonly used until the seventeenth century. The tone was very strident, and the instruments were particularly used for outdoor music. Its mechanization was minimal.

Bassoon: the bass instrument of the modern double reeds. It has not changed materially from its earlier predecessors in shape or fingering. Its long wooden pipe is doubled upon itself enabling the player to finger the instrument with comparative ease despite its great length. It has a large range, and serves as a very agile bass instrument. The contrabassoon can reach the lowest-pitched notes of all orchestral instruments.

Dulzian: the forerunner of the bassoon. It was made in a number of sizes, and differed from the bassoon in that it was made of a single block of wood.

Crumhorn, rauschpfeif, and kortholt: instruments of various sizes and shapes with encapsulated double reeds. The double reed was covered by a wooden cap into which the performer blew. The resulting wind pressure activated the reed. The range of these instruments was very limited, since they could not be overblown.

D. Wind Instruments with Cupped Mouthpieces (Brass Instruments)

These instruments, originally made of wood or animal horns, were later made of various metals. The instruments were fitted with cupped mouthpieces; the performer set the column of air into vibration with the lips pressed against the cupped shape of the mouthpiece. The single column of air could only sound the natural overtones of the basic pitch of the pipe. Early instruments solved this problem in two ways. One was by boring holes in the pipe which could be covered or opened as in a flute, and the other was by the use of a slide mechanism in metal trumpets and trombones. The introduction of valves in the nineteenth century enabled all brass instruments to play the entire chromatic scale.

Trumpet: the high pitched metal tube with a cupped mouthpiece comes pitched variously: B flat, A, E flat, and C. By the addition of three valves, either piston or rotary, the modern trumpet, with its brilliant tone, has become a versatile instrument. The cornet is a variant of the trumpet. Its shorter length and longer conical section give it a less brilliant tone than that of the trumpet.

Trombone: a lower pitched brass instrument most generally fitted with a slide mechanism, which enables the performer to shorten or lengthen the tubing and thereby play the entire chromatic scale. It has maintained its form since the fifteenth century. The predecessors of trombones were known as sackbuts and had a smaller and less brilliant tone quality due to the smaller bore of the tube and mouthpiece. Two sizes of modern trombones are generally in use today, the tenor and bass. Some use is also made of a valve trombone in brass bands.

Tuba: the largest and deepest sounding instruments of the brass family. Conically bored, it is played with a cup-shaped mouthpiece. Tubas come in various sizes, allowing them to play in different ranges. The most common are the tenor, bass, and double bass.

Zink or Cornetto: wooden tube with a cup-shaped mouthpiece and fitted with finger holes. These Renaissance and Baroque instruments were made in various sizes: soprano, alto, tenor, and bass. The latter was shaped like a letter "S" and called a serpent. It continued to be used into the nineteenth century, when it was replaced by the modern valved tuba.

Horn (French Horn): a conical metal tube wound into a spiral and played with a funnel-shaped mouthpiece. Because of its narrow bore, its playable natural tones enabled it to be one of the most versatile brass instruments even before the invention of valves. Its tone is rich and suited to solo work. It blends with other brasses and with the woodwinds.

III. PERCUSSION

A. Indefinite Pitch

Drums, tabor, and tambourin: these instruments are found among all peoples in all shapes, sizes, and in all periods of history. Those of indefinite pitch vary from very high (snare drum) to very low (bass drum). All consist of wooden or metal frames over which membranes are stretched. They are played by striking with wooden or metal sticks or by the player's hand.

Cymbals, Gong, Castanets, Triangle, Tam tam, and others: along with numerous other sound generators, these are all instruments of a single fixed pitch or sound quality made of metal or wood. Some are struck with hammers or rods as in the case of the Gong and Triangle. Others are self-sounding like the castanets or cymbals.

B. Definite Pitch

Timpani (Kettledrums): the name given to the drum whose head is stretched over a large metal, kettle-like form. They can be tuned within a limited range. They are the most important orchestral percussion instruments.

Glockenspiel, Bells, Xylophone, Marimba, Celeste, and others: these tuned bars of metal or wood form several chromatic octaves and can be played with various types of hammers: wood, metal, or rubber. The celeste is played by means of a keyboard.

Appendix 2
Recordings and Musical Examples Cited in the Text

(For more complete bibliographical information on the following sources please refer to the introduction, page xiv.)

CHAPTER 1: ANCIENT SOURCES OF WESTERN MUSIC

Rec. 1.1: 52 works of non-western cultures
HMS, vol. 1, pp. 13–38
Rec. RCA LM—6057

Further examples of recorded non-western music can be found in the UNESCO collections of Music in the Orient and Africa issued under the labels of Bärenreiter-Musicaphon and Phillips. (See Schwann Foreign Catalog.) Numerous other examples can be found under the Folkways label.

CHAPTER 2: ROMANESQUE – EARLY MIDDLE AGES (500–1100)

Rec. 2.1: Byzantine Music
HMS, vol. 2, p. 2
Rec. RCA, LM-6015

Rec. 2.2: *Ambrosian psalmellus for Quadragesima:* Redde mihi
TEM, p. 3
Rec. HSE-9100

Rec. 2.3: Ambrosian chant: Verse Eructavit
HAM, p. 11
Rec. OR-349

Rec. 2.4: Gallican Improperia for Good Friday: Popule meus
TEM, p. 8
Rec. HSE-9100

Rec. 2.5: Mozarabic Antiphon for Easter: Gaudete populi
TEM, p. 12
Rec. HSE-9100

Rec. 2.6: Gregorian hymn for Whitsunday: Veni Creator Spiritus
TEM, p. 16
Rec. HSE-9100

Rec. 2.7: Gregorian chant: Gradual: Haec dies
HAM, p. 12
Rec. OR-349

Monophonic Mass

Rec. 2.8: First Mass for Christmas
Liber Usualis
Rec. DGG, ARC-198153

Antiphon

Rec. 2.9: *Laus Deo Patri* and *Psalm 113*, Laudate pueri
MM, p. 3
Rec. HS-9038

Rec. 2.10: *Psalm 146* with Antiphon
HAM, p. 11
Rec. OR-349

Alleluia

Rec. 2.11: *Vidimus stellam*
MM, p. 6
Rec. HS-9038

Rec. 2.12: *Alleluia:* Angelus Domini
HAM, p. 12
Rec. OR-349

Trope

Rec. 2.13: *Agnus Dei*
MM, p. 18
Rec. HS-9038

Rec. 2.14: *Kyrie Jhesu dulcissime*, Fronciaco
TEM, p. 66
Rec. HSE-9101

Rec. 2.15: Kyrie-Trope: *Omnipotens*
HAM, p. 13
Rec. OR-349

Sequence

Rec. 2.16: *Victimae Paschali*
MM, p. 8
Rec. HS-9038

Rec. 2.17: *Rex caeli, Domine*
MM, p. 16
Rec. HS-9038

Rec. 2.18: *Alleluia: Dominus in Sina,* with Sequence *Christus hunc diem,* Balbulus
HAM, p. 13
Rec. OR-349

Conductus

Rec. 2.19: *Song of the Ass*
Christo psallat
Beata viscera
Sol oritur
HAM, p. 14
Rec. OR-349

Secular Monody

Rec. 2.20: *O Admirabile Veneris*
HMS, vol. 2, p. 25
Rec. RCA, LM-6015

Rec. 2.21: Sequence: *Sancti Spiritu avidit nobis gratia*
HMS, vol. 2, p. 21
Rec. RCA, LM-6015-2

Rec. 2.22: Sequence: *Victimae paschali laudes*
HAM, p. 13
Rec. OR-349

Rec. 2.23: *Alma redemptoris mater*
HAM, p. 70
Rec. Plei-251

CHAPTER 3: GOTHIC – LATE MIDDLE' AGES (ARS ANTIQUA-ARS NOVA)

Canzo

Rec. 3.1: *Be m'an perdut,* Bernart de Ventadorn
TEM, p. 27
Rec. HSE-9100

Rec. 3.2: *Reis glorios*, Guiraut de Bornelh
HAM, p. 15
Rec. OR-349

Bar Form

Rec. 3.3: *Nu al'rest*, Walther von der Vogelweide
HAM, p. 18
Rec. OR-350

Rec. 3.4: *Pour mon coeur* (rotrouenge)
HAM, p. 17
Rec. OR-349

Rec. 3.5: *C'est la fin* (virelai)
HAM, p. 17
Rec. OR-349

Rec. 3.6: *Or la truix* (virelai, trouvère song)
MM, p. 11
Rec. HS-9038

Rec. 3.7: *Gran dereit'*, Alfonso El Sabio (cantiga)
TEM, p. 33
Rec. HSE-9100

Rec. 3.8: *Ogne homo* (lauda)
TEM, p. 37
Rec. HSE-9100

Rec. 3.9: *Ey ich sach in dem trone* (lai)
HMS, vol. 2, p. 32; OM, p. 14
Rec. RCA, LM-6015-2

Rec. 3.10: *Espris d'ire*, Guillaume le Vinier (lai)
HAM, p. 17
Rec. OR-350

Rec. 3.11: *Hec dies*, attributed to Leoninus (organum with three clausulae)
HAM, p. 27
Rec. OR-351

Rec. 3.12: *Alleluya (Nativitas)*, Perotin (organum)
MM, p. 22
Rec. HS-9038

Rec. 3.13: *Viderunt omes*, Leonin (organum duplum)
TEM, p. 41
Rec. HSE-9100

Rec. 3.14: *Domino,* School of Notre Dame (clausula)
HAM, p. 25
Rec. OR-351

Rec. 3.15: *Hec Dies* (clausulae)
HAM, p. 30
Rec. OR-351

Rec. 3.16: *De castitatis thalamo* (conductus)
MM, p. 31
Rec. HS-9038

Rec. 3.17: *Hac in anni janua* (three-voice conductus)
HAM, p. 41
Rec. OR-351

Rec. 3.18: *En non Diu! Quant voi; Eius in Oriente* (Motet of the Notre Dame School)
MM, p. 27
Rec. HS-9038

Rec. 3.19: *Ave gloriosa mater-Ave Virgo-Domino* (thirteenth century motet)
TEM, p. 46
Rec. HSE-9100

Rec. 3.20: *Aucun-Lonc tans—Annuntiantes,* Petrus de Cruce (motet)
HAM, p. 36
Rec. OR-351

Rec. 3.21: *O Maria-Virgo-Davidica* (isorhythmic motet)
HMS, vol. 2, p. 53
Rec. RCA, LM-6015-1

Rec. 3.22: *S'il estoit nulz,* Machaut (isorhythmic motet)
HAM, p. 46
Rec. OR-437

Rec. 3.23: *Sumer is icumen in* (rota)
HAM, p. 44; OM, p. 17
Rec. OR-437

Rec. 3.24: *Chi più le vuol sapere,* Francesco Landini (ballata)
MM, p. 40
Rec. HS-9038

Rec. 3.25: *Notes pour moi,* Anthonello de Caserta (ballade)
TEM, p. 83
Rec. HSE-9101

Rec. 3.26: *Io son un pellegrin,* Giovanni da Florentia (ballata)
HAM, p. 54
Rec. OR-437

Rec. 3.27: *Si je chante main* (chace)
HMS, vol. 3, p. 13
Rec. RCA, LM-6016-1

Rec. 3.28: *Con brachi assai,* Giovanni da Firenze (caccia)
TEM, p. 76
Rec. HSE-9101

Rec. 3.29: *Tosto che l'alba,* Ghirardello da Firenze (caccia)
HAM, p. 55
Rec. OR-437

Ex: 3.30 *Nel mezzo a sei paon,* Giovanni da Cascia (madrigal)
HMS, vol. 3, p. 19
Rec. RCA, LM-6016-1

Ex: 3.31 *Non al suo amante,* Jacopo da Bologna (madrigal)
HAM, p. 52
Rec. OR-437

Ex: 3.32 *Messe de Nostre Dame,* Machaut
Kalmus Edition
Rec. DG, ARC-2533054

Ex: 3.33 *Agnus Dei,* Machaut (mass movement)
MM, p.38; NS, p. 3
Rec. HS-9038

Ex: 3.34 *Agnus Dei* from the *Mass of Tournai*
TEM, p. 62
Rec. HSE-9101

Ex: 3.35 *Et in terra pax,* Johannes Ciconia (mass movement)
HAM, p. 59
Rec. OR-438

Ex: 3.36 Four Dances
HMS, vol. 2, p. 43
Rec. RCA, LM-6015-1

Ex: 3.37 Instrumental Motet, *In seculum longum*
TEM, p. 54
Rec. HSE-9100

Ex: 3.38 Organ paraphrase of a Kyrie
TEM, p. 72
Rec. HSE-9101

Ex: 3.39 *Lamento di Tristan, with Rotta, Saltarello* (estampie)
HAM, p. 63
Rec. OR-438

Ex: 3.40 *Estampie*
MM, p. 33
Rec. HS-9038

Ex: 3.41 *English Dance* (estampie)
HAM, p. 43
Rec. OR-351

Ex: 3.42 *Viderunt omnes* (organum duplum)
TEM, p. 41
Rec. HSE-9100

Ex: 3.43 *Sederunt principes* (organum)
Universal, ed.
Rec. Van., HM-1

Ex: 3.44 *Le jeu de Robin et de Marion*
EM, p. 16
Rec. Turn., 34439

Ex: 3.45 Ten Secular Works
Guillaume de Machaut, Musikalische Werke
Breitkopf and Härtel, vol. 1 and 3
Rec. DGG, ARC-2533054

Ex: 3.46 *Je puis trop bien* (ballade)
HAM, p. 48
Rec. OR-437

Ex: 3.47 *Amar si le alti tue gentil costumi* (madrigal)
HMS, vol. 3, p. 21
Rec. RCA, LM-6016-1

Ex: 3.48 *Sy dolce non sono* (madrigal)
HAM, p. 57
Rec. OR-437

CHAPTER 4: RENAISSANCE (1400-1600)

Musical Forms

Isorhythmic Motet
Rec. 4.1: *Veni Sancte Spiritus,* Dunstable
TEM, p. 87
Rec. HSE-9101

Motet
Rec. 4.2: *Parce, Domine,* Obrecht
MM, p. 55
Rec. HS-9038

Rec. 4.3: *Tu pauperum refugium,* des Prez
HAM, p. 92
Rec. Plei-252

Rec. 4.4: *Tristis est anima mea,* Lassus
MM, p. 78
Rec. HS-9039

Rec. 4.5: *Magnificat octavi toni,* C. Morales
TEM, p. 108
Rec. HSE-9101

Rec. 4.6: *Sicut cervus,* Palestrina
HAM, p. 153
Rec. Plei-255

Polychoral Motet
Rec. 4.7: *Laudate Dominum,* Hassler
TEM, p. 138
Rec. HSE-9101

Hymn
Rec. 4.8: *Ave maris stella,* Dufay
SS, p. 63
Rec. Tel, S-9439

Rec. 4.9: *Beata de Genetrix,* Damett
HAM, p. 69
Rec. OR-438

Chorale
Rec. 4.10: *Komm, Gott Schöpfer, heiliger Geist,* Johann Walter
TEM, p. 120
Rec. HSE-9101

Rec. 4.11: *Aus tiefer Not,* Johann Walter
HAM, p. 115
Rec. Plei-253

Psalms
Rec. 4.12: *Mon Dieu me paist,* Goudimel
TEM, p. 126
Rec. HSE-9101

Rec. 4.13: Two Settings of *Psalm 35,* Goudimel and Claude le Jeune
HAM, p. 135
Rec. Plei-254

Anthem
Rec. 4.14: Verse Anthem: *This is the Record of John,* Gibbons
HAM, p. 195
Rec. Plei-256

Rec. 4.15: Anthem: *Heare the voyce and prayer of thy servants,* Tallis
TEM, p. 13
Rec. HSE-9101

Rec. 4.16: Verse Anthem: *Christ rising again,* Byrd
HAM, p. 165
Rec. Plei-255

Rec. 4.17: Anthem: *When David heard,* Tomkins
HAM, p. 191
Rec. Plei-256

Frottola
Rec. 4.18: *O mia cieca e dura sorte,* Cara
TEM, pp. 97 and 99
Rec. HSE-9101

Rec. 4.19: *Non vol aqua,* Tromboncini
HAM, p. 97
Rec. Plei-252

Madrigal
Rec. 4.20: *S'io parto, i'moro,* Marenzio
MM, p. 100
Rec. HS-9039

Rec. 4.21: *Thyrsis, sleepest thou?* Bennet
MM, p. 109
Rec. HS-9039

Rec. 4.22: *Io pur respiro,* Gesualdo
HAM, p. 182
Rec. Plei-256

Rec. 4.23: *Voi ve n'andat' al cielo,* Arcadelt
HAM, p. 141
Rec. Plei-254

Rec. 4.24: *Hark, all ye lovely saints,* Weelkes
HAM, p. 193
Rec. Plei-256

French Chanson
Rec. 4.25: *Adieu m'amour*, Binchois
MM, p. 48
Rec. HS-9038

Rec. 4.26: *Pour ung plaisir*, Créquillon
MM, p. 64
Rec. HS-9038

Rec. 4.27: *l'Alouette*, Janequin
HAM, p. 109
Rec. Plei-253

Polyphonic Lied
Rec. 4.28: *Oho, so geb' der Mann ein'n Pfenning*, Senfl
TEM, p. 177
Rec. HSE-9102

Rec. 4.29: *Zwischen Berg und tiefem Tal*, Isaac
HAM, p. 91
Rec. Plei-252

Quodlibet
Rec. 4.30: *Fricassée*, anon.
TEM, p. 170
Rec. HSE-9102

Rec. 4.31: *Veni sancte spiritus, Veni creator spiritus*, Finck
HAM, p. 84
Rec. Plei-251

Ayre
Rec. 4.32: *My thoughts are winged with hope*, Dowland
TEM, p. 189
Rec. HSE-9102

Rec. 4.33: *Stay, cruel, stay*, Danyel
HAM, p. 184
Rec. Plei-256

Miscellaneous Secular Forms
Rec. 4.34: Villancico: *Soy contento y vos servido*, Juan del Encina
TEM, p. 94
Rec. HSE-9101

Rec. 4.35: Meistersinger Melody: *Gesangweise*, Hans Sachs
TEM, p. 105
Rec. HSE-9101

Rec. 4.36: Virelai: *Ma bouche rit,* Ockeghem
HAM, p. 79
Rec. Plei-251

Rec. 4.37: Rondeau: *De plus en plus,* Binchois
HAM, p. 74
Rec. Plei-251

Composite Forms

Mass

Rec. 4.38: Cantus firmus Mass on a secular tune:
Missa, L'Homme armé, Kyrie I and II, la Rue
HAM, p. 95
Rec. Plei-252

Rec. 4.39: Cantus firmus Mass on a secular tune:
Missa, Se la face ay pale, Kyrie I, Dufay
MM, p. 43
Rec. HS-9038

Rec. 4.40: Cantus firmus Mass on a plainsong:
Missa Pange Lingua, des Prez
Das Chorwerk, vol. 1, Moseler Verlag
Rec. MCA-2507

Rec. 4.41: Parody Mass: *Missa Veni sponsa Christi, Agnus Dei,* Palestrina
MM, p. 86
Rec. HS-9039

Rec. 4.42: *Missa Papae Marcelli,* Palestrina
Eulenberg, ed.
Rec. DDG ARC-198182

Ricercar

Rec. 4.43: *Ricercar No. 7,* Willaert
HMS, vol. 4, p. 51
Rec. RCA, LM-6029-1

Rec. 4.44: *Ricercar arioso,* Andrea Gabrieli
HMS, vol. 4, p. 61
Rec. RCA, LM-6029-1

Rec. 4.45: *Ricercar,* Cavazzoni
HAM, p. 121
Rec. Plei-253

Canzona
Rec. 4.46: *Canzona francese deta Pour ung plaisir,* A. Gabrieli
MM, p. 64
Rec. HS-9038

Rec. 4.47: *Canzona,* Maschera
HAM, p. 201
Rec. Plei-256

In Nomine
Rec. 4.48: *In nomine,* Gibbons
TEM, p. 202
Rec. HSE-9102

Toccata
Rec. 4.49: *Toccata Quinta, Secondo Tuono,* Merulo
TEM, p. 152
Rec. HSE-9102

Rec. 4.50: *Toccata,* Merulo
HAM, p. 168
Rec. Plei-255

Fantasia
Rec. 4.51: *Three part Fantasia, No. 3,* Gibbons
HMS, vol. 4, p. 53
Rec. RCA, LM-6029-1

Rec. 4.52: *Fantasia in Echo,* Sweelinck
HAM, p. 209
Rec. Plei-256

Prelude
Rec. 4.53: *Praeludium,* Bull
HAM, p. 205
Rec. Plei-256

Variation
Rec. 4.54: *Loth to depart,* Farnaby
MM, p. 115
Rec. HS-9039

Rec. 4.55: *Goe from my window,* Munday
HAM, p. 204
Rec. Plei-256

Rec. 4.56: *Diferencias sobra O Gloriosa Domina,*
Luis de Narvaez
HAM, p. 130
Rec. Plei-254

Dance Forms

Rec. 4.57: *Pavana for the virginal,* John Bull
TEM, p. 161
Rec. HSE-9102

Rec. 4.58: *Passamezzo d'Italie,* anon.
TEM, p. 194
Rec. HSE-9102

Rec. 4.59: *Der Prinzen-Tanz; Proportz,* anon.
MM, p. 74
Rec. HS-9038

Rec. 4.60: *Paduan and Intrada,* Puerl
HMS, vol. 4, p. 51
Rec. RCA, LM-6029-1

Composite Forms

Rec. 4.61: *Three Dances,* Gervaise
HAM, p. 148
Rec. Plei-254

Composers

John Dunstable

Rec. 4.62: *O rosa bella*
HAM, p. 65
Rec. Plei-251

Rec. 4.63: Motet: *Sancta Maria*
HAM, p. 66
Rec. Plei-251

Guillaume Dufay

Rec. 4.64: *Ave Regina Coelorum*
HMS, vol. 3, p. 42
Rec. RCA, LM-6016-2

Gilles Binchois

Rec. 4.65: *Filles a marier*
HMS, vol. 3, p. 45
Rec. RCA, LM-6016-2

Johannes Ockeghem

Rec. 4.66: Chanson: *Fors seulement*
Collected Works, Breitkopf and Härtel
Rec. M. H.-1003A

Rec. 4.67: Mass: *Fors seulement*
Collected Works, Breitkopf and Härtel
Rec. M. H.-1003A

Rec. 4.68: *Sanctus* from *Missa Prolationum*
MM, p. 51
Rec. HS-9038

Rec. 4.69: Virelai: *Ma maîtresse*
HAM, p. 78
Rec. Plei-251

Josquin des Prez
Rec. 4.70: Frottola: *El Grillo*
HMS, vol. 3, p. 55
Rec. RCA, LM-6016-2

Rec. 4.71: Chanson: *Faulte d'argent*
HAM, p. 93
Rec. Plei-252

Rec. 4.72: Motet: *Tribulatio et angustia*
HMS, vol. 3, p. 58
Rec. RCA LM-6016-2

Rec. 4.73: Motet: *Ave Maria*
MM, p. 58
Rec. HS-9038

Heinrich Isaac
Rec. 4.74: *Missa Carminum*
Das Chorwerk, vol. 7, Moseler Verlag
Rec. None, 71084

Rec. 4.75: Polyphonic Lied: *Innsbruck, ich muss dich lassen*
HMS, vol. 3, p. 75
Rec. RCA, LM-6016-1

Jacob Obrecht
Rec. 4.76: Motet: *Si oblitus fuero*
HMS, vol. 3, p. 51
Rec. RCA, LM-6016-2

Rec. 4.77: Motet: *Pater Noster*
HAM, p. 80
Rec. Plei-251

Adrian Willaert

Rec. 4.78: *Ricercar No. 7*
HMS, vol. 4, p. 51
Rec. RCA, LM-6029-2

Rec. 4.79: Motet: *Victimae paschali laudes*
HAM, p. 116
Rec. Plei-253

Ludwig Senfl

Rec. 4.80: Polyphonic Lied; *Ach, Elslein, liebes Elslein*
Antiqua Chorbuch, Teil II, Edition Schott, 4256, p. 82
Rec. M. H.-929T

Rec. 4.81: Polyphonic Lied: *Da Jakob nu das Kleid ansah*
HAM, p. 114
Rec. Plei-253

Thomas Tallis

Rec. 4.82: Motet: *Adeste nunc propitius*
HMS, vol. 4, p. 34
Rec. RCA, LM-6029-2

Rec. 4.83: Responsorium: *Audivi vocem*
HAM, p. 137
Rec. Plei-254

Jacobus Clemens

Rec. 4.84: Motet: *Vox in Rama*
HAM, p. 134
Rec. Plei-254

Antonio de Cabezon

Rec. 4.85: Variations: *Diferencias Cavallero*
HAM, p. 145
Rec. Plei-254

Andrea Gabrieli

Rec. 4.86: *Canzona Francese deta Pour ung plaisir*
MM, p. 64
Rec. HS-9038

Rec. 4.87: Prelude: *Intonazione settimo tono*
HAM, p. 146
Rec. Plei-254

Philippe de Monte

Rec. 4.88: Mass: *Benedicta es*
HMS, vol. 4, p. 24
Rec. RCA, LM-6029-1

Rec. 4.89: Parody Mass: *Missa super Cara la vita*
HAM, p. 160
Rec. Plei-255

Giovanni Pierluigi Palestrina
Rec. 4.90: Madrigal: *Alla riva del Tebro*
HAM, p. 155
Rec. Plei-255

Rec. 4.91: *Missa Aeterna Christi munera*
Eulenberg, ed., AMA, p. 27
Rec. DGG ARC 2533322

Rec. 4.92: Motet: *Sicut cervus*
HAM, p. 153
Rec. Plei-255

Roland de Lassus
Rec. 4.93: Mass: *Ecce nunc benedicite Dominum*
Breitkopf and Härtel, ed.
Rec. None-71053

Rec. 4.94: Chanson: *Bon jour mon couer*
HAM, p. 159
Rec. Plei-255

Rec. 4.95: *Penitential Psalm III*
HAM, p. 157
Rec. Plei-255

William Byrd
Rec. 4.96: Motet: *Ego sum panis vivus*
MM, p. 91
Rec. HS-9039

Rec. 4.97: Motet: *Non vos relinquam*
HAM, p. 164
Rec. Plei-255

Tomás Luis de Victoria
Rec. 4.98: *Missa Quarti Toni*
Breitkopf and Härtel
Rec. M. H.-612H

Rec. 4.99: Motet: *O vos omnes*
HAM, p. 163
Rec. Plei-255

Re. 4.100: Motet: *O Domine Jesu*
HMS, vol. 4, p. 23
Rec. RCA, LM-6029-1

Luca Marenzio
Rec. 4.101: Madrigal: *Scendi dal Paradiso*
HMS, vol. 4, p. 14
Rec. RCA, LM-6029-1

Rec. 4.102: Madrigal: *Madonna mia gentil*
HAM, p. 173
Rec. Plei-255

Giovanni Gabrieli
Rec. 4.103: from the Sacrae Symphoniae: *In ecclesiis*
HAM, p. 175
Rec. Plei-255

Rec. 4.104: *Sonata pian'e forte*
HAM, p. 198
Rec. Plei-256

Thomas Morley
Rec. 4.105: Madrigal: *Thyrsis and Milla*
HMS, vol. 4, p. 48
Rec. RCA, LM-6029-2

Rec. 4.106: Ballett: *My bonny lass*
HAM, p. 180
Rec. Plei-256

Don Carlo Gesualdo
Rec. 4.107: Madrigal: *Moro lasso*
TEM, p. 181
Rec. HSE-9102

Rec. 4.108: Madrigal: *Io pur respiro*
HAM, p. 182
Rec. Plei-256

Hans Leo Hassler
Rec. 4.109: Polyphonic Lied: *Ach Schatz*
HAM, p. 187
Rec. Plei-256

Rec. 4.110: Motet: *Quia vidisti me*
HAM, p. 186
Rec. Plei-256

Claudio Monteverdi
Rec. 4.111: Madrigal: *Amor*
Ricordi: Complete Works
Rec. DGG. ARC 2533146

Thomas Weelkes
Rec. 4.112: Madrigal: *O care thou wilt dispatch me*
HMS, vol. 4, p. 17
Rec. RCA, LM-6029-1

CHAPTER 5: BAROQUE (1575-1750)

Music for Voices

Recitativo Accompagnato
Rec. 5.1: *Comfort Ye* from *Messiah,* Handel
NS, p. 117
Rec. Col. MS-6928

Recitativo Secco
Rec. 5.2: *Al valor del mio brando* from *Rinaldo,* Handel
MM, p. 189
Rec. HS-9040

Aria
Rec. 5.3: *Cara sposa* from *Rinaldo,* Handel
MM, p. 189
Rec. HS-9040

Rec. 5.4: *Every Valley* from *Messiah,* Handel
NS, p. 120
Rec. Col. MS6928

Arioso
Rec. 5.5: *O jour affreux* from *Dardanus,* Rameau
HMS, vol. 5, p. 23
Rec. RCA, LM-6030

Rec. 5.6: *Ach Golgotha,* from the *St. Matthew Passion,*
J. S. Bach
MM, p. 226
Rec. HS-9040

Chorus
Rec. 5.7: Scene from *Venus and Adonis,* Blow
L'Oiseau Lyre Press
HMS, vol. 5
Rec. RCA, LM-6030-2

Motet
Rec. 5.8: *Ich lasse dich nicht*, J. C. Bach
Moseler Verlag
HMS, vol. 5
Rec. RCA, LM-6030-1

Spiritual Concerto
Rec. 5.9: Sacred Cantata: *O Herr, hilf*, Schütz
MM, p. 135
Rec. HS-9040

Rec. 5.10: Chorale concerto: *Erschienen ist der herrliche Tag*, Schein
TEM, p. 217
Rec. HSE-9102

Rec. 5.11: Verse Anthem: *Hear, O Heavens*, Humfrey
HMS, vol. 5, p. 38
Rec. RCA, LM-6030-2

Solo Song
Rec. 5.12: *Meine Seufzer, meine Klagen*, Erlebach
HMS, vol. 5, p. 18
Rec. RCA, LM-6031-1

Italian Opera
Rec. 5.13: *Orfeo*, Monteverdi
Bärenreiter, ed. No. 2031a
Rec. DGG ARC. 270015

Rec. 5.14: Opera buffa: *La Serva Padrona*, Pergolesi
Ricordi, ed.
Rec. None. 71043

Rec. 5.15: Opera seria: *Giulio Cesare*, Handel
Aria and Recitative; *V'adoro, pupille*
HMS, vol. 5, p. 17
Rec. RCA, LM-6030-1

French Opera
Rec. 5.16: *Scene infernale* from *Alceste*, Lully
HMS, vol. 5, p. 20
Rec. RCA, LM-6030-2

Rec. 5.17: *Séjour de l'éternelle paix* from *Castor et Pollux*, Rameau
MM, p. 172
Rec. HS-9040

Rec. 5.18: *Chaconne* from the opera-ballet, *Les Fetes Vénitiennes*, Campra
TEM, 270
Rec. HSE-9103

English Opera

Rec. 5.19: *Dido and Aeneas,* Purcell
Oxford University Press, Piano Score
Rec. DGG, ARC-198424

German Opera

Rec. 5.20: *Ach! Nero ist nicht Nero mehr,* from *Octavia,* Keiser
HMS, vol. 5, p. 26
Rec. RCA, LM-6030-2

Rec. 5.21: *Hoffe noch* from *Croesus,* Keiser
TEM, p. 277
Rec. HSE-9103

Oratorio

Rec. 5.22: *Jephte,* Carissimi
GMB, p. 244
Rec. M. H.-3137H

Rec. 5.23: *Draw the tear from hopeless love,* from *Solomon,* Handel
MM, p. 200
Rec. HS-9040

Rec. 5.24: *Via, via, false Sirene* from *Rappresentazione di Anima e di Corpo,*
Cavalieri
TEM, p. 208
Rec. HSE-9102

Passion Music

Rec. 5.25: *St. Matthew Passion,* J. S. Bach
Eulenburg, ed.
Rec. DGG, ARC-2712001

Cantata

Rec. 5.26: *Laudate Dominum,* Buxtehude
Bärenreiter, ed.
Rec. None. 71258

Rec. 5.27: *Wachet Auf,* Cantata No. 140, J. S. Bach
N. S., p. 219
Rec. None. 71029

Rec. 5.28: *Ein feste Burg,* Cantata No. 80, J. S. Bach
OM, p. 149
Rec. Sera. S-60248

Rec. 5.29: Chorale and Chorus from *Christ lag in Todesbanden,* Cantata No. 4,
J. S. Bach
MM, pp. 208, 215
Rec. HS-9040

Rec. 5.30: Recitative and aria, *Amor tu sei,* from *Stravaganze d' Amore,* Marcello
TEM, p. 304
Rec. HSE-9103

Mass
Rec. 5.31: *Messe de Minuit,* Charpentier
Concordia Publishing House
Rec. ANG-S-36528

Instrumental Compositions

Toccata
Rec. 5.32: *Toccata in e minor for Organ,* Pachelbel
MM, p. 156
Rec. HS-9039

Prelude
Rec. 5.33: *Prelude and Fugue in E flat major for Organ,*
J. S. Bach
Peters, ed.
Rec. Col. MS-6748

Rec. 5.34: *Toccata and Fugue in d minor for Organ,*
J. S. Bach
Peters, ed.
Rec. Col. MS-6261

Rec. 5.35: *Prelude and Fugue in c minor* from *Das Wohltemperierte Klavier,*
J. S. Bach
NS, p. 207
Rec. DGG, 2714004

Ricercar
Rec. 5.36: *Ricercar dopo il Credo,* Frescobaldi
MM, p. 144
Rec. HS-9039

Fugue
Rec. 5.37: *Das Wohltemperierte Klavier,* J. S. Bach
OM, p. 182; AMA, p. 100
Rec. DGG, 2714004

Rec. 5.38: *Contrapunctus III,* from *Kunst der Fuge,*
J. S. Bach
MM, p. 230
Rec. HS-9040

Rec. 5.39: *Capriccio über dass Hennengeschrey,* Poglietti
TEM, p. 232
Rec. HSE-9102

Fantasia

Rec. 5.40: *Fantasies for 3, 4, 5, 6, 7, Viole da Gamba,*
Purcell
Nagels Musik-Archiv
Rec. DGG ARC 2533366

Rec. 5.41: *Fantasie for violin solo,* Telemann
TEM, p. 297
Rec. HSE-9103

Overture

Rec. 5.42: *Overture to Armide,* Lully
MM, p. 152
Rec. HS-9039

Rec. 5.43: *Sinfonia* to the opera, *La Caduta de Decem Viri,*
A. Scarlatti
Rec. HSE-9103

Theme and Variation

Rec. 5.44: *La Follia,* Corelli
Schott, ed.
Rec. DGG ARC 2533133

Rec. 5.45: *Goldberg Variations,* J. S. Bach
Eulenburg, ed.
Rec. DGG, ARC-198020

Passacaglia and Chaconne

Rec. 5.46: *Passacaglia and Fugue in c minor,* J. S. Bach
NS, p. 158
Rec. Col. MS-6261

Rec. 5.47: *Chaconne for Violin,* Vitali
Schirmer, ed.
Rec. DGG ARC 2533086

Chorale Prelude

Rec. 5.48: *In dulci jubilo,* Buxtehude and J. S. Bach
HMS, vol. 6, p. 26
Rec. RCA, LM-6031-2

Rec. 5.49: *Christ lag in Todesbanden,* J. S. Bach
MM, p. 212
Rec. HS-9040

Rec. 5.50: *Nun komm, der Heiden Heiland,* Buxtehude
TEM, p. 237
Rec. HSE-9102

Composite Forms

Suite
Rec. 5.51: *Suite in e minor,* Froberger
MM, p. 147
Rec. HS-9039

Rec. 5.52: Lute piece: *Tombeau de Mademoiselle Gaultier,*
D. Gaultier
TEM, p. 227
Rec. HSE-9102

Orchestral Suite
Rec. 5.53: *Suite no. 3 in D major for Orchestra,* J. S. Bach
Eulenburg, ed. NS, p. 211
Rec. DGG 924005

Sonata da Chiesa
Rec. 5.54: *Sonata da chiesa in e minor,* op. 3, No. 7, Corelli
MM, p. 162; NS, p. 77
Rec. HS-9040

Rec. 5.55: *Violin Sonata in g minor,* Tartini
Schirmer, ed.
Rec. None. 71361

Sonata da Camera
Rec. 5.56: Trio Sonata: *Concert Royal,* Couperin
Editions de l'Oiseau Lyre, Complete Works of Couperin, vol. 7
Rec. DGG ARC 2712003

Rec. 5.57: *Violin Sonata in E Major,* J. S. Bach
Schirmer, ed.
DGG—2709028

Keyboard Sonata
Rec. 5.58: *Sonata in c minor,* D. Scarlatti
MM, p. 179
Rec. HS-9040

Concerto and Concerto Grosso
Rec. 5.59: *Violin Concertos, nos. 1 and 2,* J. S. Bach
Schirmer, ed.
Rec. DGG ARC 2533075

Rec. 5.60: *Concerto Grosso in C major* (first movement), Handel
MM, p. 182
Rec. HS-9040

Rec. 5.61: *Brandenburg Concerto no. 2*, J. S. Bach
NS, p. 171
Rec. Ang. S-3627

Rec. 5.62: *La Primavera, Op. 8, no. 1* (first movement),
Vivaldi
TEM, p. 286
Rec. HSE-9103

Composers

Giulio Caccini
Rec. 5.63: Madrigal: *Dovrò dunque morire*
MM, p. 120
Rec. HS-9039

Jacopo Peri
Rec. 5.64: Three pieces from the opera *Euridice*
GMB, p. 186
Rec. Tel. 2635014

Jan Pieterzoon Sweelinck
Rec. 5.65: Chorale Variation: *Ach Gott, von Himmel sieh' darein*
HMS, vol. 4, p. 62
Rec. RCA-6029-1

Claudio Monteverdi
Rec. 5.66: *Orfeo*
Chester, ed; OM, p. 72; NS, p. 46
Rec. Tel. 3635020

Michael Praetorius
Rec. 5.67: *Wie schön leuchtet der Morgenstern*
HMS, vol. 4, p. 39
Rec. RCA, LM-6029-2

Rec. 5.68: *Vater unser im Himmelreich*
HAM, p. 189
Rec. Plei-256

Girolamo Frescobaldi
Rec. 5.69: Organ Music
Bärenreiter, ed.
Rec. Col MG 32311

Heinrich Schütz
Rec. 5.70: *Die Sieben Wortte*
Eulenburg, ed.
Rec. Turn-34521

Hermann Schein
Rec. 5.71: *Banchetto musicale*, Suite no. 5
Moeck, ed.
Rec. DGG, ARC-198166

Samuel Scheidt
Rec. 5.72: *Tabulatura nova*
Ugrino, ed.
Rec. Orion 77264

Pier Francesco Cavalli
Rec. 5.73: Duet from *Egisto, Musici della selva*
HMS, vol. 5, p. 11
Rec. RCA, LM-6060-1

Jacques Champion Chambonnières
Rec. 5.74: Keyboard Music
HMS, vol. 6, p. 20
Rec. RCA, LM-6031-2

Giacomo Carissimi
Rec. 5.75: *Afferte gladium*, from *Judicium Salomonis*
MM, p. 129
Rec. HS-9039

Johann Jakob Froberger
Rec. 5.76: *Suite in e minor*
MM, p. 147
Rec. HS-9039

Marc' Antonio Cesti
Rec. 5.77: *E dove t' aggiri* from *Il Pomo d'oro*
HMS, vol. 5, p. 12; OM, p. 81
Rec. RCA, LM-5030-1

Jean-Henri d'Angelbert
Rec. 5.78: *Prelude, Allemande, Sarabande* from a suite for harpsichord
HAM, vol. 2, p. 96
Rec. Vic, Vics-1370

Jean-Baptiste Lully
Rec. 5.79: *Scene infernale* from *Alceste*
HMS, vol. 5, p. 20
Rec. RCA, LM-6030-2

Marc-Antoine Charpentier
Rec. 5.80: Oratorio scene from *Le Reniement de St Pierre*
TEM, p. 242
Rec. HSE-9103

Rec. 5.81: Motet: *Ave regina coelorum*
SS, p. 175
Rec. None-71040

Dietrich Buxtehude
Rec. 5.82: *Chorale Prelude: In dulci jubilo*
HMS, vol. 6, p. 26
Rec. RCA, LM-6031-2

Johan Pachelbel
Rec. 5.83: *Toccata in e minor*
MM, p. 156
Rec. HS-9040

Arcangelo Corelli
Rec. 5.84: *Concerto grosso Op. 6, no. 8* "Christmas Concerto"
Eulenburg, ed.
Rec. DGG 2530070

Rec. 5.85: *Violin Sonatas Op. 5*
Schott, ed.
Rec. DGG ARC 2533132/3

Henry Purcell
Rec. 5.86: *Dido and Aeneas*
Oxford University Press, ed., OM, p. 102
Rec. DGG, ARC—198424

Rec. 5.87: *A New Ground*
MM, p. 159
Rec. HS-9040

Johann Kuhnau
Rec. 5.88: *Biblical Sonata No. 2*
Broude, ed.
Rec. M. H.-879T

Alessandro Scarlatti
Rec. 5.89: Quartet: *Idolo mio ti chiamo Tito* from *Tito Sempronio Gracco*
HMS, vol. 5, p. 16
Rec. RCA, LM-6030-1

François Couperin
Rec. 5.90: *Concerts Royal*
Editions de l'Oiseau Lyre. Complete edition, vol. 7
Rec. DGG ARC 2712003

Rec. 5.91: *La Galante*
MM, p. 169
Rec. HS-9040

Antonio Vivaldi

Rec. 5.92: *Concerto for Flute and String Orchestra,*
Op. 10, no. 3 *Il gardellino*
Schott, ed.
Rec. DGG 2533044

Rec. 5.93: *Concerto Grosso Op. 3 no. 11 in d minor*
NS, p. 84
Rec. LON. STS. 15364

Georg Telemann

Rec. 5.94: *Concerto in D major for Trumpet, 2 Oboes and Continuo*
Sikorski, ed.
Rec. None. 71132

Rec. 5.95: Opera: *Pimpinone*
Bärenreiter, ed.
Tel. 2635285

Jean-Philippe Rameau

Rec. 5.96: *Pièces de Clavecin*
Durand et Fils, ed.
Rec. Turn-34243

Rec. 5.97: *Les Indes galantes*
Durand et Fils
Rec. Col. M-32973

Johann Sebastian Bach

Rec. 5.98: *Goldberg Variations,* S.988
G. Schirmer, ed.
Rec. DGG, ARC-198020

Rec. 5.99: *Kunst der Fuge,* S.1080
Peters, ed.
Rec. DGG, ARC-2708002

Rec. 5.100: *Brandenburg Concertos,* S.1046/51
Eulenburg, ed.
Rec. DGG, ARC-2709016

Rec. 5.101: Cantata: No. 21 *Ich hatte viel Bekümmernis,*
Eulenburg, ed.
Rec. Tel. 2635032

Rec. 5.102: *The Passion According to St Matthew,* S.244
Eulenburg, ed.
Rec. DGG, ARC-2712001

Domenico Scarlatti
Rec. 5.103: Sonatas
G. Schirmer, ed.
OM, p. 92; AMA, p. 144; NS, p. 278
Rec. DGG, ARC-2533072

Georg Frideric Handel
Rec. 5.104: *Concerti Grossi, Op. 6*
Bärenreiter, ed.
Rec. Vox-SVBX558 (Q)

Rec. 5.105: *Messiah*
G. Schirmer, ed.; NS, p. 113
Rec. ANG-S-3657

Rec. 5.106: *Giulio Cesare*
Bärenreiter, ed.; NS, p. 110
Rec. RCA, LSC-6182

Giovanni Battista Pergolesi
Rec. 5.107: Opera Buffa: *La Serva padrona*
Ricordi, ed.
Rec. None. 71043

Rec. 5.108: Recitative and Aria from the opera buffa, *Livietta e Tracollo*
TEM, p. 314
Rec. HSE-9103

CHAPTER 6: CLASSIC (1725-1800)

(Until this chapter, specific recordings have been suggested for all listening examples. Because of the large number of recordings available for many works from the Classic period to the present, beginning with chapter 6 the authors have chosen to recommend compositions, but not specific recordings for these more readily available examples.)

Music for Voices

Recitative
Rec. 6.1: *Hai già vinta la causa* (the Count), from *Le Nozze di Figaro*, Mozart

Aria
Rec. 6.2: *Che farò senza Euridice* (Orfeo), from *Orfeo ed Euridice*, Gluck

Choruses and Ensembles
Rec. 6.3: *Le Nozze di Figaro* (Marriage of Figaro), Mozart

Vocal Polyphony

Rec. 6.4: *Der Greis*, Haydn
Rec. 6.5: *Piu non si trovano*, K. 549, Mozart

Lied

Rec. 6.6: *An Chloë*, K. 524, Mozart
Rec. 6.7: *My mother bids me bind my hair*, Haydn

Composite Vocal Forms

Opera

Rec. 6.8: *Orfeo ed Euridice*, Gluck
Rec. 6.9: *Don Giovanni*, Mozart
Rec. 6.10: *Die Entführung aus dem Serail* (The Abduction from the Seraglio), Mozart

Oratorio

Rec. 6.11: *Die Schöpfung*, Haydn
Rec. 6.12: *Die Jahreszeiten*, Haydn

Mass

Rec. 6.13: *Missa Solemnis in d minor* (Nelson Mass), Haydn
Rec. 6.14: *Mass in C major* (Coronation), K. 317, Mozart

Music for Instruments

Sonata Form

Rec. 6.15: *Symphony no. 101, D major* (Clock), first movement, Haydn
Rec. 6.16: *Piano Sonata no. 14, c minor*, K. 547, first movement, Mozart
Rec. 6.17: *String Quartet no. 1, F major*, Op. 18, no. 1, first movement, Beethoven

Rondo

Rec. 6.18: *String Quintet in g minor*, K. 516, last movement, Mozart
Rec. 6.19: *Piano Sonata no. 2, A major*, Op. 2, last movement, Beethoven

Variation Form

Rec. 6.20: *Clarinet Quintet, A major*, K. 581, last movement, Mozart
Rec. 6.21: *String Quartet in C major*, Op. 76, second movement, Haydn
Rec. 6.22: *Variation for piano in f minor*, Haydn

Three-Part Song Form

Rec. 6.23: *Piano Sonata no. 1 in f minor*, second movement, C. P. E. Bach
Rec. 6.24: *Symphony no. 101, D Major* (Clock), second movement, Haydn

Minuet and Trio, and Other Dance Forms

Rec. 6.25: *Eine Kleine Nachtmusik*, K. 525, Menuetto, Mozart
Rec. 6.26: *Symphony no. 101, D major* (Clock), third movement, Haydn

Overture

Rec. 6.27: *Overture to Orfeo ed Euridice*, Gluck
Rec. 6.28: *Overture to Le Nozze di Figaro*, Mozart

Polyphonic Instrumental Forms

Rec. 6.29: *String Quartet, B major*, K. 387, last movement, Mozart
Rec. 6.30: *Symphony no. 41, C major*, K. 550, last movement, Mozart

Composite Instrumental Forms

Sonata

Rec. 6.31: *Sonata no. 10 in C major for Piano*, K. 330, Mozart
Rec. 6.32: *Sonata in G major for Violin and Piano*, K. 301, Mozart
Rec. 6.33: *Sonata no. 44 for Piano*, Haydn

Symphony

Rec. 6.34: *Symphony no. 1 in C major*, Opus 21, Beethoven
Rec. 6.35: *Symphony no. 92 in G major* (Oxford), Haydn
Rec. 6.36: *Symphony in D major*, Op. 5, no. 2, Johann Stamitz

Concerto

Rec. 6.37: *Cello Concerto in B flat major*, Boccherini
Rec. 6.38: *Piano Concerto no. 20 in d minor*, K. 466, Mozart
Rec. 6.39: *Concerto no. 10 in E flat major for Two Pianos*, K. 365, Mozart

Chamber Music

Rec. 6.40: *Piano Trio no. 1 in G major*, Haydn
Rec. 6.41: *Piano Quartet no. 2 in E flat major*, K. 493, Mozart
Rec. 6.42: *String Quartet no. 19 in C major*, K. 465, Mozart

Serenades, Divertimenti, Cassations, Notturni

Rec. 6.43: *Divertimenti*, Haydn
Rec. 6.44: *Serenata Notturna in D major*, K. 239, Mozart

CHAPTER 7: ROMANTIC (1800–1910)

Music for Voices

Art Song

Rec. 7.1: *Dichterliebe*, Opus 48, Schumann
Rec. 7.2: *Die Winterreise*, D. 911, Schubert
Rec. 7.3: *Without Sun*, and *Songs and Dances of Death*, Mussorgsky
Rec. 7.4: *Five Poems of Charles Baudelaire*, Debussy

Choral Music

Rec. 7.5: *Te Deum,* Verdi
Rec. 7.6: *Ein Deutsches Requiem, Op. 45,* Brahms
Rec. 7.7: *Mass in F major,* Bruckner
Rec. 7.8: *Symphony no. 9 in d minor, Op. 125* (choral), Beethoven
Rec. 7.9: *Schicksalslied, Op. 54,* Brahms

Opera
Italian Opera

Rec. 7.10: *Lucia di Lammermoor,* Donizetti
Rec. 7.11: *La traviata,* Verdi
Rec. 7.12: *Tosca,* Puccini
Rec. 7.13: *Pagliacci,* Leoncavallo

French Opera

Rec. 7.14: *Les Hugenots,* Meyerbeer
Rec. 7.15: *Carmen,* Bizet
Rec. 7.16: *Pellas et Mlisande,* Debussy

German Opera

Rec. 7.17: *Der Freischütz,* Weber
Rec. 7.18: *Tristan and Isolde,* Wagner
Rec. 7.19: *Parsifal,* Wagner

Nationalistic Opera

Rec. 7.20: *Boris Godunov,* Mussorgsky
Rec. 7.21: *Bartered Bride,* Smetana

Oratorio

Rec. 7.22: *Elijah, Op. 70,* Mendelssohn
Rec. 7.23: *L'enfance du Christ, Op. 25,* Berlioz
Rec. 7.24: *La Damoiselle lue,* Debussy

Music for Instruments

Sonata Form

Rec. 7.25: *Piano Sonata no. 23, Op. 57* (Appassionata), Beethoven
Rec. 7.26: *Symphony no. 3 in E flat major, Op. 55* (Eroica), first movement, Beethoven
Rec. 7.27: *Symphony no. 3 in F major, Op. 90,* first movement, Brahms

Two-Part and Three-Part Song Forms

Rec. 7.28: *Nocturnes,* Chopin
Rec. 7.29: *Caprices for Violin,* Opus 1, Paganini
Rec. 7.30: *Ballade no. 4,* Opus 52, Chopin
Rec. 7.31: *Ballade, Op. 10 no. 1,* Brahms

Variations

Rec. 7.32: *Enigma Variations, Op. 36,* Elgar
Rec. 7.33: *Variations on a Theme by Handel, Op. 24,* Brahms
Rec. 7.34: *Variations in D major, Op. 76,* Beethoven

Dance Movements

Rec. 7.35: *Polanaise Fantasie, Op. 61,* Chopin
Rec. 7.36: *Mephisto Waltz,* Liszt
Rec. 7.37: *Danse Macabre,* Opus 40, Saint-Saëns

Rhapsody

Rec. 7.38: *Hungarian Rhapsody no. 2,* Liszt
Rec. 7.39: *Rhapsody in E flat major, no. 4, Op. 119,* Brahms
Rec. 7.40: *Spanish Rhapsody, Op. 70,* Albeniz

Etudes

Rec. 7.41: *Études, Op. 25,* Chopin
Rec. 7.42: *Transcendental Études for Piano,* Liszt

Concert Overture

Rec. 7.43: *Hebrides Overture,* Opus 26, Mendelssohn
Rec. 7.44: *Academic Festival Overture, Op. 80,* Brahms

Symphonic Poem

Rec. 7.45: *Les Préludes,* Liszt
Rec. 7.46: *Vltava* (Moldau), Smetana
Rec. 7.47: *Till Eulenspiegels* lustige Streiche, Richard Strauss

Sonata and Symphony

Rec. 7.48: *Sonata for Violin and Piano in c minor, Op. 30,* Beethoven
Rec. 7.49: *Sonata for Cello and Piano in F major, Op. 90,* Brahms
Rec. 7.50: *Sonata no. 2, Op. 35,* Chopin

Rec. 7.51: *Symphony no. 3 in E flat major, Op. 55* (Eroica), Beethoven
Rec. 7.52: *Symphony no. 2 in c minor (Resurrection),* Mahler
Rec. 7.53: *Symphony no. 5 in e minor, Op. 64,* Tchaikovsky
Rec. 7.54: *Symphonie Fantastique, Op. 14,* Berlioz

Concerto

Rec. 7.55: *Piano Concerto in a minor, Op. 54,* Schumann
Rec. 7.56: *Violin Concerto in D major, Op. 77,* Brahms

Chamber Music

Rec. 7.57: *String Quartet no. 16 in F major, Op. 135,* Beethoven
Rec. 7.58: *Piano Quintet in E flat major, Op. 44,* Schumann
Rec. 7.59: *Clarinet Quintet in b minor, Op. 115,* Brahms

Ballet

Rec. 7.60: *Creatures of Prometheus,* Beethoven
Rec. 7.61: *Swan Lake,* Tchaikovsky

Symphonic Suite
Rec. 7.62: *Nutcracker Suite*, Op. 71A, Tchaikovsky
Rec. 7.63: *Peer Gynt Suite no. 1*, Op. 46, Grieg

CHAPTER 8: EARLY TWENTIETH CENTURY MUSIC

Music for Instruments

Overture and Symphonic Poems
Rec. 8.1: *Outdoor Overture* (1938), Copland
Rec. 8.2: *Big Ben Overture* (1934), Toch

Variation
Rec. 8.3: *Variations for Orchestra*, Op. 31 (1938), Schoenberg
Rec. 8.4: *Variations for Piano*, Op. 27 (1936), Webern

Short Forms: Dances, Poetic Pieces
Rec. 8.5: *Three Pieces in the Shape of a Pear* (1890–1903), Satie (piano)
Rec. 8.6: *Mikrokosmos* (1926–37), Bartók (piano)
Rec. 8.7: *Sarcasms* (1912–14), Prokofiev (piano)

Sonata, Chamber Music, and Symphony
Rec. 8.8: *Sonata for Violin and Piano* (1921–22), Bartók
Rec. 8.9: *Piano Sonata* (1941), Copland
Rec. 8.10: *Sonata for Trombone and Piano* (1941), Hindemith
Rec. 8.11: *Sonata for Cello Unaccompanied* (1909–10), Kodály
Rec. 8.12: *String Quartet No. 6* (1939), Bartók
Rec. 8.13: *Sonata for Violin and Cello* (1920–22), Ravel
Rec. 8.14: *Ode to Napoleon* (1942), Schoenberg
Rec. 8.15: *London Symphony* (1914, rev. 1920), Vaughan Williams
Rec. 8.16: *Symphony for Chamber Orchestra*, Op. 21 (1928), Webern

Concerto
Rec. 8.17: *Piano Concerto* (1942), Schoenberg
Rec. 8.18: *Violin Concerto* (1936), Berg
Rec. 8.19: *Violin Concerto No. 2* (1935), Prokofiev
Rec. 8.20: *Concerto Grosso No. 1* (1924–25), Bloch
Rec. 8.21: *Concerto for Orchestra* (1944), Bartók

Suite
Rec. 8.22: *Lyric Suite* (1927), Berg (string quartet)
Rec. 8.23: *Appalachian Spring Suite* (1945), Copland (orchestra)
Rec. 8.24: *Lieutenant Kije Suite* (1934), Prokofiev (for orchestra)
Rec. 8.25: *Suite No. 2 for Orchestra* (1902, rev. 1943), Bartók
Rec. 8.26: *Suite*, Op. 25 (1924), Schoenberg (piano)

Ballet

Rec. 8.27: *El Sombrero de tres picos* (1919), de Falla
Rec. 8.28: *Le Sacre du printemps* (1913), Stravinsky
Rec. 8.29: *Le Création du monde* (1923), Milhaud
Rec. 8.30: *The Golden Age* (1930), Shostakovitch

Incidental Music for Film and Drama

Rec. 8.31: *Of Mice and Men* (1939), Copland (film)
Rec. 8.32: *Quiet City* (1939), Copland (film)
Rec. 8.33: *Major Barbara* (1941), Walton (film)
Rec. 8.34: *Divertissement* (1930), Ibert (drama)

Music for Voices

Rec. 8.35: *Songs*, Ives
Rec. 8.36: *Chansons madécasses* (1926), Ravel
Rec. 8.37: *Das Marienleben*, Op. 27 (1923, rev. 1948), Hindemith
Rec. 8.38: *Pierrot Lunaire* (1912), Schoenberg

Short Choral Works

Rec. 8.39: *The Peaceable Kingdom* (1936), Randall Thompson
Rec. 8.40: *Mörike Lieder*, Op. 19 (1938–39), Distler
Rec. 8.41: *Dirge for Two Veterans* (1914), Holst
Rec. 8.42: *Twelve Welsh Folk Songs* (1931), Holst

Opera

Rec. 8.43: *Wozzeck* (1931), Berg
Rec. 8.44: *Mathis der Mahler* (1938), Hindemith
Rec. 8.45: *Moses and Aron* (begun 1932, incompl.), Schoenberg
Rec. 8.46: *Die Dreigroschenoper* (1928), Weill
Rec. 8.47: *Porgy and Bess* (1935), Gershwin

Musical Theater

Rec. 8.48: *Die lustige Witwe* (1905), Lehar
Rec. 8.49: *Desert Song* (1926), Romberg
Rec. 8.50: *Showboat* (1927), Kern
Rec. 8.51: *Anything Goes* (1934), Porter

Oratorio/Choral Works with Orchestra

Rec. 8.52: *Symphony of Psalms* (1930), Stravinsky
Rec. 8.53: *Psalmus Hungaricus* (1923), Kodály
Rec. 8.54: *Belshazzar's Feast* (1931), Walton
Rec. 8.55: *Carmina Burana* (1937), Orff

Liturgical Music

Rec. 8.56: *Sacred Service, "Avodath Hakodesh"* (1934), Bloch
Rec. 8.57: *Choral-Passion* (1933), Distler

CHAPTER 9: MUSIC SINCE WORLD WAR II

Music for Instruments

Traditional Genres

Rec. 9.1: *Double Concerto for Harpsichord and Piano,* Carter (1961)
Rec. 9.2: *Concerto for Piano and Woodwinds,* Riegger (1954)
Rec. 9.3: *Violin Concerto,* Penderecki (1967)
Rec. 9.4: *Symphony No. 2* (Mysterious Mountain), Hovhannes (1955)
Rec. 9.5: *Symphony in Three Movements,* Stravinsky (1946)
Rec. 9.6: *Baroque Variations,* Foss (1967)
Rec. 9.7: *Variazione per Orchestra,* Dallapiccola (1954)
Rec. 9.8: *Landrover,* John Cage (1972) (ballet)
Rec. 9.9: *Winterbranch,* La Monte Young (1964) (ballet)
Rec. 9.10: *The Labyrinth,* Henze (1952) (ballet)
Rec. 9.11: *Piano Trio,* Kirchner (1954)
Rec. 9.12: *Quintet for Brass,* Carter (woodwind quartet) (1974)

Nontraditional Musical Forms Using Traditional Instruments

Rec. 9.13: *Threnody for the Victims of Hiroshima,* Penderecki (1959–60)
Rec. 9.14: *Pithoprakta,* Xenakis (1957)
Rec. 9.15: *Dance Four Orchestras,* Cage (1981)
Rec. 9.16: *A Collection of Rocks, Orchestra Without Conductor,* Cage (1984)
Rec. 9.17: *Fontana Mix,* Cage (1958)
Rec. 9.18: *Chronochromie,* Messiaen (1960)

Electronic Music

Rec. 9.19: *Silver Apples of the Moon,* Subotnik
Rec. 9.20: *Computer Piece,* Ussachevsky (1965)
Rec. 9.21: *And God Created Great Whales,* Opus 229/1, for taped whale sounds and orchestra, Hovhannes (1970)
Rec. 9.22: *Synchronisms No. 7,* Davidovsky (1974)
Rec. 9.23: *Orfeo,* for dancer, flute, and tape, Musgrave (1975)

Music for Voices

Art Song

Rec. 9.24: *Six Songs,* Op. 62, Shostakovich (1942, orchestrated, 1971)
Rec. 9.25: *Goethe-Lieder,* for voice and three clarinets, Dallapiccola (1953)
Rec. 9.26: *Still Falls the Rain—The Raids, 1940, Night and Dawn,* for tenor, horn, and piano, Britten (1954)
Rec. 9.27: *Poems of Love and the Rain,* Rorem (1962–63)
Rec. 9.28: *Philomel,* for voice and magnetic tape, Babbitt (1964)
Rec. 9.29: *Eight Songs for a Mad King,* for baritone and instruments, Davies (1969)

Rec. 9.30: *Recital I (for Cathy)*, sop. solo with seventeen instruments, Berio (1972)
Rec. 9.31: *Final Alice*, for sop., folk group, and orchestra, del Tredici (1976)
Rec. 9.32: *In the Theater of Night: Dream Songs on Poems of Karl Shapiro*, Zaimont (1983)

Short Choral Works
Rec. 9.33: *Five Flower Songs*, Britten (1950)
Rec. 9.34: *Ave Maria*, Davies (1961)
Rec. 9.35: *Sound Patterns*, Oliveros (1961)
Rec. 9.36: *Motetti per la Passione*, Petrassi (1965)
Rec. 9.37: *Lux Aeterna*, Ligeti (1966)
Rec. 9.38: *Campian Suite*, Stevens (1967)
Rec. 9.39: *Ecloga VIII*, Penderecki (1972)
Rec. 9.40: *Three Evangelienmotetten*, David (1971)
Rec. 9.41: *Sacred and Profane—Mediaeval Lyrics*, Op. 91, Britten (1974–75)

Opera and Musical Theater
Rec. 9.42: *Peter Grimes*, Britten (1945)
Rec. 9.43: *Consul*, Menotti (1950)
Rec. 9.44: *The Rake's Progress*, Stravinsky (1951)
Rec. 9.45: *My Fair Lady*, Loewe (1956)
Rec. 9.46: *Sound of Music*, Rodgers (1959)
Rec. 9.47: *Fiddler on the Roof*, Bock (1964)
Rec. 9.48: *The Midsummer Marriage*, Tippett (1965)
Rec. 9.49: *West Side Story*, Bernstein (1965)
Rec. 9.50: *A Water Bird Talk*, Argento (1974)
Rec. 9.51: *The Mask of Orpheus*, Birtwistle (1974–77)
Rec. 9.52: *We Come to the River*, Henze (1974–76)
Rec. 9.53: *Chorus Line*, Hamlisch (1975)
Rec. 9.54: *Mary, Queen of Scots*, Musgrave (1977)
Rec. 9.55: *Satyagraha*, Glass (1980)
Rec. 9.56: *Cats*, Webber (1981)
Rec. 9.57: *Phantom of the Opera*, Webber (1987)
Rec. 9.58: *Into the Woods*, Sondheim (1987)

Oratorio and Liturgical Music
Rec. 9.59: *Mass*, Stravinsky (1948)
Rec. 9.60: *Messe de la Pentacôte*, Messiaen (1950)
Rec. 9.61: *Christmas Cantata*, Honneger (1953)
Rec. 9.62: *Canti di Liberazione*, Dallapiccola (1955)
Rec. 9.63: *War Requiem*, Britten (1962)
Rec. 9.64: *Passion According to St. Luke*, Penderecki (1962–65)
Rec. 9.65: *The Vision of St. Augustine*, Tippett (1963–65)
Rec. 9.66: *Mass*, Bernstein (1971)
Rec. 9.67: *A Polish Requiem*, Penderecki (1980–84)

Appendix 3
Further Source Readings

(Additional recommended readings are found at the end of the preface to this volume.)

Chapter 1: Ancient Sources of Western Music

Borenstein, Itzy. *Ancient Music.* Wolfeboro, N.H.: Longwood Pub. Group, 1978.

Brandel, Rose. *The Music of Central Africa.* The Hague: M. Nijhoff, 1961.

Idelsohn, Abraham. *Jewish Music in Historical Development.* New York: Schocken, 1967.

Kunst, Jaap. *Ethno-Musicology.* The Hague: M. Nijhoff, 1959.

Malm, Wm. P. *Music Cultures of the Pacific, The Near East, and Asia.* Englewood Cliffs, N.J.: Prentice-Hall, 1967.

May, Elizabeth, ed. *Music of Many Cultures—An Introduction* (20 Essays, 3 Recordings). Berkeley: University of California Press, 1980.

Merriam, Alan P. *The Anthropology of Music.* Evanston, Ill.: Northwestern University Press, 1964.

Nettl, Bruno. *Folk and Traditional Music of the Western Continents.* 2nd ed. New York: Prentice-Hall, 1973.

———. *Music in Primitive Culture.* Cambridge: Harvard University Press, 1956.

Prajnanananda, Swami. *A Historical Study of Indian Music.* Calcutta: Anandadhara Prakashan, 1965.

Sachs, Curt. *The Wellsprings of Music.* ed. by Jaap Kunst. Jersey City: Da Capo, 1977.

Winnington-Ingram, R. P. *Mode in Ancient Greek Music.* Cambridge: Cambridge University Press, 1936.

Chapter 2: Romanesque — Middle Ages (500-1100)

Apel, Willi. *Gregorian Chant.* Bloomington: University of Indiana Press, 1958.

Fenlon, Ian, ed. *Early Music History.* 7 vols. Cambridge, England, Cambridge University Press, 1981 and following.

Hoppin, Richard H. *Medieval Music.* Ch. I-VII. New York: W. W. Norton, 1978.

————. *Anthology of Medieval Music*. New York: W. W. Norton, 1978.
Phillips, Elizabeth V. & Jackson, John-Paul. *Performing Medieval &
     Renaissance Music: An Introductory Guide*. New York: G. Schirmer, 1986.
Seay, Albert. *Music in the Medieval World*. Englewood Cliffs: Prentice-Hall,
     2nd ed., 1975.

Chapter 3: Gothic — Late Middle Ages (Ars Antiqua-Ars Nova)

Apel, Willi. *The Notation of Polyphonic Music*. Cambridge: Medieval
     Academy of America, 1949.
————. *French Secular Music of the Late Fourteenth Century*. Cambridge:
     Medieval Academy of America, 1950.
Arnold, John. *Medieval Music*. New York: Oxford Univ. Press, 1986.
Boorman, Stanley. *Studies in the Performance of Late Medieval Music*. New
     York: Cambridge Univ. Press, 1984.
Cattin, Giulio. *Music of the Middle Ages*. Translated by Steven Botterill. New
     York: Cambridge Univ. Press, 1985.
Collins, Fletcher, Jr. *A Medieval Songbook: Troubadour and Trouvère*.
     Charlottesville: University Press of Va., 1982.
Hoppin, Richard H. *Medieval Music*. Ch. VIII-XX. New York: W. W. Norton,
     1978.
————. *Anthology of Medieval Music*. New York: W. W. Norton, 1978.
Hughes, Andrew. *Medieval Music: The Sixth Liberal Art*. 2nd ed. Toronto:
     Univ. of Toronto Press, 1980.
Marocco, W. Thomas and Nicholas Sandon. *Medieval Music*. New York:
     Oxford Univ. Press, 1977.
McGee, Timothy J. *Medieval and Renaissance Music: A Performer's Guide*.
     Toronto: University of Toronto Press, 1985.
Seay, Albert. *Music in the Medieval World*. Englewood Cliffs: Prentice-Hall,
     2nd ed., 1975.
Stevens, John. *Words and Music in the Middle Ages: Song, Narrative, Dance and
     Drama*. New York: Cambridge University Press, 1986.

Chapter 4: Renaissance (1400-1600)

Andrews, H. K. *An Introduction to the Technique of Palestrina*. London:
     Novello, 1958.
Bukofzer, Manfred. *Studies in Medieval and Renaissance Music*. New York:
     W. W. Norton, 1950.
Carpenter, Nan Cooke. *Music in the Medieval and Renaissance Universities*.
     Norman: University of Oklahoma Press, 1958.
Einstein, Alfred. *The Italian Madrigal*. Princeton: Princeton University Press,
     1949.
Fellowes, E. H. *The English Madrigal Composers*. London: Oxford, 1950.
Gray, Cecil and Philip Heseltine. *Carlo Gesualdo, Prince of Venosa. Musician
     and Murderer*. London: Paul, Trench, Trubner, 1926.

Greenberg, Noah and Paul Maynard, eds. *Anthology of Early Renaissance Music.* New York: W. W. Norton, 1975.

Harmon, Alec, ed. *Oxford Book of Italian Madrigals.* New York: Oxford Univ. Press, 1983.

Jeppeson, Knud. *The Style of Palestrina and the Dissonance.* London: Oxford, 1927.

Ledger, Philip, ed. *Oxford Book of English Madrigals.* New York: Oxford Univ. Press, 1978.

Lowinsky, Edward E. *Secret Chromatic Art in the Netherlands Motet.* New York: Columbia University Press, 1946.

Reese, Gistav. *New Grove High Renaissance Masters.* Edited by Stanley Sadie. New York: W. W. Norton, 1984.

Stevens, J. E., ed. *Music and Poetry in the Early Tudor Court.* New York: Cambridge Univ. Press, 1979.

Walker, Ernest. *A History of Music in England.* London: Oxford, 1952.

Chapter 5: Baroque (1575-1750)

Anthony, James, et al. *New Grove French Baroque Masters.* New York: W. W. Norton, 1987.

Anthony, James R. *French Baroque Music.* New York: W. W. Norton, 1981.

Arnold, Denis. *New Grove Italian Baroque Masters.* New York: W. W. Norton, 1984.

Bianconi, Lorenzo. *Music in the Seventeenth Century.* Translated by David Bryant. New York: Cambridge Univ. Press, 1987.

David, Hans T. and Arthur Mendel. *The Bach Reader.* New York: Norton, 1945.

Flower, Newman. *Handel.* London: Cassell and Co., 1959.

Geiringer, Karl. *The Bach Family.* New York: Oxford, 1954.

Gleason, Harold and Warren Becker. *Music in the Baroque.* 3rd ed. Van Nuys, Calif.: Alfred Pub. Co., 1979.

Grout, Donald J. *A Short History of Opera.* 3rd ed. New York: Columbia University Press, 1973.

Hutchings, Arthur. *The Baroque Concerto.* New York: Norton, 1965.

Newman, William S. *The Sonata in the Baroque Era.* Chapel Hill: University of North Carolina Press, 1959.

Palisca, Claude V. *Baroque Music.* Englewood Cliffs: Prentice-Hall, 1968.

Rifkin, Joshua, et al. *New Grove North European Baroque Masters.* New York: W. W. Norton, 1985.

Smither, Howard E. *A History of Oratorio.* 3 vols. Chapel Hill: University of North Carolina Press, 1977–87.

Chapter 6: Classic (1725-1800)

Burney, Dr. Charles. *An Eighteenth Century Musical Tour in Central Europe and the Netherlands.* New York: Oxford, 1959.

———. *An Eighteenth Century Music Journey in France and Italy.* New York: Oxford, 1959.

Carse, Adam. *The Orchestra in the Eighteenth Century.* Cambridge, England: W. Heffer, 1940.

Dent, E. J. *Mozart's Operas.* rev. ed. New York: Oxford, 1947.

Einstein, Alfred. *Mozart: His Character and Work.* New York: Oxford, 1945.

Geiringer, Karl. *Haydn, A Creative Life in Music.* New York: W. W. Norton, 1946.

————. *The Bach Family.* New York: Oxford, 1954.

Grout, Donald J. *A Short History of Opera.* 3rd ed. New York: Columbia University Press, 1973.

Kirby, F. E., ed. *Music in the Classic Period: An Anthology with Commentary.* New York: G. Schirmer, 1979.

Landon, H. C. Robbins. *Haydn's Chronicle and Works.* Bloomington: Univ. of Indiana Press, 1976.

Newman, William S. *The Sonata in the Classic Era.* Chapel Hill: University of North Carolina Press, 1963.

Pastelli, Giorgio. *Age of Mozart and Beethoven.* Translated by Eric Cross. New York: Cambridge Univ. Press, 1984.

Pauly, Reinhard G. *Music in the Classic Period.* Englewood Cliffs: Prentice-Hall, 2nd ed., 1973.

Rosen, Charles. *The Classical Style.* New York: Viking, 1971.

Chapter 7: Romantic (1800-1910)

Abraham, Gerald. *A Hundred Years of Music.* New York: Knopf, 1938.

Barzun, Jacques. *Berlioz and the Romantic Century.* 2 vols. New York: Little, Brown, 1950.

Chase, Gilbert. *America's Music.* New York: McGraw-Hill, 1955.

Cooper, Martin. *French Music from the Death of Berlioz to the Death of Fauré.* New York: Oxford Univ. Press, 1951.

Grout, D. J. *A Short History of Opera.* 3rd ed. New York: Columbia University Press, 1973.

Kirby, F. E., ed. *Music in the Romantic Period: An Anthology with Commentary.* New York: G. Schirmer, 1986.

Kramer, Lawrence. *Music and Poetry: The Nineteenth Century and After.* Berkeley: Univ. of Calif. Press, 1984.

Landau, Annaliese. *Lied: The Unfolding of Its Style.* Lanham, Md.: Univ. Press of America, 1980.

Longyear, Rey M. *Nineteenth-Century Romanticism in Music.* 2nd ed. Englewood Cliffs: Prentice-Hall, 1973.

Newman, Ernest. *The Wagner Operas.* New York: Knopf, 1949.

Plantinga, Leon. *Romantic Music.* New York: W. W. Norton, 1987.

Prawer, S. S. *Penguin Book of Lieder.* New York: Penguin, 1982.

Soloman, Maynard. *Beethoven.* New York: Schirmer, 1977.

Thayer, A. W. *Life of Ludwig van Beethoven.* Princeton: Princeton University Press, 1964.

Wagner, Richard. *Prose Works.* 8 vols. Translated by W. W. Ellis. London: 1892-1899.

Zetlin, Mikhail O. *The Five, the Revolution of the Russian School of Music.* New York: International Universities Press, 1959.

Chapter 8: Early Twentieth Century Music (1900-1945)

Eimert, Herbert and Karlheinz Stockhausen. *Anton Webern.* Valley Forge: European-American Press, 1958.

Kislan, Richard. *The Musical: A Look at the American Musical.* Englewood Cliffs: Prentice-Hall, 1980.

Leibowitz, René. *Schoenberg and His School.* New York: Philosophical Library, 1949.

Martin, George. *The Companion to Twentieth Century Opera.* New York: Dodd, 1984.

Martin, William R. and Julius Drossing. *Music of the 20th Century.* Englewood Cliffs: Prentice-Hall, 1980.

McVeagh, Diana, et al. *New Grove Twentieth Century English Masters.* New York: W. W. Norton, 1986.

Modern Music Quarterly (1923-1946). Published by the League of Composers, New York.

Pleasants, Henry. *The Agony of Modern Music.* New York: Simon and Schuster, 1955.

Prendergast, Roy M. *Film Music: A Neglected Art.* New York: W. W. Norton, 1978.

Reihe, Die. (An intermittently appearing journal dealing exclusively with serial and electronic music.) Bryn Mawr: Presser, 1955.

Salzman, Eric. *Twentieth-Century Music: An Introduction.* 2nd ed. Englewood Cliffs: Prentice-Hall, 1974.

Sessions, Roger. *The Musical Experience of Composer, Performer, Listener.* Princeton: Princeton University Press, 1950.

Somfai, Laszlo, et al. *New Grove Modern Masters: Bartók, Stravinsky, Hindemith.* Edited by Stanley Sadie. New York: W. W. Norton, 1984.

Stuckenschmidt, H. H. *Twentieth Century Music.* Translated by Richard Deveson. New York: McGraw Hill, 1969.

Chapter 9: Music Since World War II

Boehm, Laszlo. *Modern Music Notation.* New York: G. Schirmer, 1961.

Cage, John. *Silence.* Middletown, Conn.: Wesleyan University Press, 1961.

Carlson, Effie B. *Bio-Bibliographical Dictionary of Twelve Tone and Serial Composers.* Ann Arbor: UMI, n.d.

Cope, David. *New Directions in Music.* Dubuque, Iowa: Wm. C. Brown Company Publishers, 1984.

Dorter, Tom and Greg Arbruster. *The Art of Electronic Music.* New York: Morrow, 1985.

Ernst, David. *The Evolution of Electronic Music.* New York: G. Schirmer, 1987.

Ligeti, György. *Ligeti in Conversation.* Jersey City: Da Capo Press, 1985.

Manning, Peter. *Electronic and Computer Music.* New York: Oxford University Press, 1987.

Meyer, Leonard B. *Music, The Arts and Ideas.* Chicago: University of Chicago Press, 1967.

Nyman, Michael. *Experimental Music: Cage and Beyond.* New York: G. Schirmer, 1981.

Perspectives of New Music (A biannual journal). Princeton University Press for the Fromm Music Foundation, 1962.

Read, Gardner. *Music Notation: A Manual of Modern Practice.* New York: Taplinger, 1972.

Schwartz, Elliott and Barney Childs, eds. *Contemporary Composers on Contemporary Music.* New York: Holt, Rinehart and Winston, 1967.

Stone, Kurt. *Music Notation in the Twentieth Century: A Practical Guidebook.* New York: W. W. Norton, 1980.

Strange, Allen. *Electronic Music Systems, Techniques and Controls.* Dubuque, Iowa: Wm. C. Brown Co. Publishers, 1982.

Xenakis, Iannis. *Formalized Music: Thought and Mathematics in Composition.* Ann Arbor: UMI, n.d.

Chapter 10: Popular Music in the Twentieth Century

Berendt, Joachim. *The Jazz Book.* Westport, CT: Lawrence Hill, 1975.

Brown, Charles T. *The Art of Rock and Roll.* 2nd ed. New York: Prentice-Hall, 1987.

Ewen, David. *All the Years of American Popular Music.* Englewood Cliffs: Prentice-Hall, 1977.

Feather, Leonard. *The Encyclopedia of Jazz in the 60s.* New York: Horizon, 1967.

Feather, Leonard & Ira Gitler. *The Encyclopedia of Jazz in the 70s.* New York: Horizon, 1976.

Haralambos, Michael. *Soul Music: Birth of a Sound in Black America.* Jersey City: Da Capo, 1985.

Hintoff, Nat. *Jazz Is.* New York: Limelight Editions, 1984.

Hodier, André. *Jazz, Its Evolution and Essence.* New York: Grove Press, 1986.

Jone, LeRoi. *Blues People: Negro Music in White America.* New York: Morrow, 1963.

Kaufman, Fredrick and John P. Guckin. *The African Roots of Jazz.* Van Nuys: Alfred, 1979.

Marcus, Greil. *The Aesthetics of Rock.* Jersey City: Da Capo, 1987.

Oliver, Paul, et al. *New Grove Gospel, Blues and Jazz.* New York: W. W. Norton, 1988.

Pattison, Robert. *The Triumph of Vulgarity: Rock Music in the Mirror of Romanticism.* New York: Oxford, 1987.

Shestack, Melvin. *The Country Music Encyclopedia.* New York: T. Y. Crowell, 1977.

Schuller, Gunther. *Early Jazz: Its Roots and Musical Development.* New York: Oxford, 1968.

Tanner, Paul O. W. and Maurice Gerow. *A Study of Jazz.* 5th ed. Dubuque, Iowa: Wm. C. Brown, 1984.

Whitcomb, Ian. *After the Ball: Pop Music from Rag to Rock.* Rev. ed. New York: Limelight Ed., 1986.

Williams, Martin, ed. *The Art of Jazz: Ragtime to Bebop.* Jersey City: Da Capo, 1981.

Wilder, Alec. *American Popular Song: The Great Innovators, 1900–1950.* New York: Oxford, 1972.

Glossary

A CAPPELLA—A term used to designate choral music without accompaniment.

ALEATORIC MUSIC—A type of composition based on the element of chance in both the selection of sounds and their performance.

AGRÉMENTS—A French term applied to small melodic ornaments.

BALLET de COUR (Ballet of the Court)—A dramatic presentation in dance at the seventeenth century French Royal Court.

BASSO CONTINUO—The bass part in music of the Baroque period usually performed by a harpsichord or organ together with viol, bassoon, or cello. It was normally read from a figured bass.

BINARY FORM—A form consisting of two sections: A-B.

CADENCE—A melodic or harmonic ending of a phrase or movement. Authentic, plagal, and deceptive are terms used to describe the degree of repose.

CANON—The musical term denoting strict imitation within a polyphonic texture.

CANTUS FIRMUS—A basic melody, either composed or taken from another source, upon which certain polyphonic works are constructed.

CHORD—A combination of three or more tones sounded simultaneously.

CHROMATIC ALTERATION—Altering a tone of the diatonic scale by means of accidentals.

CLAVECIN—The French term for harpsichord.

COLORATURA—Virtuoso ornamentation and embellishment on a melodic line, normally referring to the human voice.

CONCERTATO STYLE—A style of musical performance associated with the seventeenth century that commonly features a basso continuo with melodies shared among several voices in alternation.

CONSONANCE—In traditional harmony, an interval or chord which produces an effect of repose or agreeableness.

CONTRAPUNTAL—See COUNTERPOINT

CONTRARY MOTION—The movement of two voices in opposite directions.

CONTRATENOR—The third voice, added to the tenor and discant in fourteenth and fifteenth century vocal compositions.

COUNTERPOINT—The combination of two or more distinctive melodic lines into a single musical fabric. It is often used synonomously with polyphony.

DIATONIC—The scale made up of five whole tones and two semitones. The term is also used to describe melodic motion in scales without chromatic alterations.

DISSONANCE—In traditional harmony, an interval or chord which produces an effect of harmonic tension.

DOMINANT—The fifth degree of the diatonic scale or, in harmonic practice, a chord built upon the fifth degree.

DOUBLE-STOP—The simultaneous playing on two strings of a bowed instrument.

DRONE BASS—A sustained bass note that is retained throughout a section or a whole piece. The note is usually the tonic, but it sometimes alternates between the tonic and dominant.

DYNAMICS—Signs, abbreviations, and words used to indicate degrees of loudness and volume of sound.

EMPFINDSAMER STIL SENSITIVE STYLE—A mid-eighteenth-century style that emphasized melodic simplicity and refined expression. See GALANT STYLE.

EPISODE—A secondary passage or section which digresses from the main theme. Episodes are frequently found in rondos and fugues.

EQUAL TEMPERAMENT—A system of tuning in which the octave is divided into twelve equal semitones.

FALSETTO—A style of singing by the male voice in which a very high head tone is produced.

FIGURATION—Stereotyped chordal patterns used in the realization of a figured bass.

FIGURED BASS—The numerical symbols placed beneath the staff from which continuo players realize the harmonic intent of the composer.

GALANT STYLE—An eighteenth-century style noted for its regularity of phrase, lightness of texture, inclination to ornamentation, and simple harmonies. The music of Louis Couperin is in this style.

HARMONY—A simultaneous sounding of two or more tones; the theory and practice of chord construction and progressions.

HOCKET—A medieval musical device in which notes alternated rapidly between two (or among three) voices, resulting in an unusual, prominent rhythmic pattern.

HOMOPHONY—Music in which one dominant melodic voice is supported by an accompaniment.

IMITATION—The repetition, exact or with minor variations, of a melodic, rhythmic, or harmonic entity in music.

INCIPIT—The opening line of text or music or both from a composition.

INTERVAL—The distance in pitch between two tones played either successively (melodic interval) or simultaneously (harmonic interval).

INTONATION—The degree of accuracy of pitch.

INVERSION—(1) An interval is inverted by transferring its lowest tone to the octave above, or by transferring its highest tone to the octave below. (2) A chord is inverted by placing any other than its root or fundamental tone in the bass. (3) A melody is inverted by changing each descending interval to the same ascending interval.

LIED—The German term for Art Song.

LITURGY—The official order of service in the Roman Catholic church. The word also applied to authorized services in most Christian churches.

MELISMA—An elaborate, flowing ornament sung on one syllable in a melody. It normally refers to medieval music.

MELODRAMA—A work or part of a work in which spoken parts are performed in alternation with instrumental passages, or in some cases together with such instrumental accompaniment. There are examples from the time of J. J. Rousseau to Stravinsky.

METER—The organization of time in music by means of accented and unaccented beats.

MODULATION—The process of moving from one tonal center to another in the course of a single composition.

MONOCHORD—An instrument consisting of a single string stretched over a resonating body.

MONOPHONY—A single melodic line without accompaniment.

MONOTHEMATIC—A composition based on only one melody or theme.

MOTIVE—A short melodic or rhythmic figure that is repeated to give design to a melodic or rhythmic phrase.

MUSIQUE CONCRETE—Sounds from the natural world that are recorded and manipulated electronically.

MUTATION—The transition used by a voice in moving from one hexachord to another in medieval music.

ORNAMENTATION—Added notes, such as trills or turns, to a melody.

OSTINATO—A short melodic figure that is repeated in one voice, usually the bass, throughout a section, movement, or composition. This is also known as ground bass.

PARALLEL MOTION—Two or more voices moving in the same direction at the same interval.

PERIOD—A group of measures that makes a natural division of the melody, usually two phrases, analogous to a sentence in speech or writing.

PHRASE—A segment of melody that has a natural pause or ending. It is analogous to a phrase in speech or writing.

PITCH—The aspect of a tone determined by the number of vibrations per second.

PIZZICATO—To pluck the string of a bowed instrument.

POLYPHONY—A musical texture made of two or more simultaneous melodies sounded by independent voices or instruments.

POLYRHYTHMS (cross-rhythms)—The use of different rhythmic patterns simultaneously.

POLYTHEMATIC—A composition based on more than one melody or theme of equal importance.

PROGRAM MUSIC—Music of a descriptive character, especially but not exclusively of the nineteenth century, often designed to follow a specific pictorial narrative. It often employs imitative or evocative (representative) sounds.

RANGE—The distance between the highest and lowest pitch of a melody, voice, or instrument.

REFRAIN—One or two melodic phrases repeated at the end of each stanza.

RITORNELLO—(1) An instrumental interlude before or after an aria or scene; (2) the tutti section of a concerto grosso; (3) the last two lines of the stanza in the fourteenth-century madrigal.

RUBATO—Elasticity of tempo in performance.

SCALE—A series of adjacent tones arranged according to whole and half steps, or any other regular increment of pitch.

SEQUENCE—The repetition of a melodic motive in the same part above or below the original.

SONG CYCLE—A series of art songs connected by a central poetic idea.

STILE RAPPRESENTATIVO—The style of presentation employed in the performance of the earliest operas and oratorios of the seventeenth century. It was characterized especially by free rhythmic declamation.

STROPHIC—A song of which all stanzas are sung to the same music.

SYNCOPATION—A rhythmic device that displaces the accent from a strong beat to a weak beat or a weak portion of the beat.

TABLATURE—Name for the various early systems of notation in which symbols, letters, or figures were used instead of notes on the staff.

TEMPO—The rapidity with which beats succeed each other in a musical texture. Tempo marks are words and abbreviations used to indicate degrees of speed.

TENOR—(1) designation for a high male voice. (2) the melody upon which medieval masses and motets were constructed. See CANTUS FIRMUS.

TERNARY FORM—A form consisting of three sections: A-B-A.

TETRACHORD—A scale-series of four tones, the highest and lowest of which form the interval of a perfect fourth.

TEXTURE—The density of melodic and harmonic elements designated by such terms as homophonic, polyphonic, chordal.

THEME—A distinctive melody, or musical idea, that serves as a basis for musical composition. Also, a melodic gesture that is transformed variously, by the composer.

THROUGH-COMPOSED—The opposite of strophic; a song that has different music for each stanza.

TIMBRE—Quality (color) of a tone as produced on a specific instrument or voice; also referred to as tone color.

TONALITY—The result of harmonic organization around a central tone, called the tonic or keynote.

TONE COLOR—See TIMBRE.

TONIC—The first note of the scale, also called the keynote.

TRANSCRIPTION—A composition originally written for one medium that has been transcribed for another.

TREMOLO—(1) The rapid repetition of a single note a number of times; (2) the rapid alternation between two different notes.

TRIAD—A chord consisting of three tones.

TRI-TONE—The interval made up of three whole tones, also called the augmented fourth.

TUNING (temperament)—A system of determining the intervals of the octave. Various methods are known as: Pythagorean, just intonation, mean-tone, equal-tempered.

TUTTI—Marking in a score that indicates entrance of all instruments or voices after a solo passage.

VIBRATO—A minute fluctuation of pitch both below and above the tone for the purpose of tonal coloring.

VIRTUOSO—A performer with superior technical facility.

Index